The Best of Friends

THE BEST OF FRIENDS

Profiles of Extraordinary Friendships

David Michaelis

WILLIAM MORROW AND COMPANY, INC.
New York · 1983

Grateful acknowledgment is made for permission to quote from the following:

Unpublished letters of John F. Kennedy, Joseph P. Kennedy, Kathleen Kennedy; permission granted by Stephen E. Smith, President, John Fitzgerald Kennedy Library Incorporated.

Unpublished letters, telegrams, and papers of Kirk LeMoyne Billings, and unpublished telegrams of John F. Kennedy and Kathleen Kennedy, reprinted by permission of Sally F. Carpenter, Executor of the Estate of Kirk LeMoyne Billings.

Unpublished letters of David Ambrose Knowles, reprinted by permission of Rob Taylor.

Excerpts from the quartermaster's log of George Cadwalader, first published by George Cadwalader in "Transatlantic by Cal-20" in *Yachting,* reprinted by permission of George Cadwalader.

Buckminster Fuller: At Home in the Universe by Alden Hatch. Copyright © 1974 by Alden Hatch. Used by permission of Crown Publishers, Inc.

Lines from "We Open in Venice" by Cole Porter, copyright © 1949 by Cole Porter. Copyright renewed, assigned to John F. Wharton as Trustee of the Cole Porter Musical and Literary Property Trusts. Chappell & Co., Inc., Publisher. International copyright secured. All Rights Reserved. Used by permission.

Lines from "Rocket Eighty-Eight" by Jackie Brenston, copyright © 1951 by Hill & Range Songs, Inc. Copyright renewed, all rights controlled by Unichappell Music, Inc. (Rightsong Music, Publisher). International copyright secured. All Rights Reserved. Used by permission.

From "New South Burn" by Dan Aykroyd and John Belushi from *Rolling Stone* #230, 1/13/77. Reprinted by permission of Straight Arrow Publishers, Inc., copyright © 1977. All Rights Reserved. Reprinted by permission.

Lines from "I'm No Angel" with words by Gladys Du Bois and Ben Ellison and music by Harvey Brooks, copyright © 1933 by Paramount Productions Inc. Copyright assigned to Shapiro, Bernstein & Co. Inc., Capitol Theater Building, Corner Broadway and 51st Street, New York. International copyright secured. All Rights Reserved including public performance for profit. Used by permission.

Library of Congress Cataloging in Publication Data

Michaelis, David.
     The best of friends.

     1. United States—Biography.   2. Friendship.
I. Title.
CT220.M53   1983   920'.073   83–973
ISBN 0–688–01558–1

Printed in the United States of America

First Edition

1 2 3 4 5 6 7 8 9 10

BOOK DESIGN BY ELLEN LO GIUDICE

To my father
Michael Michaelis
and
To the memory of
my mother
Diana Tead Michaelis

Preface

T his book is about the importance of friendship in the lives of fourteen contemporary men.

From the start, my thought was to tell a series of stories based on the recollections of men to whom a close friendship with another man mattered as much as a romance with a woman.

So it has turned out to be a book about another kind of romance. In these profiles you will find men whose friendships have been strong, enduring, and intimate, yet not complicated by sexual love; men whose lives have been lived together in university dormitories and on naval destroyers, in barren hotel rooms and on high mountain peaks, in preparatory school-rooms and on Hollywood sound stages, in boats at sea and on the boards of corporations, in sculpting studios and on the seventeenth floor of 30 Rockefeller Plaza, in dilapidated bars and on the third floor of 1600 Pennsylvania Avenue.

These are men who have illustrated, with their respective recollections, the issues, conflicts, and pleasures of intensely close male friendships; men who have characterized, in the language of their particular friendship, the personal history they share, and the strengths and weaknesses of personality upon which these friendships have grown—some for more than half a century; men who have been, by turns, as honest and perplexed when trying to define their loving admiration of their best friend as Michel Eyquem de Montaigne was when he wrote in 1580 of his friend, Étienne de La Boétie: "If you press me to say why I loved him, I can say no more than it was because he was he and I was I."

I intended to press such men, hoping they would say more. Yet when I began the interviews for this book in 1981, I had no idea whether one man—let alone his best friend, and the women in their lives—would talk candidly, and at length, about a relationship which, though obviously important, was perhaps difficult to describe. Moreover, men living in a culture and an era that offer us such disappointing descriptions of the nature of physical and emotional attraction—heterosexuality, homosexuality, bi-sexuality, *uni*-sexuality, *latent*-homosexuality—might be understandably reluctant to reveal, on the subject of their most intimate friendship, emotions into which a pejorative analysis could be read.

When the world was younger, men expressed unhesitatingly their sentiments about the kind of friendship in which two men's love for one another was profound. Listen to David, the son of Jesse the Bethlehemite, lamenting the death of Jonathan, the son of Saul: "I am very distressed for you, my brother Jonathan; very pleasant have you been to me: your love to me was wonderful, passing the love of women." Listen to Achilles pledging to avenge the death of Patroclus, calling his fellow warrior: "The friend of all my friends whom I most loved, dear to me as life—Him I have lost." Listen to the young Persian soldier in the fifth century B.C. who was asked by his king, Cyrus the Great, whether he would trade for a kingdom the horse on which he had just won a race: "Certainly not, Sire," he replied, "but I would gladly part with him to gain a friend, if I could find anyone worthy of such fellowship." Listen to the Scottish philosopher David Hume having the same kind of problem in 1740: "The difficulty is not so great to die for a friend, as to find a friend worth dying for." And to Balzac, who had it all figured out by 1835: "Well, for me, and I have turned life inside out, only one real sentiment exists—friendship between man and man." And to Emerson, who spurred me on: "When a man becomes dear to me, I have touched the goal of fortune. I find very little written directly to the heart of this matter."

Today, friendship between men is still one of the most important, least examined, relationships in America. During the last two decades, we have seen a seemingly inexhaustible supply of studies of marital relationships, divorce, and mother-

daughter and father-son relationships. Yet the relationship between two close male friends has been shoved into the outskirts of journalism, the side streets of biography. Beyond a
small shelf of contemporary novels, and a knee-high stack of
sociological literature, very little remains written about "the
heart of this matter."

Perhaps this is because in America a man's success is almost
always seen in terms of his roles as a professional, as a lover,
as a husband, and as a father. A man's success in love seems to
be viewed only inasmuch as it pertains to his wife or lover.
Rarely do we gauge a man in terms of his success as a friend.
American men are celebrated not for the achievement of a
loyal, lasting, and significant friendship with another man but
for the achievement of a significant professional career, and
possibly for the achievement of a loyal, lasting, and fruitful
marriage. A famous man is often measured by a journalistic
yardstick the marks of which show us three feet of his professional ability, ten inches of his marriage, one sixteenth of an
inch of his emotional reliance on, and need for support from,
another man who is his best friend. Assuming that this celebrated man does indeed have one such important friendship
(in some cases, the unexplored assumption is that the man's
wife is his best friend), it is curious that the degree of intimacy
that this man has shared with his closest male friend does not
receive as much attention as that which he has shared with his
wife. The result is that we usually have to wait until after a man
has died to recognize the role that a particular friendship has
played in his life. Then, in the eulogy delivered after death, the
best friend at last steps forth to articulate the qualities and
experiences that have made the deceased such an important
friend to him.

Even more rare is another kind of testimony concerning
the value that one man's friendship has had to another: Where
today, outside of the armed forces, would one find the kind of
friendship in which one man is willing to die for his friend?
Damon and Pythias, the two Syracusan friends of the fourth
century B.C., would have been excellent subjects for a profile
in this book if at least one of them had been alive to be inter-

viewed. Their friendship would have satisfied the first require-
ment I made when I began to seek pairs of great friends about
which to write: That one would have enjoyed being with those
two men on the day when their faith in each other mattered
to them most, or on the day when their friendship was at
its best.

In the case of Damon and Pythias, the first would have
been the day when Pythias, condemned to death by the tyrant
Dionysius, was freed to put his house in order, and Damon
agreed to stay in his place as a pledge. The second would have
been the day when, instead of leaving Damon to die, Pythias
returned to stand for his own execution, whereupon Dionysius
was so moved that he freed them both and asked to be their
friend.

The matters of friendship reported in the following seven
profiles are specifically those of fourteen men. Therefore, this
book does not claim to be a definitive study of men's friendships in America today. These stories are simply intended to
illustrate the importance of friendship as a particular and enduring kind of romance in American life. For if these men all
have one thing in common, it is that they have committed
themselves to a close friendship as if to a romantic, but unconditional, pledge of love.

Contents

. . . because he was he and I was I.
        —MONTAIGNE

I : ROOMIES

Donold B. Lourie / George H. Love

I t was Love at first sight.

In September 1916, on the first day of the school year at Phillips Exeter Academy in New Hampshire, when the students were assigned to sit by alphabetical order in Chapel, Donold Bradford Lourie was directed toward George Hutchinson Love. Lourie, a new junior from Peru, Illinois, had never been east before. For luck, he carried a dime in his wallet. He had transferred to Exeter from the LaSalle-Peru Township High School, and there was about him a look of rawness and inexperience. All the same he boldly pushed his way into the pew and claimed his seat beside Love, who seemed to possess the effortless poise of a boy sophisticated in the ways of the school, if not the world. For the next few minutes, they sat shoulder to cold shoulder.

Lourie felt conspicuously new. For one thing, he was wearing a green suit—the kind of garment that seems more impressive in the mirror of a clothing store than in front of classmates on the first day at a new school. Yet here in the Exeter chapel, it was neither the cut of the suit, nor its dark shade of green that made Lourie stand out; it was the Norfolk-style belt that encircled the jacket, cinched tightly below Lourie's ribs, and buckled in front.

On the recent summer day when Lourie's father had accompanied him from Peru (pronounced "Pee-roo") to Herman, Mandis & Bogan, a swank men's store in Chicago, there had been general agreement among the trio of father, son, and salesman that that belted jacket was the latest item for a boy going east to school. Lourie now noticed that his neighbor, who was wearing a beltless, three-button suit, was eyeing him with humorous distaste.

"Pretty fancy suit you got there," said George Love. "Where'd you get it?"

"My father gave it to me," Lourie replied. "Do you want to make something out of it?"

Evidently, Love could not make anything more of it. His stifled laughter was already in danger of disrupting the entire chapel—all very disconcerting to Lourie, who decided on the spot to get rid of the suit as soon as possible. But the destiny of alphabetical order persisted in placing Lourie and Love at one another's side throughout the day's classes. Having been at Exeter since freshman year, Love casually conferred on Lourie the power of his campus wisdom, revealing bit by bit, mostly with humorous asides, the crucial facts of preparatory school life. By dinnertime, they were both laughing about the belt on the green suit, and by the time Lourie had stowed the suit away in the far reaches of his closet that night, they were fast friends.

They were a contrasting, but complementary pair. If Love was the more sophisticated of the two, Lourie was the more innocent—the shy boy from the midwestern high school. ("I didn't tell him I'd been to high school," Lourie remembers, "—didn't want him to know.") Lourie was five feet eight inches tall ("a little fellow," Love recalls) with dark, neatly slicked-back hair, a friendly grin, and large ears which stuck out with the aerial impishness of kites in a high breeze. Though small in size, Lourie was large in strength, endowed with a trim build and exceptional muscular coordination. He was wiry, athletic, rough and ready.

By comparison, Love was smooth-mannered and even then, at age sixteen, debonair. Blond and slender, he was about an inch taller than Lourie ("a cute little guy," says Lourie, "who had lots of hair") and enough boyish charm to have earned himself the nickname "Cupe" (pronounced *kewp*, as in *Kewpie* doll). A dapper dresser, Love had a statesmanlike way of carrying himself that made him seem almost elegant. The locutions of his speech were refined and droll.

Both young men had been raised in families that were Republican, Episcopalian, well-to-do (Lourie's father was the director of the Peru Plow and Wheel Company in Illinois;

Love's father was president of the Union National Bank in Johnstown, Pennsylvania). Both were easygoing, gregarious, and quick-witted. Both enjoyed the other's sense of humor, which in Love's case tended toward the biting, satiric comment, and in Lourie's case, the well-timed crack, turned on himself, or on Love. There was between them the constant presence of laughter.

Together, or apart (which they rarely were), they achieved enormous popularity among their classmates. They became leaders. During senior year, according to one classmate, "they pretty well took over the Class of 1918." Lourie was elected president; Love, secretary and treasurer. Lourie, who had been an outstanding sprinter back home in Illinois, became a star on the Exeter track team of which Love was manager. On the football field, Lourie's triumphs were legendary: As quarterback and captain of the varsity, he led his squad to victory over arch-rival Andover Academy two years in a row, scoring by himself the only points in both games. Love, the managing editor of the weekly *Exonian,* devoted lavish six-column spreads to Lourie's feats of glory.

Lourie had immense respect for Love's scholastic victories. ("Cupe was a star student, while I had a hard time passing Latin.") For Lourie, Love had unqualified admiration. Years later, when asked what qualities had initially caused them to become such close friends, Love replied: "I really don't know how to answer that except to say that I have always been a hero worshipper. All through Exeter, Lourie was the outstanding hero at all times." The rest of their class almost unanimously shared Love's admiration. In the class elections before graduation, Lourie received every vote except one in the "Most Popular" category. So Love, joined by a member of the football team, "went to see the rather insignificant bird who got one vote because we wanted Lourie to be chosen unanimously. We found that this little fellow had voted for himself because his father told him he wouldn't get a vote for anything, so he felt he had no choice. However, he was very happy to change his vote because I was accompanied by one of the big football players."

After Exeter, Lourie and Love enrolled at Princeton University, entering in the autumn of 1918 with a generation of young men who had been born with the century, raised in the horse-and-buggy era, and now destined to inherit the responsibilities of the thousands of slightly older young men who were being killed in the trench warfare of the Great War. Much as it occupied the center of their thoughts, the "war to end all wars" was not to be fought by the 475 men in the Class of 1922.

That autumn, they did not travel on troop trains bound for coastal ports for transport overseas; rather, their travels took them to Princeton aboard the one Pennsylvania Railroad train (consisting of an engine, a single passenger coach, and a baggage car) that departed Manhattan every day late in the afternoon. By twilight, their view of the passing countryside was growing ever more splendid as the inessential parts of New Jersey fell behind, revealing lush dairy pastures dotted with cows, and flat country lanes bordered by corridors of stately sycamores, and long lazy fields sweeping straight toward Princeton, where at last was offered their first glimpse of Blair Hall Tower—its majestic turrets and crenelated battlements suddenly rising out of the trees; its triple-lancet windows reflecting the last light from the west—conjuring up expectations of something proud, mediaeval, and mysterious.

The train came to an abrupt and final halt beside a small railroad depot at the foot of the Blair steps. This was the end of the line. Out on the low platform, the sooty, creosote odor of the car and the clattering of the train were now replaced by the vigorous evening air and the dignified sound of a distant bell tolling the hour across the tops of fluted spires and rustling elms. Lourie and Love were among the contingent of newcomers who stiffly ascended the thirty-two steps leading up to the shadowy, vaulted archway of Blair, through which lay the campus itself. The freshmen fanned out along the dusky paths, walking uncertainly toward cloistered courtyards and the pinnacled outlines of gothic dormitories whose darkened rooms were, as always, awaiting new life with the arrival of autumn.

But this year was to be different, for as Lourie and Love moved into a two-bedroom suite in 181 Little Hall, the last mournful notes of a bugler sounding taps from beyond the sequestered courtyard struck away Lourie's hopes for a winning freshmen football season. The Princeton that welcomed them was, in fact, more military camp than university. The campus had been requisitioned by the War Department to train men to fight overseas. The dormitories had been turned into barracks for undergraduates as well as for transient, uniformed army and navy personnel preparing to go the Western Front. The upper-class eating clubs had been closed, the 1918 football season canceled, the traditional college activities given over to martial order and discipline.

Each chilly autumn morning at 5:45 A.M., Lourie and Love, privates in the Students' Army Training Corps, fell in line for reveille and marched by rank to classes. They performed military drills every afternoon and stood retreat every evening in front of Witherspoon Hall. A fervent desire to serve in battle swept through the class, but for these men even the college war regimen was short-lived. On November 11, the bell atop Nassau Hall pealed the news of the armistice in Europe. Lourie and Love joined the triumphant columns of uniformed men parading up and down Nassau Street.

After Christmas, the campus returned to normalcy. Settling into the seasonal cycle of college life, Lourie and Love once again established themselves as important figures in their class. These were the days when it was common for undergraduates to speak of having a college *career.* Each man felt a sense of duty to raise his level of accomplishment year by year, to distinguish himself for the honor of the class, the glory of the university. This was a serious, passionate business, *the honor of the class:* Four hundred and seventy-five men—nearly all white, mostly Protestant, Republicans outnumbering Democrats three to one—finding satisfaction in individual achievement for the collective greatness of *1922.* "Why is 1922 Princeton's Greatest Class?" a class poll asked.

"Self-evident," replied one man.

"Just look at us," wrote another.

Look at Lourie and Love: By the time they graduated, their names were linked together at the head of the rolls of nearly all the class organizations and committees. They served together on the Senior Council (along with another Illinois classmate, Adlai E. Stevenson). They joined clubs together: Tiger Inn, the Right Wing Club (a campus political organization), the Varsity Club. Lourie seemed to be president of everything: Sophomore Class, Senior Class, Varsity Club, Exeter Club, St. Paul's Society, University Store, Honor Committee, Discipline Committee, Tiger Inn.

They roomed together in 181 Little all four years. "Although Lourie was always in training for either track or football and I was living a completely different life style," Love remembers, "we never had a real argument." What few disagreements they had were settled quickly by one man's saying to the other: "You may be right, but I don't think so." Lourie often attempted to get Love to quit smoking cigarettes: "I'd try to get the cigarette out of his mouth when he was lying down on his bed, but it never worked. Cupe was a stubborn guy." They were low-voltage humorists, never failing to keep each other alert to humility with a gentle shock. They understood one another with a kind of sweet simplicity. Theirs was a friendship uncomplicated by demands, jealousy, competition. Their emotions could be fused absolutely by, say, the anticipation of Saturday's game.

Autumn was their greatest season. Football was a matter of the gravest concern, the highest importance. ("On the presidential campaign of 1920 interest second only to that in football was displayed," the class historian would write for the 1922 *Nassau Herald*.) Their priorities were not surprising: In that pre-television, twilight era of professional football, college football was the arena of national heroes. Ivy League teams were often of the highest caliber in the country. The outcome of the Harvard-Yale and Princeton-Yale games were given bold headlines and extensive coverage in national newspapers and magazines. The quarterback of a championship Big Three team was an authentic star, famous throughout the forty-eight states; his greatest feats were told and retold until they had assumed mythic dimensions.

Enter: Donold Bradford Lourie, the star quarterback of

Princeton's undefeated 1920 team, with his best pal, Cupe Love, working the sidelines as the team's assistant manager. At 158 pounds, Lourie was the lightest man on the team, a fact which Cupe Love, a shrewd manager, made certain to alter before each game: "In the official football program we put his weight up ten pounds because we didn't want the opposition to know how light he was, and we put his age down a year so he wouldn't appear as if he were older than the average of the class. . . . During the years that have passed since that time, Don has come to believe that the age we published was the correct one."

Suiting up in the changing room before the last game of the season—against Yale—on November 13, Lourie discovered that he had left his lucky dime in his room. Since starting away to school in the East in 1916, Lourie had never been without the coin—not even during the football games at Exeter. He had always carried it in his hip pads; and now, here he was in the varsity changing room, only moments before the most important contest in his life, and the dime was far across the campus in his dormitory room. When Coach Bill Roper and the rest of the team were quietly informed of this fact by Lourie at the conclusion of Roper's fiery pregame lecture, Roper was immediately beseiged by every member of the nation's only undefeated football team—volunteering to retrieve the coin. Roper sent Cupe Love on one of the most important missions of *his* life: an all-out sprint, of over a mile, from the field-house changing room to 181 Little Hall, and back to Palmer Stadium, the enormous horseshoe-shaped arena on the outskirts of the campus.

It was a snappy, sunny day. At 2 P.M., Lourie took the field with his lucky dime tucked in his hip pads. (Lourie still carries that dime today—next to a plastic Hertz charge plate in his wallet.) From the sidelines, Love watched Lourie make a spectacular 47-yard touchdown run in the second quarter. It is remembered by a number of their classmates that the favorite and most oft-repeated cheer that day was: "R-r-r-ay, Lourie!" Working from a spread formation, Lourie was unsurpassed as a field tactician. His generalship during the game was characterized by Walter Camp in *Collier's Weekly* as "almost uncanny in its accuracy in disclosing every weak point of his opponents." It was a perfect game. The final score was Princeton 20, Yale 0.

Princeton could now claim the football championship of the United States. That night, Lourie was carried on the shoulders of his teammates in a wild, torch-lighted procession, which included the entire undergraduate population, winding through the shadowy campus and up to the central greensward behind Nassau Hall where, after the afternoon's victory, a massive heap of wood—chairs, desks, almost anything that was combustible—had been spontaneously foraged and donated to the pile, which now rose as high as the ivy vines clinging to embrasures of the dark third-story windows in stately Nassau Hall. There, Lourie was given the honor of tossing the torch that would set ablaze this bonfire of bonfires —seen only on cold November nights after Princeton has beaten Yale.

Afterward, the team was rated the best in the country, and Lourie was named First Quarterback on Walter Camp's All-American team (a lineup that included Notre Dame's legendary fullback "the Gipper," George Gipp). The best quarterback in the country, Lourie was also an international star in track and field. In England during the summer of 1920, the Princeton track team defeated the Oxford University team, and in another meet, Lourie won the long-jump championship of England, Scotland, and Wales with a jump of 22 feet 4 inches. When he was awarded the cup, one of his teammates loudly declared that Lourie would have also won the 100-meter dash—"if only his ears had been pinned back. . . ." He was expected to win the long jump again the next summer when the combined teams of Oxford and Cambridge came to America for an international track meet with Princeton and Cornell, but he was beaten, by three inches, by his top rival in the long-jump event, an intense, dark-eyed Cambridge sprinter named Harold Abrahams (who would later become a legend after winning the gold medal in the 100-meter dash at the 1924 Olympic Games in Paris).

Lourie was characteristically modest about his various accolades and his national celebrity. It was not until Love was elected manager of the football team in the spring of 1921 that he raised a glass in celebration: The eighteenth Amendment, prohibiting the sale of alcoholic beverages, had gone into effect on January 16, 1920. Lourie, however, was not the least bit chagrined by the new constitutional law because he had never drunk a drop of liquor in his life—at least not until this late spring evening when a friend of theirs named Edward K. Miller (whom everyone called "Dopey") came over to 181 Little, carrying a bottle of gin which was elaborately hidden in his book satchel. Lourie was reluctant to drink. Dopey made a persuasive case: "Your roommate is going to win his letter as manager of the team," he said to Lourie. "Besides, here's the last bottle of gin you'll ever see, so let's drink to Cupe." They all drank; it was not, however, "the last bottle of gin we ever saw," recalls Lourie.

Of other pursuits they shared in those days, Lourie remembers, "we liked girls"—though, of course, none was allowed to visit the campus, much less their room, unchaperoned. By the autumn of 1921, 181 Little had begun to feel like home. For the fourth year in a row, they had not bothered to put a rug down. The All-American quarterback and the manager of the best football team in the land had no time (and little money) for housekeeping details; and until long after each football game was over, they had not one free moment to get a date with the Swarthmore girls who came chaperoned to Palmer Stadium.

Their last season was disappointing. During the second quarter of the second game Lourie was injured in a running play. Love raced out and helped him off the field. When Lourie returned to command the backfield for the Harvard game in November, Princeton's 3–2 record had wiped out all expectations of another championship season. Lourie played brilliantly against the Crimson Tide, but he could not spark the team in its final defeat to the Bulldogs from New Haven. Nevertheless, Lourie was awarded Princeton's highest football honor, the Poe Cup, for his outstanding career as a student-athlete.

At the Senior Dinner that April, a candlelit, black-tie affair, Lourie received multiple honors from his classmates. The results of the traditional Class Vote (which gave recognition to the "Biggest Fusser" and the "Finest Legs" and the "Most Likely To Succeed," among other superlative categories) were announced, naming Lourie "Best All-Around Man," and "Best All-Around Athlete," and "Most Popular" (a category which involved a future presidential candidate: Lourie, 134; Trimble, 7; Stevenson, 6 . . .). Lourie was also recognized as the senior who had "Done Most for Class" and "Done Most for Princeton." Cupe Love was elected the second "Prettiest" and seventh "Most Brilliant" man of 1922.

During the banquet, Lourie and Love sat side by side, applauding and kidding one another. Celebrated individually, they had also become famous among their classmates as an inseparable pair. "It was like a diphthong," says John Reynolds, the class secretary. "We always thought of them together." There was no category among the senior statistics for "Best Friends" so the class devised a farewell gesture especially for Lourie and Love.

The nineteenth of June was a brilliant, sunny day. Gathered for their Class Day Exercises, the men in the Class of 1922 were embowered by the great trees on the perimeter of Cannon Green behind Nassau Hall. They formed a circle around the Revolutionary War cannon that was two-thirds sunk, muzzle down, in the center of the green. Within the circle, the Presentation Orator, a man of theatrical flair, was awarding prizes— some serious, some humorous. His name was Louis Edward Tilden, and together with his best friend, Russell Forgan, he had written the music and lyrics for this year's Triangle Club musical comedy. Tilden and Forgan were another well-known pair in the Class of '22; they had been named by their classmates as the first and second "Most Original," "Most Entertaining," and "Wittiest." The idea for the special tribute to Lourie and Love had been proposed by Tilden, seconded by Forgan, and passed after a secret, random polling of the class.

A roguish grin was now buttoned up in Tilden's jolly face as he called for Don Lourie and Cupe Love to step forward together.

Naturally, the legendary duo were already in tandem—a sight so familiar that it drew from the class a warm laugh, which turned into applause when Tilden suddenly slapped a pair of steel handcuffs on Lourie and Love, joining them together at the left and right wrists, respectively.

Lourie grinned, Love laughed, and Tilden announced that in recognition of Don and Cupe's extraordinary loyalty and devotion to each other, the Class of 1922 was hereby shackling them together so that even graduation would not separate them in their lives after college. There were more cheers. Lourie and Love raised their linked hands and gave a friendly wave. The steel cuffs flashed in the sun.

When the class seemed to have fully absorbed the joke, Lourie and Love quietly asked Tilden to release them. Tilden replied that the key to the cuffs had been misplaced. He announced that with all the excitement of the last days of Senior Spring, he had simply *lost* the key. So, following an even bigger laugh now, the handcuffed roommates returned to their places in the circle.

In fact, Lourie and Love spent the next six hours wandering the campus, side by side, captive to one another. In part, they spent the time looking for a way to get unhooked, and in part, they just strolled around, enjoying this last unexpected walk together before their commencement the next day. It was going to be strange, they agreed, to leave Princeton after four years among these people and these places and these things that they had grown to know so well: their cozy, rugless room in Little . . . the town kids whom they always helped sneak in to watch the varsity basketball games by boosting the little guys up to a gymnasium window near their room . . . the Victorian stained-glass windows in the School of Science on the way to meals at Tiger Inn . . . the clomp-clomp of the duck boards underfoot on the paths in winter . . . the wearing of black "dink" caps as freshmen . . . their first autumnal "cane spree" tournament—the pitched battles against the sophomore class, illuminated by the flickering light of burning brooms . . . the night when old Dickinson Hall burned down during houseparties weekend of sophomore year—they and their classmates had stayed up until dawn, trying to fight the towering flames as they spread to the Marquand Chapel . . . the bottle of gin Dopey Miller brought over during Prohibition, junior year . . . the wearing of golf knickers—their privilege now as upperclassmen . . . the Senior Singing on the steps of Nassau Hall in the spring dusk . . .

Mainly, however, their minds were on the future as they made their final round of the sultry, summery campus. Love was bound for the Harvard Graduate School of Business Administration next fall; Lourie was hoping to find a summer job in Chicago to earn enough money to buy an engagement ring for his sweetheart out in Athens, Illinois. It was time to separate.

They sauntered down Nassau Street to the police station, where, after the better part of an hour's work with a file, a sweaty officer managed to split the links of the handcuffs in two.

Forty-two years later, on November 7, 1964, Lourie and Love were again walking the campus, side by side. Since their graduation they had come back to Princeton together many times —for football games and class reunions and meetings of the university's Board of Trustees, on which both men had served, first as Alumni Trustees, and then as Charter Trustees. When there were board meetings, Lourie and Love always took a room together at the Nassau Inn.

Even in 1964, they were still two of the most inseparable companions to be found anywhere on the campus. Love remembers that one of their classmates who saw them together at Princeton that day "talked at great length about the Damon-Pythias relationship between the two of us." This visit was different from the others because they had come back to dedicate a new dormitory which was to be christened in a formal ceremony later that morning. The story of how it had come to be built had begun when the two young graduates had set out to make their mark on American industry back in 1922.

On his way home to Peru, Illinois, that summer, Lourie was hired by the Quaker Oats Company. He started as a trainee clerk in the accounting department. During the Depression and World War II he rose from the position of advertising manager in 1930 to executive vice-president in 1945. He was named president of Quaker Oats in 1947. According to the company historian, Arthur F. Marquette, "Lourie was an innovator, although not a believer in change for its own sake. Neither employees nor outside observers sensed any break with tradition when he became president. Throughout the period of mid-century growth and change, he sought to preserve the atmosphere of personal management."

As a chief executive, Lourie was much admired, not only by business colleagues at Quaker Oats (they describe him as a warm, modest, affectionate man), but also by leaders outside of industry. In 1953, John Foster Dulles persuaded Lourie to serve as his undersecretary of state for administration, a new post created by Congress. At first, Lourie was reluctant; the job involved a complete administrative streamlining of the State Department. In other words, Lourie would have to relocate, or fire, thousands of employees. After fifteen months in Washington, Lourie had turned a bloated, postwar roster of 42,000 employees into an efficient policy-making team by abolishing 6,000 jobs and transferring 17,000 more employees to other agencies. "I'd better get back to rolling oats before the company finds out how well it can get along without me," Lourie told reporters in April 1954, after submitting his resignation to President Eisenhower. In 1962, Lourie was elected chairman of the board of Quaker Oats.

Meantime, in Pittsburgh, after a start in the investment business, George Love had gone into coal. He became president of a bituminous coal-mining concern, Union Collieries Company, and then founded his own enterprise, the Consolidation Coal Company. He became its president in 1945, and a year later, chairman of the board. The company was fabulously successful; when a planned merger with the $125 million Pittsburgh Coal Company was announced in March 1946, Consolidation Coal was valued at $32 million. "I used to tell him that the coal business was decadent," Lourie remembers, "and he used to tell me that the oats business was decadent, so we didn't invest anything into the other's business. I never bought any Consolidation Coal stock, and Cupe never bought any Quaker Oats. But he was a very astute businessman."

Love was also a formidable negotiator. He became a major figure during the labor disputes of the middle nineteen-forties, earning the respect of both industry and labor leaders. A Princeton classmate once said of him: "Cupe is the only Coal Baron I ever heard of who took on John L. Lewis [president of the United Mine Workers, 1920–1960] in behalf of the entire industry, got what he wanted from him, and made the old war horse like it!" As an industrial catalyst, Love was much in demand. He became chairman of the board of the Chrysler Corporation, successfully reorganizing the company during the early nineteen-sixties.

As a manager of money, Love was even more shrewd than he had been as manager of the Princeton varsity football team. In 1926, he started a trust fund with the intention of someday giving to Princeton a memorial to his best friend, the outstanding All-Around Man and All-American quarterback, Don Lourie. Love neither told Lourie about the fund (he expected that Lourie, ever modest, would object to any kind of monument to himself) nor did he mention it to anyone else over the years. Through decades of Wall Street's ups and downs—collapses even—the Lourie memorial trust fund just kept growing.

Though they never went into business together, the two chairmen often compared notes (they talked by telephone at least once a month), shared opinions, and sat together on the Board of Trustees of their alma mater. (Even a partial list of the corporate boards of directors on which one or the other man has served reads like a hefty chunk from the *Fortune* 500: Chrysler Corporation, Consolidation Coal Company, General Electric Company, Hanna Mining Company, Illinois Central Railroad, International Harvester Company, International Paper Company, Mellon National Bank and Trust Company,

Northern Trust Company, Pullman Company, Pure Oil Company, Quaker Oats Company, Union Carbide Corporation.)

Characteristic of both men is their tendency to minimize their achievements in business. Lourie, for instance, refers to a laudatory, but rather straightforward profile of his career (published in the company magazine, *The Quaker,* on the occasion of his retirement as chairman in 1970) as being "pretty flowery." Love talks about getting "mixed up" with Consolidation Coal and Chrysler. "Those are the kind of euphemisms they use," says Lourie's son, Donold. "They would never say they were president of anything, or had won a ball game, or been captain, or anything. They just *never* talk about themselves. It's one thing they have in common. They have a tremendous sense of humility to the point of something more than humility. They simply do not talk about themselves or blow their own horns. And when they talk about each other, they sort of knock each other, kiddingly."

For two lives that had begun with the century, witnessing every major technological advance of an expanding, mobile society—from the advent of the automobile to the supersonic transport—theirs remained close to home, a pleasant pasture for frequent companionship. One of the happiest circumstances of their ongoing friendship was that they had married two charming and energetic women who got along well together. (Lourie married Mary Edna King in Athens, Illinois, in 1923; Love married Margaret "Peg" McClintic in Pittsburgh in 1929.) According to Lourie, "Marriage didn't change our friendship at all. Mary and Peg were very fond of each other."

The births of children—each family had one son and two daughters—were occasions for joint celebration and godfatherhood. Lourie's son, Don, is Love's godson; Love's son, Pete, is Lourie's godson. "The relation among the four of us," says Love, "has been close all these years." Donold K. Lourie, who graduated from Princeton in 1947 (the same year Lourie and Love celebrated their 25th Reunion), recalls the vivid impression made by his father and godfather's friendship when he was growing up: "I heard a lot about their friendship. In fact, I saw it in course of action because they really would hardly go anyplace, the one without the other, or the one without the mention of the other. It was a fascinating friendship. They were really very close, but I would say that outsiders, even family, weren't a part of it. I think it was something between them, not even between their wives, not really shared with an awful lot of others, except that other people would always see them together and think of them as Love and Lourie, Lourie and Love. Even the families were not that close —for example, I never have even *met* Pete Love, although I knew his sister quite well. It was just them really, sort of to the exclusion, in some ways, of others."

Every year (without exception), beginning in the nineteen-fifties, they went down to Love's country place in Miccosukee, Florida, where the two men hunted quail and duck near the Georgia border. Sometimes they went shooting with their wives, but mostly alone. Love, an avid hunter, was the better shot of the two. (Lourie tells of the day when there was some dispute about this: "The dogs were up on a point. And up came the quail. We blasted away, both of us—twice—we each got off two shots. I hollered over to Cupe and said, 'I got a double.' And Cupe said, '*I* got a double.' The dogs came up with two birds instead of four, and we had a big argument about who got the double.") When they entered golf tournaments as partners, there was, according to Love, nothing to argue about: "We are both poor golfers," he says. (Love will, however, admit to having won one tournament together.)

By the end of the nineteen-fifties, Cupe Love's secret trust fund had grown to a considerable size. Princeton had inaugurated a $53 million capital campaign. Although the alumni directors of the campaign did not know about Love's fund for the Lourie memorial, they paid a visit to Love in Pittsburgh. When Love heard their proposal—a substantial quantity of money that they hoped he could contribute to the campaign —he replied, "Gentlemen, this is the greatest compliment I have ever had. Imagine me being able to give an amount like that!" The meeting was adjourned; the matter left open for consideration. After a while, Love decided that it was finally time to release the trust fund, and, with an additional large contribution, to donate the sum to Princeton for a specific purpose.

Telephoning the campaign director, Love told him: "I've been thinking it over, and I think I can make a donation of that size, but there is one string attached to it—the money must go towards a facility on the campus named for Don Lourie."

So the time had also come to tell Lourie about the plan. Love telephoned him at home in Winnetka, Illinois. He was not at all sure whether Lourie would cotton to the notion of a building with L-O-U-R-I-E chiseled in its cornerstone. Lourie's reaction was instantaneous: He simply said that if any building were going to be built with his name on it, he would naturally want to put up enough additional money to have Love's name right there on the cornerstone beside his own.

In all the years of nurturing the secret trust fund, Love had never thought of that. He agreed that it would be a fine thing.

Lourie then telephoned the campaign director and pledged a substantial contribution of his own, specifying that his gift was to be added to Love's donation. The aggregate sum of $600,000 (roughly $1.8 million in current dollar value) would be used for the exclusive purpose of constructing a new dormitory named Lourie-Love Hall.

And so, in 1964, on this cool November Saturday morning before the Harvard game, the two former roommates were walking down to the south end of the campus to christen a dormitory that would be used by centuries of future room-mates. It was an unprecedented gift to the campus: Princeton had no other building which bore the names of *two* men, and for that matter, no two men had ever before given a dormitory in commemoration of a lifetime of close friendship.

And there it was: a low-lying, rectangular, grayish-brown, brick building, rising two stories high on the site of the old Goldie field. It had nineteen two-man rooms and fifty-five one-man rooms, which were arranged, by small groups, in the university's traditional multi-entry system. By Princeton's standards, the building's appearance was modern; there were neither spires nor gargoyles, yet an attempt had been made, with the entry system and the brick exterior, to design a dormitory that would be, in architect Hugh Stubbins's words, "a contemporary neighbor" of the older dormitories. All in all, considering the personalities of its two donors, Lourie-Love Hall looked appropriately unadorned, perhaps even modest.

At the outdoor dedication ceremony, Lourie and Love were seated with their wives in the front row. Along with the university's president, Robert F. Goheen, assorted deans, United Nations Ambassador Adlai E. Stevenson, and other members of the Class of 1922 and their families, they listened to their classmate, Russell Forgan, tell the story of their long friendship—particularly the highlights of their days at Princeton:

"Forty-three years ago this June," Forgan remembered, "the Class Day exercises were being conducted . . . and the Presentation Orator—a wolf in sheep's clothing if there ever was one—innocently asked Don Lourie and Cupe Love to step forward. Whereupon he slipped a pair of handcuffs on them to demonstrate how inseparable they had been through the four long years of college. After an appropriate period of time they asked to be released, only to be told by the sadistic emcee that he had lost the key. Some six or eight hours later, after various embarrassing experiences, they managed to find a policeman who sawed the links in two. . . ."

Though neither Lourie nor Love recalled having been especially embarrassed by their predicament on that afternoon in 1922, they both smiled, remembering the policeman who had labored to separate them—sweating in the sultry June heat at the police station, long before the days of air conditioning—and at the memory of the astonished look on the Presentation Orator's face when they returned his "keyless" cuffs to him later that day.

"The Presentation Orator who was responsible for their discomfort is here today," Forgan announced, peering over the rows of mostly silver-haired heads, which turned to look at Forgan's old pal, Louis Edward Tilden, who was himself now a distinguished-looking, gray-haired man. For a moment, Forgan and Tilden, the renowned Triangle Club duo, exchanged a merry, conspiratorial look which registered in the audience like the visual equivalent of a stage whisper. Then, reaching into his pocket, Forgan removed, and held aloft, two rounded, metal objects which might have flashed in the November sunlight had they not been somewhat tarnished with age.

Forgan disclosed that he would now read from an accompanying document which had been prepared by Tilden a few days ago:

> On June 19, 1922, Don Lourie and Cupe Love were shackled together with these handcuffs to perpetuate their friendship as roommates through Exeter and through Princeton. This was done during the Class Day Exercises. The key was inadvertently lost and file marks are evident on the handcuffs where they were severed. However, through the years, no handcuffs have ever been necessary for them to become even closer and more loyal friends and jovial companions.

The applause, which was led by Lourie and Love, resounded through the courtyard of the new dormitory. Grinning, the two old friends rose and gave a salute to the other pair of famous friends in the Class of '22.

"So we are here today to dedicate this building," Forgan declared, after telling the story of how Cupe Love's secret trust fund, along with Don Lourie's additional large gift, had become a dormitory named Lourie-Love Hall, "and through it to commemorate a very remarkable friendship between two very remarkable men. And now, in closing, will you please let your imaginations wander with mine to the year 2064. Two young Princetonians are roommates in Lourie-Love Hall, and their conversation might be as follows:

" 'Say, Bill, how come they named this building after two guys? There isn't anything else like it on the campus. Do you know the story?'

" 'Sure I know, and you could know too if you studied the history of Princeton in the library. But actually I learned the whole story in Professor Shorty McNab's course on the Demo-cratic System of the Twentieth Century: In those days, things were very different from now. For one thing, they had *two* political parties—the other one was called Republican. And in those days goods and services were provided mainly through private corporations—a misnomer, because most of them were owned by the public and had literally millions of stockholders. In those days when a fellow got out of college, if he wanted to go into business he often started at the bottom with one of these corporations, and if he had brains and ability, and stick-to-it-iveness, and integrity and guts, he could work his way to the top. And when he got there he was amply rewarded and he made money, and after he had paid his taxes he could do anything he wanted to with his money. And that's what these two guys did. They rose to the top of large companies. They had roomed together through prep school and college, just as we have—and because they were devoted to each other and devoted to Princeton they gave this dormitory as a lasting monument to their friendship.'

" 'Gee,' the other boy says, 'what a wonderful story! Maybe those old guys and that democratic system had something. Wouldn't it be great if we could do that some day?'

"And their voices fade away in the distance," Forgan con-cluded, looking up from his text. He scanned the faces in the courtyard, and his gaze came to rest on the two men in the front row. "In this uncertain world there is one thing about which I am completely certain," Forgan declared, "—and that is, that good deeds and the memories of good deeds are eter-nal. And, therefore, I am absolutely sure that the legend of Lourie-Love Hall will go resounding down the corridors of time, and that it will warm the hearts and enrich the lives of untold generations of future Princetonians—just as Don and Cupe have warmed the hearts and enriched the lives of all of us."

After the ceremony, Lourie and Love, and their wives and classmates, toured the hall, stopping for a celebration in Room 121, where three pairs of roommates in the Class of '66 were hosting a cocktail party in honor of the two roommates from

'22. One of the undergraduates asked Lourie and Love to step forward into the center of the room. Then, in a reenactment of Louis Edward Tilden's finest performance, the young man handcuffed Lourie and Love together again, this time with a pair of 29-cent toy handcuffs purchased from Marsh's, a drugstore on Nassau Street.

The two old roomies stood there beaming—four sets of crow's feet wrinkling the skin around their eyes—and then raised their linked wrists. The smile on Don Lourie's face made his ears stick out all the more. The hair on Cupe Love's head was now mostly gone.

At the end of that November day, the cornerstone of Lourie-Love Hall was sealed. Sunk in a vault inside the rectangular block of limestone was the original pair of steel handcuffs with which the two old friends had been shackled together when they were young. Engraved on one of the cuffs was an inscription that will be read—perhaps by archaeologists, perhaps by the great-great-great grandchildren of Lourie and Love, perhaps by another pair of roommates living in Lourie-Love Hall —when the cornerstone is opened in the year 2064:

> *Presented to D. B. Lourie and G. H. Love.*
> *Class Day Exercises Princeton 1922.*
> *So that graduation would not separate them*
> *nor interfere with their splendid friendship.*

II : INDEPENDENTS

Isamu Noguchi / Buckminster Fuller

1: The Nude in the Bedroom

There was a naked woman in the house of the future. Guests staying at the Roger Smith Hotel at 501 Lexington Avenue in 1932 were able to peep through her large window, directly into her bedroom. The Peeping Toms had to crane their necks, but what a view they had: She was slim and alone, lying belly down on her bed. Her left shin rested cozily on her right calf; her dark hair fell over her bare shoulders; her slender buttocks and thighs were completely nude. There wasn't a trace of clothing or bedcovers anywhere in the bedroom. It was hard to tell exactly what she was *doing* in there. Propped up on her elbows, she seemed to be reading, or performing some kind of peculiar exercise, or just lolling about, quietly reveling in her total nudity and the perfection of her house. Perhaps she was waiting for someone.

The hotel peepers looked on with varying degrees of suspicion. What kind of *house* was that anyway? They had been told that it was an ideal dwelling in which a family of five could live with minimum daily drudgery. The woman, apparently, could lie around on her bed all day because every household function was automatically taken care of by machines: Dishes were washed, dried, and returned to revolving shelves. Laundry was cleaned, pressed, folded, and stored. The toilets used no water; wastes were packed, stored, and cartoned for recycling by a splashless, waterproof, hermetic packaging system. The ten-minute "fog-gun" atomizer bath and shower required only a quart of water which was filtered, sterilized, and recycled.

Teeth were cleaned with a "vacuum brush." The firmness of beds was adjusted by compressed air. Doors were opened by a flick of the hand through a light beam. Floors were sucked free of dust by a comprehensive compressed-air and vacuum system. Air, drawn from the outside and centrally circulated, was cooled or heated to the ideal temperature—which was why the prototypic woman of the house could comfortably relax in the nude.

Still, to some of the hotel peepers, the spectacle of the naked woman was, if not quite eerie, considerably unsettling . . . *with all those machines stacking dishes, vacuuming teeth, sucking floors, and folding shirts, why wasn't there a single machine to put some clothing back on that woman?* This was 1932. And despite the fact that the house they were observing was only a beautifully detailed, dollhouse-sized, tabletop model of the eventual paradise—and even though the alarming figure on the bed was just a four-inch nude doll, illustrating the pleasures of climate control—there was something *freakish* about a house that would be prefabricated, transportable, hexagonal, cable-supported, suspended, automated, dustless, soundproof, bugfree, climate-controlled, air-breathing, light-distributing, floor-sucking, and, in the inventor's words, "high-standard functioning." *High standard?*—my God, the place looked like a nudist colony, possibly French, obviously the work of a crackpot inventor gone amok. *(A house that sucked floors!)* What kind of *proper* hotel, they wanted to know, would exhibit this kind of thing in public?

The Roger Smith Hotel was having hard times. Most of their rooms were vacant, a common plight in that era. Since the stock-market crash of 1929, the hotels in New York City had been deserted. Now, they had to bait their hooks. Hoping to attract customers, the Roger Smith public-relations men had converted the hotel's Grand Suite into an exhibition salon. They removed all the furniture from the suite except one table upon which was exhibited the large model of the revolutionary family dwelling known as the Dymaxion House. Even if the future did not look promising (went the wisdom of the public-relations men) people could still be lured in to look at the house of the future. And if potential customers didn't want to see the future, there was always the nude in the bedroom.

The hotel had an arrangement with the inventor of the Dymaxion House: Each day, he was to stand beside the tabletop model, discussing his patented invention with anyone who happened to wander into the exhibition salon. At night, when the curious had departed and the weary had presumably checked into the hotel, the inventor was free to go. But Richard Buckminster Fuller, the bespectacled, thirty-seven-year-old inventor, had no place else to go in the city. He had no luggage, no bed or bedclothes, no pillow, and very little money. So, each night, unbeknownst to the hotel management, he simply lay down on the floor under the exhibition table and took short naps, like a dog. Fuller had, in fact, developed a pattern of sleeping (one half hour in every six) by observing the way dogs slept at brief intervals whenever they were tired. In this manner, he was able to work around the clock. He needed neither much sleep, nor a change of clothes. He washed his shirt, socks, and underpants, by hand, in the evenings. He brushed his teeth without toothbrush or paste; a finger and a pinch of salt sufficed. He shaved with hotel soap. Like a living definition of his trademark—*Dymaxion*—Fuller was trying to do *the most with the least*. Mostly, he was trying to survive.

These nocturnal habits were observed by his friend, Isamu Noguchi, a twenty-eight-year-old sculptor who also had nowhere else to go. Despite good critical notices for Noguchi's recent show at the Rheinhardt Gallery, nothing had sold. He had been evicted from his studio, his work seized and impounded by a sheriff. Temporarily out of lodgings and money, Noguchi shared the Roger Smith exhibition salon with Fuller, sleeping on an air mattress while Fuller dozed under the table. It turned out to be such a good arrangement that when the Roger Smith public-relations men changed exhibitions, Fuller and Noguchi and the tabletop model of the Dymaxion House moved over to the Winthrop Hotel, and later, the Hotel Carlyle. Living rent-free, they were able to save a little money, but still not enough to afford three square meals a day. Between them, Fuller and Noguchi had just enough cash to buy doughnuts from a Lexington Avenue coffee shop, every other day. They never loaned money to one another; they shared whatever they had. It had been that way since their first meeting in October of 1929.

2: The Geography of World Men

Down a crooked stairway, in a basement below Washington Square South, there was a tavern called Romany Marie's, jointly owned and run by Puck Durant and Romany Marie. Marie was an exotic woman with a wise, gypsy smile and dark eyebrows arched like the zodiacal sign of Aries. She wore colorful, puff-sleeved dresses, and gold hoops in her ears; her wristwatch was strapped halfway up her left forearm to make room for an array of bright, jangling bracelets. Her place had the feel of an outlaw-gypsy caravan on the frontier of Bohemia. Smoky and dark, it was always jammed with artists, writers, radicals, mystics, Communists, and intellectual pioneers who came from abroad, and from all over the city, to engage in esoteric idea-slinging and political shoot-'em-ups. In its heyday, Romany Marie's was the main attraction of the event known as Greenwich Village. If you were an artist, fresh from a trip abroad, you went straight to Marie's to find out what was happening.

Isamu Noguchi was one of the regulars. He had recently returned from Paris after two years on a Guggenheim fellowship, studying, sculpting abstractions in metal, and working as a stonecutter and polisher in the studio of Constantin Brancusi. He was twenty-five and flat broke. He could no longer afford the luxury of making abstractions that didn't sell. To make a living, he began sculpting clay-and-bronze portrait heads of the people he was now meeting, among them, George Gershwin, Martha Graham, and others to whom he was introduced by Romany Marie. While abstractions had brought him insolvency and solitude, heads had the combined advantage of bringing income and new friends to his studio.

One night in October, Romany Marie introduced Noguchi to Buckminster Fuller. They shook hands just before Fuller began lecturing about his Dymaxion House to the intelligentsia at the tavern. The scale model was perched on a table beside Fuller. It was, the inventor explained to his audience, the prototype of a dwelling that would be economically mass-produced and deliverable, ready for instant use, like a telephone or an automobile. Suspended by cables from a central, Duralumin mast, the hexagonal structure seemed to be floating, free of the earth: *a house on a pole.*

Sitting on the floor of Romany Marie's, Noguchi was sizing up Buckminster Fuller's head. It seemed too large for the short, compact body to which it was attached, and too small for the exploding, fertile population of ideas it contained. Noguchi listened avidly to Fuller's proposal for a definitive solution to mankind's need for shelter. There was a kind of scientific poetry in Fuller's diction, a childlike simplicity in his manner. He had a voice like a Maine lobsterman: axiomatic, prosaic, yet oddly lyrical. Using terms little known in 1929—*ecological patterning . . . environment control . . . ecosystems . . . Spaceship Earth*—Fuller described the industry he envisioned: Thousands of Dymaxion Houses would come off assembly lines, whence they would be individually airlifted by zeppelins to any location in the world, remote or populous—even the North Pole (to which an Italian dirigible had made the first successful flight in 1926). At the proposed "building site," the hovering zeppelin would drop an explosive charge to the earth, forming a crater into which the mast of the house would be planted like a tree. Through the pioneering use of air transport, a forest of houses could be sown around the globe. "Ergo," Fuller remarked, "making possible World Citizenry."

World Citizens . . . comrades!— The Communists at Romany Marie's applauded Fuller's Dymaxion House. To others less radical, the house seemed like a technological Trojan horse from whose six-sided belly would leap who-knew-how-many unclothed, un-American World Citizens. In Noguchi's eyes, the most fascinating, revolutionary, and prescient part of the house was the technology that made it function as an independent machine, unattached to local resources such as reservoirs, sewage disposal, electrical power grids. Noguchi could see that Fuller was even more technically advanced than Europe's avant-garde architects. While LeCorbusier, for instance, had succeeded in embodying his "machine-for-living" aesthetic only in the visual structure and style of individual buildings, Fuller was proposing not one house that actually *functioned* like a machine, but a whole industry of such dwellings. The Dymaxion House was, in every sense, a truly mechanized shelter, designed like a self-sufficient ship—destination: the world. *Anywhere* in the world. More than all other features of the house, it was this triumph of adaptability that appealed to Noguchi.

Half-American and half-Japanese, and not quite at home in either country, but somewhat at home in both, Isamu Noguchi had spent twenty-five years adapting to the changes of terrain in his peripatetic life. He was born in Los Angeles in 1904. His father was the Japanese poet Yone Noguchi. His American mother, Leonie Gilmour, was an intellectual, blond, Bryn Mawr graduate of Irish-Scottish descent. At the age of two, Noguchi was taken by his mother to Japan—first to his father's house in Tokyo, and then to the seaside town of Chigasaki when his parents officially separated. His mother hoped to enroll him at Cheltenham, a British school. The headmaster, however, considered the purity of the English language a racial matter; children of mixed blood were not permitted to matriculate. Noguchi attended the local Japanese school.

In the afternoons, while waiting for his mother to return home from her job as an editor of *The Far Eastern Review* in Tokyo, his strongest impressions were of solitude and the danger of the nearby sea. He dreaded the thought of abandonment. He developed a keen sensitivity and devotion to nature; he knew where to find eels, and how to make whistles from willow twigs, and what to do with rose clippings, pump water, and rocks to build a garden of brooks and fifty rosebushes. At ten, apprenticed to the local cabinetmaker in Chigasaki, he became a skilled wood-carver, and learned to handle tools in the Japanese manner. His alienation from Japan began with a move to Yokohama, where his mother began teaching at Miss Manders School for Girls. Noguchi enrolled in a French Jesuit grammar school, St. Joseph's College, where he suddenly felt more foreign than the foreigners. (He so envied the security of the Catholic children who belonged to their faith and to God that he often secretly joined them in early morning Mass.) His mother recognized his difficulties as a child of mixed nationality. She decided, when Noguchi was thirteen, that he should continue his education in America, as an American, on his own.

For Noguchi, the renunciation of his Japanese citizenship (enacted on departure from Yokohama, he recalls, by the American consul mumbling over a Bible) seemed like banishment. He felt he had no choice in his dispossession; when his father, whom he had not seen for years, suddenly appeared at the boat to prevent him from leaving, his mother's will prevailed. The pattern of travel between East and West would continue throughout his life. When he met Buckminster Fuller at Romany Marie's in 1929, his deeply felt desire to belong somewhere had not diminished with time. He told Fuller about his envy of people who belonged to their native lands, and he would later write: "With my double nationality and double upbringing, where was my home? Where my affections? Where my identity? Japan or America, either, both—or the world?" Even as a full-fledged American citizen, Noguchi remained a wanderer, in his words, "a citizen of nowhere."

Buckminster Fuller, he discovered, had wrestled with similar questions (albeit for different reasons) and had resolved the issue by choosing *the world* as his home and laboratory. Although Fuller belonged to America, specifically to Boston and its elite institutions (Milton Academy, Harvard, the Somerset Club), he had philosophically renounced his regional ties in favor of a global allegiance which Noguchi found both reassuring and compelling.

In 1929, the geographic coordinates of Fuller's life were pinpointed by local places, but the course of his mind had already begun to girdle the globe in ever-widening degrees of latitude. One might expect the champion of World Citizenry to have been an exile, ashamed of his antecedents, embarrassed by his roots in privileged ground. Instead, Fuller was—and is—proud of his origins.

He was born in Milton, Massachusetts, in 1895 to the ninth generation of a New England family in which greater store was set by an individual's intuition than by societal tradition. The Fuller genealogy is a paradoxical document, featuring strong-willed men and women who were dissenters as well as up-holders of tradition (a contradiction carried down to Richard Buckminster Fuller, Jr., who inherited, at birth, both an innate mistrust of conformity, and the sponsorship of a Longfellow and an Agassiz for membership in the Somerset Club). Genera-tional continuity went hand in hand with the resolute New England conscience that sent forth Fuller's ancestors to vo-cally and actively raise their objections to the British Crown; to Harvard College's oppressive rules; to slavery; to the Con-federacy; to European domination of arts and letters; and to any doctrine that confined the power of independent thinking or restricted the rights of man. The ancestor in whom Fuller takes greatest pride (perhaps because he shares with her a strong philosophical affinity) is his great-aunt, Margaret Fuller —"The High Priestess of Transcendentalism," historians like to call her. As independent and advanced in her era as Fuller would be in his, she was a pioneer feminist, social reformer, author, critic, the first female foreign correspondent in Ameri-can journalism, and, as co-founder of the Transcendentalist magazine *Dial,* the first to publish Emerson and Thoreau. Her conviction that "a man should stand unpledged, unbound" became her great-nephew's birthright.

Four consecutive generations of Fuller sons had attended Harvard, but in 1912 the Yard did not keep the fifth one bound for long. By midyear exams of freshman year, Fuller was frus-trated by formal curricula and disillusioned by the impending doom, the sheer social catastrophe of not being invited to join the important Harvard clubs, most especially, the Porcellian. He was an athletic bust (he broke his knee in football practice because his legs were of unequal length) and a social outcast (*"Bucky, you're going to be a disgrace to the family. You're not going to get into any of the clubs!"* said his sister, Leslie, who was married to a Porcellian man). And with his large head, squat body, crossed eyes, and seltzer-bottle spectacles, he seemed to the clubable young aristocrats . . . *Let's face it, gentlemen* . . . an oddball.

To get even with his classmates, he began showing off by taking sexy chorus girls to supper at the Touraine Hotel in Boston. He accomplished this daring feat by appearing after a show at the stage door, equipped with Mitzi, his sister's alluring white Russian wolfhound. Mitzi was a tireless recruit, submitting to the eager hands of every showgirl who, naturally, stopped to fondle her. One of the girls who accepted Mitzi's owner's dinner invitation was Marilyn Miller, the beautiful *première danseuse* of the "Passing Show of 1912." However instrumental Mitzi was to the scheme's success, Fuller himself was not entirely lacking in charm or persuasive powers. Marilyn became his constant dinner companion. When the show moved to New York, Fuller cut all his exams, took Mitzi in tow, and arrived backstage at the Winter Garden theater. Agog with the glory of opening night, he invited not just Marilyn Miller but every girl in the chorus line to dinner at Churchill's, blowing his entire year's allowance in one shot. Harvard kicked him out for "general irresponsibility." He was readmitted the following year and promptly redismissed, not to return until 1962 when he was named Charles Eliot Norton Professor of Poetry, a post that T. S. Eliot had held.

Before his wedding, in 1917, to Anne Hewlett (the eldest of ten children of a prominent, energetic, Long Island family), Fuller joined the navy. As the commander of a crash-boat flotilla during the war, and afterward as an assistant export manager for the Armour and Company meat-packing firm, he became preoccupied with the problems humanity would face in the new, technological, postwar world he foresaw.

His final conversion to global thinking was precipitated by a series of personal tragedies and crises that altered his course forever. In 1923, his three-year-old daughter, Alexandra, caught influenza and spinal meningitis, then infantile paralysis. She died within hours of contracting pneumonia in November.

Fuller was demolished. He felt responsible for her death, which he believed could have been prevented if he had provided adequate housing and a properly designed environment. Nothing could assuage his guilt. He drank heavily and buried himself in his work at the Stockade Building Company, a business he had founded with his father-in-law, James Monroe Hewlett. Then, in 1927, the loss of the company, coupled with personal bankruptcy, brought Fuller close to suicide. He was living with his wife and newborn daughter, Allegra, in tenement housing on Chicago's Northwest Side, a slum area virtually controlled by Al Capone. Drinking, shambling along the shore of Lake Michigan in the long afternoons, Fuller considered himself an utter, abject failure. One afternoon, he faced what he later called "a jump or think decision." New England conscience stepped forward in that moment while he stood beside the lake. Instead of taking his life, he vowed then and there to dedicate it forever after to the service of his fellowman. He swore he would give up speech until he understood exactly what was in his mind and how it would be best expressed. Adopting a phrase Margaret Fuller had written in the nineteenth century—"I must start with the universe and work down to the parts"—he quietly began formulating the blueprint for a comprehensive design revolution. Fuller's brother, Wolcott, was not alone when he wrote to Bucky in 1928, saying: "I don't understand you. . . ."

In silence and contemplation (speaking to no one but his wife and daughter), Fuller continued to live locally—in Chicago, Manhattan, Long Island, and Maine—but he was no longer perceiving himself as a local man. His absolute commitment to global problem-solving, particularly the worldwide distribution of prefabricated shelter by air transport, led him to think about the world as if it were one town, connected by air routes, surrounded by one ocean. Fuller's comprehensive plan integrated the history, geography, industry, and economics of every nation—including the entire human race . . . *every girl in the chorus line*—into one "omni-crossbred world society." National boundaries were irrelevant to his grand strategy. "He was looking," Noguchi remarked later, "for new ways of experiencing the world; new ways, let's say, in living, in housing, in friendship for that matter."

By the time Fuller met Isamu Noguchi, he was ready for a

friendship that could exist, like his Dymaxion House, any-where in the world, free of boundaries, unfixed in time or place. In Noguchi, he saw an independent thinker who shared the vision of the one-town world, and who, like himself, had become a dispossessed, one-town-world man. "We were both independent thinkers," says Fuller. "That's the only thing that makes really strong friendships. Neither of us was homosexual. Our relationship was intellectual, not physical, right from the beginning. I was completely an independent kind of thinker, dealing in conceptuality and technology. And the technology I talked about absolutely fascinated Isamu, particularly what I had to say about light."

3: The Light in Seven Sittings

On a sunny day, there was so much light in Noguchi's studio that one could get a tan just by standing near the large win-dows which faced south and west. A converted laundry room at the top of the corner building at Madison Avenue and Twenty-ninth Street, the studio was neat and sparsely equipped on that morning in 1929 when Noguchi was prepar-ing his clay for Buckminster Fuller's arrival. At Romany Marie's, Fuller had responded enthusiastically to Noguchi's proposal to make a portrait of his head. The next day he came up to the studio for the first of seven sittings. "And that's where our long friendship began," Fuller recalls. "Those seven sit-tings gave us the opportunity to build up a friendship that just continued on and on."

They talked about light. At Fuller's suggestion, Noguchi painted the entire studio, including the ceiling, with alumi-num paint. Suddenly, it was a room without shadows, smooth and brilliant as an uncrinkled sheet of foil. Light was reflected everywhere. Bedazzled, Noguchi began work on the head. "I could hardly see what I was doing," he recalls. "All the light practically blinded me." Fuller sat soberly in the silver glare, posing. As Noguchi molded the clay (intending later to cast the piece in bronze), he mentioned to Fuller that he had been thinking about the negative and positive of light. Throughout history, Noguchi observed, sculptors had relied on negative light—shadows—to produce definition. Jewelers had been able to produce positive light reflections with the permanently reflective surface of nonoxidizing gold, a metal too expensive for sculpting. If cost were not a factor, said Noguchi, he would like to sculpt a head the surface of which was absolutely reflective, shadowless, and therefore, like the still surface of a pond, almost invisible but for its outline and whatever nearby objects happened to be reflected on it.

"Henry Ford," replied Fuller, "has just made a breakthrough for you." With excitement, he described to Noguchi the new, commercially available alloy known as chrome-nickel steel, which Ford had recently used on the radiator grille of the Model A car. The metal's surface was completely reflective, Fuller explained—its finish was permanent. Noguchi was enthralled. When he finished modeling the head of Fuller, he plated it with chrome-nickel steel. The result was a startling likeness, the surface of which continually changed depending on the environment in which it was placed. When a white sheet was hung around the sculpture, the head seemed to be a flat silhouette. When the sheet was removed, the high, gleaming dome of Buckminster Fuller's head reflected the world around it and seemed to radiate a light of its own.

4: The Geometry of Ladies' Men

To the casual observer of appearances, they were a puzzling duo. The Yankee Brahmin had a jawbone like the prow of a schooner. The Nisei hybrid somehow managed to appear Italian; his facial bone structure was elegant, angular, and fine. ("It was amazing," says Fuller, "that he came out like a Neapolitan boy. He looked like some of the figures you see in Michelangelo's work. Physically, he was very beautiful.") Fuller had a tendency, at times, to put on weight; Noguchi was perpetually reed-thin. Fuller almost always wore a ministerial three-piece black suit and a look of dialectic engagement with a superior intelligence somewhere in the cosmos; Noguchi, though mannerly and refined, was more casual in dress and demeanor.

Two thirds of Fuller's accent came from Maine, one third from the helms of handsome yachts; Noguchi's accent could have been fractionally divided among a half-dozen travelers in an international airport. And there were similarities: Both men stood five feet five inches tall; both were self-reliant, aloof, and vigorous; both were readily adaptable to any environment or predicament. Together, they were like a pair of cats who always landed on their feet.

They loved to prowl the city after dark. ("We walked everywhere," Noguchi remembers. "New York was a fantastic no-man's-land, especially at night.") Fuller liked the smells of the metropolis, the fruit stands, fish markets, leather goods, spices, and less so, the subway, to which access was difficult in that Depression era because of the homeless people sleeping in the stairwells. Their walks were long and brisk: Starting downtown at Romany Marie's; up Fifth Avenue, passing the Flatiron Building (a favorite of Fuller's); traversing Central Park; then up the West Side to the rocks and ledges of Washington Heights. From there, they had a view across the river to the glowering New Jersey Palisades, recently connected to Manhattan Island by Othmar Ammann's great suspension bridge, which was still nameless in its third year under construction. If it was day, they would spend a few hours on a rock, reverently watching the boomers spinning the steel cables back and forth across the silvery skeleton of the two magnificent towers and the 3,500-foot span that would soon be christened the George Washington Bridge.

Bridges thrilled them both. Combining their mutual interest in new technology, engineering, geometry, and poetry, bridges were, for Noguchi and Fuller, majestic symbols of aesthetic purity and structural integrity. More than any other, the Brooklyn Bridge captured the romance of skyward-soaring stress and tension. Fuller once said that he made it his "cathedral," the place where he "could get closest to the Almighty." He and Noguchi made frequent pilgrimages, crossing the wooden footway between the gothic arched sandstone towers. The spires of Manhattan churches were visible, the docks were full; the age of skyscraper and airplane had not yet transformed lower Manhattan. In the sunlight, the harbor seemed full of chrome. On the bridge, flanked by the tracery of steel cables, Fuller felt as if he and his friend were on top of the world, ascending the aisle of a sky-high temple. He was energized. Ideas came bubbling into his head, and he explained them to Noguchi as if to a throng.

Fuller's grand strategy for bettering mankind, quietly percolating since the suicidal hour beside Lake Michigan in 1927, was suddenly at full boil. Having cleared his mind of "other men's words," Fuller had emerged from silence and contemplation determined to explain nothing less than man's relation to the patterns and structure of the Universe. Like a publicist with mankind as a client, he was ready to tell everyone how, for instance, his Dymaxion House was going to provide shelter for people around the world. The question was: Who was going to listen to the ideas of a man who had been discredited by the academic, business, and architecture establishments, who hadn't spoken a word to anyone but his wife and daughter for nearly two years, and who was now speaking a myriad of incomprehensible words with a compulsion that approached messianic proportions? Not a few listeners dismissed him as an amiable lunatic. Even his brother, Wolcott, an engineer at the General Electric Company, considered his theories "nonsense."

At Romany Marie's, where Fuller was doing a lot of his explaining, one third of the table-sitters were intellectuals who believed that Communism—not a house on a pole—was the panacea for the world's problems. They were a lively but limited group on which to test out his ideas; Fuller could always tell when someone, with whom he had previously conversed freely, had become a Communist because they now had to talk the party line. A radical and a dissenter by nature, Fuller was nevertheless apolitical . . . *unpledged, unbound.* Doctrine of any kind was anathema to him. Politics were irrelevant to his grand strategy. He believed that world problems should be solved by "artifacts yielding maximum performance from available technology." The Dymaxion credo was based on his assumption that if you improve man's environment, mankind will improve.

To that end, he was tireless. Because his process of thinking was often dialectical, he needed someone with whom to investigate the truth of his ideas; someone who would give him a good, logical fight; someone who had the energy to listen commensurate with his own desire to explain. Noguchi fit the profile. Fuller recognized that Noguchi, though radical and sympathetic to his friends on the Left, was too independent in his thinking to join up with the Communists at Romany Marie's. Noguchi was adventuresome, unaffiliated, open to prophecy, ready to listen. Fuller was obviously ready to talk. "He *had* to talk," Noguchi recalls. "He may have thought an idea, but until he said it, he didn't quite know the shape of it. It was through the process of words that he found, gradually, what he was really saying."

Fuller's prophecies had the density of fissionable material. They were unstable with respect to polite society. Split apart in discussion with Noguchi, his supercritical mass of ideas produced a runaway chain reaction, yielding a fireball of words in the kiloton range. He could speak at a rate of seven thousand words an hour (almost two words per second) and continuously maintain that pace for sixteen-hour stretches over a three-day period. "He could also," says Noguchi, "drink anyone under the table. He was a habitual bar hound, and he was very disarming because, of course, no one ever suspected it of him." During frequent three-day-and-three-night dialogues, Noguchi was unable to keep pace with Fuller's marathon talking and drinking. ("It would never stop. I couldn't stand it. I would fall off.") Even so, Noguchi became Fuller's constant listener. Much later, he would regard the time he was spending with Fuller as his real education.

Like Fuller who refers to schools as "ignorance factories," Noguchi is predominantly self-educated. He considers his schooling in Japan, at La Porte High School in Indiana, and as a premed student at Columbia University to have been a waste of time. "I don't recollect a thing about it," he says now, "but I recollect very distinctly all the things I learned from Bucky." Noguchi also speaks with fondness about an educator named Edward Rumely who founded Interlaken, a boarding school

for boys near La Porte, Indiana. Modeled after European ex-
perimental schools, Interlaken emphasized minimum classroom experience combined with maximum exposure to
nature. The school's "daily ideal" was "to learn to know by
doing." Sent by his mother from Japan in 1917, Noguchi arrived at the school with a bag of tools under his arm, and
immediately began constructing a frieze of waves and shells on
a breadboard. He flourished under Rumely's guidance and
convictions, among them that "the greatest works of the world
have been wrought by the artist-artisan." Noguchi stayed at
Interlaken through the summer until the school was shut down
when Rumely was indicted for concealing the fact that he
shared ownership of the New York *Evening Mail* with the
German government.

Though Rumely was found guilty on December 8, 1920, of
wartime propagandizing for Germany (and later pardoned by
President Coolidge after serving a one-month sentence), he
continued to act as Noguchi's mentor, a relationship which
Noguchi valued. ("I have been very fortunate in having the
friendship of older people. Partly because I was never close to
my father, never really knew him well, I had these substitutes,
these friends, people who were interested in me.") Noguchi's
habit of using a formal appellation when talking with Rumely
was carried over to his friendship with Fuller. "No matter how
intimate we were," Fuller remembers with a smile, "Isamu
always called me Mr. Fuller. I would ask him to call me Bucky,
and he would say, 'No, you are *Mister* Fuller.' He felt that I
took the place of Dr. Rumely." Noguchi persistently acknowledged Fuller's status as the revered elder friend until the late
nineteen-forties when their nine-year age difference began to
seem less significant; Noguchi began calling Fuller, "Bucky."
During the following thirty years, the process of aging gradually equalized what had been for Noguchi "a considerable
difference." By the time Fuller was eighty-six, and Noguchi,
seventy-seven, both men would feel little or no disparity in
their ages.

In 1929, the nine-year contrast of ages did not inhibit Noguchi from occasionally contradicting *Mister* Fuller's inexorable

explanations of the Universe. He felt that it was crucial to maintain his own identity through skepticism and rebuttal. Having returned from Europe under the strong influence of Brancusi, Noguchi was determined to make his own way, philosophically and artistically. ("You can't be submerged by one person," he insists. "Bucky rescued me from Brancusi in the same way that Brancusi rescues me from Bucky. With Brancusi I had to object. With Bucky also I had to object.") As a foil to Fuller, he performed in the dual role of listener and contradictor. He was nervy and direct. Fuller responded to Noguchi's candor. "Bucky would take it from me. I don't know that he always takes it. I am not a yes man, but I am also an appreciator." Fuller agrees: "Isamu, being independent, would like to parry my thoughts, but he was terribly impressed with my technical thinking. Many times I advised him on what to do. When he was doing sculpture I often suggested that he do this or that and he would pay attention to my thoughts about how he could alter his sculpture. If I was saying something that appealed to him, he would do it."

Fuller came to Noguchi's studio at any hour of the day or night. He was living with his wife and daughter on Long Island, but his work kept him in the city during the week. His income was almost zero. The little money he possessed was spent on his family. (Noguchi occasionally went out to visit the Fullers, but, says Bucky, "He usually didn't like it; my world seemed to be too conventional for him. My family has liked Isamu very much through all the years, but in the early days they didn't understand each other too well.") In Manhattan, Fuller was usually flat broke. Food was a problem.

Romany Marie had offered him unlimited free meals in recompense for the furniture and aluminum cornucopia lighting he had designed for her restaurant, but Fuller, the prudent New Englander, was cautious about overstepping his welcome. He ate a bowl of Marie's vegetable soup every other day. And there were other guardian angels. One was K. Halle, a resourceful, attractive blond woman from a Cleveland department-store family who developed a technique for feeding Fuller and Noguchi, both of whom she admired and cared about.

If she was invited out to dinner by a rich suitor, she would ask Fuller and Noguchi over to her apartment at the Elysée Hotel for a drink beforehand. When the suitor arrived, she would whisk him out of earshot, apologizing for her mistake . . . *but you see, darling* . . . she had *forgotten* the dinner engagement she had made earlier with the struggling artists . . . and now, not wanting to embarrass them, they would *all* have to go out to . . . *some horrible little cheap restaurant.* Invariably, the rich suitor took the whole group to a fancy place and picked up the tab. That solved the food problem for the next forty-eight hours.

For housing, there was Noguchi's studio. Fuller slept on the floor. It was not unusual for him to awaken to the sound of classical music filling the luminous silver room, and the sight of a gorgeous woman posing for Noguchi. One of Noguchi's sitters was a rich girl whom Noguchi had persuaded to pose for a full-length figure, in the nude. The girl had agreed somewhat reluctantly, and because she did not possess a professional model's lack of inhibitions, Noguchi discreetly cloaked her in a sheet whenever Fuller was in the studio. Fuller came to think that the figure was more aesthetically appealing cloaked than nude. Noguchi agreed with him. Finally, when he executed the piece, he also did away with the girl's head and feet, much to her annoyance.

A serious artist with a sheaf of good reviews from his first exhibition at Eugene Schoen's gallery, Noguchi was also something of a ladies' man. He could be charming and witty, independent and cool; many women considered him sexy. "He was," says Fuller, "an extraordinarily beautiful young man. He appealed very much to very beautiful women. He sculpted about a dozen heads, and some of them were of great actresses who then immediately fell in love with him." Fuller himself had considerable charm with women. If Noguchi's artistic nature attracted a coterie of beautiful actresses, Fuller's energetic philosophizing drew to him a cult of admiring followers, mostly female. Their adoration embarrassed him. Social movements, political parties, cults of any kind, were repugnant to Fuller. He made a conscious decision to get rid of his "devotees." Deliberately, he began to drink excessively, and to act as obnoxiously as possible in their presence. By his own admission, he was downright offensive.

Though he successfully divested himself of cult worship, Fuller did not retreat into another period of silence and contemplation. He was a restless partygoer. He became a familiar figure at the artists' and models' balls of the Kit Kat Club, and at the famous Beaux Arts Balls at the Hotel Astor. Late on Saturday nights, if the mood seized him, he would come into town from Long Island, and round up a merry group for dancing and carousing in Greenwich Village. Sometimes Noguchi joined in the revels. The geometry of their respective social lives often ran parallel, intersecting the uptown and downtown circles of Society and Bohemia. ("We were independents," says Fuller, "so we had our own sets of friends, but we seemed to like the same people.") Rumors inevitably developed around their reputations as ladies' men. It was said that Noguchi, once returning to town after a trip, was upset to discover that Fuller had fallen in love with his girl friend. Today, Noguchi dismisses that suggestion. Their friendship, he says, though not always free from public innuendo, has never been hampered by private entanglements. "We never had any conflict with girls. We went our own way. And there was the age difference; nine years was sort of a protection. Friendship needs to be free of all those petty things which are likely to gum up friendship. I'm told, for instance, that money is one of the worst destroyers of friendships. I don't doubt it. I think that it is. But with Bucky and me, there is none of that. We are free of obligation and dependence to one another."

5: The Snows of Indiana

Independence is a word that recurs constantly in the vocabulary of their friendship. Individually, both men have striven for independence, lived by it, made it an essential component in the evolution of their work and the order of their lives. They share, as Noguchi puts it, "the idea of freedom—freedom from the restraints of the established way of looking at things." Freedom, too, from institutions, labels, formulas, and conventional methods of achieving success. Their respective careers demonstrate a persistent effort to elude categorization. Neither man fits a mold. Both have challenged the standard pattern of professional specialization as a means to success. Labels don't stick to their multifaceted careers. Architects have said that Fuller is a mathematician; mathematicians have said he's an engineer; one retired dean of engineering at an Ivy League university once called him "a punk who has appropriated the icosahedron." Fuller prefers to characterize himself as "a random element," "a comprehensive generalist," "a new former," or simply, "a verb."

He refers to Noguchi as "a visio-tactile formulator" or "a scientist-artist," but not as a sculptor. "Isamu," he points out, "learned that in the Orient there was historically no general concept of 'sculptor' as we know the word." Indeed, the diversity and abundance of Noguchi's accomplishments defy easy classification; no museum could ever exhibit more than three or four parts of the whole. Critics, commenting on Noguchi's "extraordinary range and scope," have called his career "the most varied and far-reaching in the history of American sculpture." His work encompasses furniture design, fountains, stage décor, portrait and abstract sculpture, small-scale objects, gardens, cemeteries, lanterns, public plazas, playgrounds, parks, and outdoor sculpture. Like Fuller's geodesic domes, Noguchi's "akari" lamps are acknowledged around the world as modern design classics that are accessible to multitudes of people. Yet to know Noguchi and Fuller only by their most famous creations is to understand them in part while offending the integrity of the whole. In the same way that they resist allegiance to one locality ("We both live in Universe," Fuller says repeatedly), their faith in the conception of their work as a continuously evolving *whole* is absolute. Their accomplishments, Fuller will tell you, are part of an evolutionary process. The moment Fuller and Noguchi achieve popular, critical, or commercial success with one phase of their work, they shake off the homage of followers, molt the approval of critics, and migrate, like birds, to another part of the creative world, as if acclamation—or loss of independence—were a harsh climate.

Though they achieve different results, the artifacts left behind after each molting season share a similar spirit of intimate service to mankind and nature. Noguchi's realized vision of "sculpture as environment" is so close to Fuller's Dymaxion philosophy of "creating artifacts to improve the environment," that one wonders why in fifty-two years they have never collaborated on a single project. Even occasions when they have simply contributed to one another's work are rare. In 1934, Fuller asked Noguchi to make the small-scale plaster models for his Dymaxion Car. In 1936, Noguchi was in Mexico City, sculpting his first major work, a seventy-two-foot-long wall, part of which would be a figure of an Indian boy observing Einstein's equation for energy. Having forgotten the equation, Noguchi wired to Fuller who sent back a telegram explaining $E = MC^2$ in precisely fifty words. Fuller published a cover photograph of a Noguchi sculpture on the November 1932 issue of his *Shelter* magazine, and later gave the name to Noguchi's sculpture *Miss Expanding Universe*. Elements of Fuller's tensegrity spheres and icosahedrons can be found in the tensile web of at least one Noguchi public monument.

"Why run the risk of jeopardizing a good friendship by doing something together?" asks John Dixon, a former associate and close family friend of Fuller's, who believes, "There was a deep intuition on the part of both men that their egos might be too overdeveloped for a joint effort." Yet joint exhibitions of their work in 1929 at the Harvard Society of Contemporary Art in Boston and the Arts Club in Chicago did not compromise their strict sense of independence. ("It was," says Fuller, "a beautiful coincidence: we were growing along together, people were getting to know about us as independents, and then they'd suddenly find that we were friends, and have us both show at the same time.") To get to the Boston and Chicago exhibitions, they piled Noguchi's portrait heads and Fuller's Dymaxion House model into the back of Fuller's Dodge station wagon, and drove straight through with Bucky at the wheel. Their single prolonged stop during the Chicago drive (and perhaps their only "collaboration") came during a heavy snowstorm in Indiana. The highway was impassable. Cars had skidded off the road. No tow trucks could get through to pull the cars back onto the highway. So, together, Fuller and Noguchi went out into the blizzard to devise, with every available resource, the simplest, most dynamically efficient, omnibipedal, regenerative energy system for securing the renewed forward motion of the now immobile transports: In other words, they organized motorists into teams behind the stranded cars, lowered their shoulders, and pushed. . . .

Shoji Sadao, a partner in the architectural firm of Fuller and Sadao, P.C., has been an associate of both men at various times since his graduation, *summa cum laude,* from the Cornell School of Architecture in 1954. He closely assisted with, among other projects, Fuller's Expo '67 dome for the United States Pavillion and Noguchi's 1958 aluminum sculptures, and he has, on occasion, provided architectural drawings for Noguchi's large public projects. He is in charge of Fuller's New York office which shares the same floor of a converted warehouse building on Long Island City with Noguchi's studio and office. The two large studio spaces are separated by a door. ("Isamu and I stay very close together that way," says Fuller, who does not, however, work in New York on a regular basis because his main office is in Philadelphia. "My partner," he adds, "really does a whole lot more for Isamu, almost, than he does for me.") Having been with the two men in a variety of social circumstances, and having seen them work individually, Sadao feels that it is best that Fuller and Noguchi never joined forces professionally: "When they are talking about philosophy and about their work on an independent basis, they can always keep it abstract. But if they were working on something together, and they got down to that point where it had to be either this way or that way, then I think there might have been quite a clash of personalities. With Bucky and Isamu being very strong and independent personalities, there might have been a conflict which would have been very difficult to resolve, or there might have been a parting of the ways."

Sadao, who is polite, reserved, and perhaps sensitive to the delicate balance of his close working relationship with both men, smiles when he says: "In a sense, too, I'm glad that a collaboration didn't happen because I would have been right in the middle of it."

Seeing Noguchi in his Long Island City studio, one does not envision a second creative mind naturally taking part in the sculptor's work. Noguchi dominates the wide, sunny room like an austere leopard, thoughtfully considering the prime moment to spring into action. When he does, his movements are quick and decisive. If he is interrupted by a request from someone on the telephone, his voice rises sharply, filling the room with the uncompromising, tart, exacting phrases of his reply. He bristles at intrusion. Time is precious. He is quick to express his impatience with the wrong turn of an assistant's hand. Things must be done just so. His manner is, by turns, brusque and cheerful. He seems delighted with his independence. In fact, so much so that the enjoyment of his own freedom allows him to contribute to someone else's work if the opportunity arises.

Noguchi has collaborated with his friend Martha Graham, creating sets and décor for her dances *Frontier, Appalachian Spring, Herodiade, Cave of the Heart,* and *Judith.* He says his contributions to her work have given him pleasure. "But with Bucky, curiously, there is no such thing. I don't know that he ever expects any kind of input from me. There's no demand on his part, or my part, that we should do something together. In a way, I have regretted that he's never suggested that I could contribute something to what he's been doing. There have been certain small things that I've been able to do for him. I wish there had been more. On the other hand, he's having this dialogue with the Universe and my subject is a far more constrained one. That's *his* way. So let him be. I don't try to interfere with him, and he doesn't try to interfere with me."

Like frontiersmen, they maintain their independence and high mutual regard for one another by staking separate claims. Still, their professional territories have subtle boundaries. For his part, Fuller does not regret the absence of full-fledged collaboration. He is acutely sensitive about the possibility of encroaching on Noguchi's artistic terrain. While acknowledging their mutual employment of new technology, industrial apparatus, advanced metal alloys, architectural craft, and similar geometric shapes in their respective projects, Fuller insists that he is the technologist, Noguchi, the artist. Whereas Noguchi readily declares that Fuller is an artist, Fuller, out of respect for Noguchi's talent, regards himself otherwise.

"I'm never going to infringe on what you're doing," he has told Noguchi more than once. "I'm never going to call what I'm doing an art."

Fuller is conscious, too, of refraining from declarations—even witty ones—that might lead to personal affront. He possesses a knack for writing humorous lyrics and verse suited to special occasions, often among family and friends, such as the verse he wrote about his wife's grocery shopping during their days of poverty in Chicago during the nineteen-twenties:

> *Lady Anne went to the store*
> *To buy food for a week or more.*
> *She bought an egg and half a roll*
> *And a nice red apple that she stole.*

Yet he has never written a single comic couplet for, or about, Noguchi. "That would be the kind of thing I wouldn't do because that would offend him. I would not make jokes about Isamu. My humorous poems have to do with idiosyncrasies and I would not discuss his idiosyncrasies."

Why?

"Because," Fuller explains, "I just honor him that way. That's his right to be that way—to have the imagination that he can fly."

6: The Greatest of Ease

Red-faced, sweaty, and exuberant, Isamu Noguchi was swinging on a trapeze in his studio one day in 1934. He propelled himself higher and higher, pumping hard with his arms, giving an extra kick on each backswing. The trapeze hung from the ceiling which was two stories above the floor in this corner studio at Fifty-seventh Street and Sixth Avenue. Fuller, something of an aerialist himself, had encouraged Noguchi to install the apparatus earlier that year. Fuller liked to keep his body strong; he was disciplined about fitness, regularly performing a series of gymnastic exercises he had developed. Noguchi had a routine, too. He loved the trapeze. He swung on it every day, back and forth in graceful arcs that made the suspended ropes creak and sing. Today, he felt as if he could fly. And he did: Rushing to the height of a swing, his back arched and his arms full of flight, he suddenly let go of the trapeze, and soared across the studio—straight into a wall. The impact smashed his collarbone.

Fuller tells that story, and another one like it, to demonstrate a point about the disagreements he has had with Noguchi. In the second story, Noguchi was driving to Mexico in 1935. He was driving a car that had, in fact, belonged to Fuller —a Hudson. Going broke again, Fuller had been forced to get rid of the Hudson. Noguchi had offered to buy it. He had never owned a car before. It was a great feeling to begin a journey west in his first car. He had a terrific trip. As he got farther and farther across the continent, and the horizon expanded, and the sky was suddenly huge, he got to thinking that he could fly again. He pushed the accelerator to the floor, and, reports Fuller, he got arrested time and time again.

"These were," Fuller explains, "the impractical sides of Isamu. His imagination could take him out of reality. He would use the same thing in our talks about politics. He'd go into these flights of the imagination. He supported ideas which I didn't think made much sense. I've always felt that he was unsound in his political thinking."

Political opinions have been the only recurrent source of discord between Fuller and Noguchi. Whereas Fuller maintains a resolutely apolitical world view, Noguchi has at times embraced the spirit of revolution. During the nineteen-thirties Noguchi believed that sculpture could be "socially useful." The wall he sculpted in Mexico City in 1936, for example, was intended to be a "Leftist, if not communist," political statement. In addition to the figure of the Indian boy observing

Einstein's energy equation, the wall depicted representations of a "fat capitalist" being murdered and of "labor triumphant." (Noguchi shared a laugh with a professor who watched him sculpt the wall: The professor's explanation of $E = MC^2$ was $Estado = Muchos\ Cabrones^2$ or "the State equals Many Sons of Bitches.") That year, the September 15 issue of *The New Masses* quoted Noguchi: "Capitalism everywhere struggles with inevitable death. All the machinery of war, coercion, and bigotry are as smoke from their fire. Labor awakens with the red flag."

The only revolution that Fuller deemed logical and effective was a comprehensive design-science revolution. To him, Noguchi's political beliefs in the thirties seemed impulsive and unsound. He took exception to Noguchi's rhetoric. But during World War II, when Fuller was appointed head of mechanical engineering on the Board of Economic Warfare, Noguchi came to see him in Washington and Fuller applauded Noguchi's dogged fight with the War Relocation Authority on behalf of the Nisei groups that had been interned in camps after the Japanese attack on Pearl Harbor.

Noguchi had been in Los Angeles on December 7, 1941, but, being a New Yorker, he was exempt from California's evacuation of Japanese-Americans to the relocation camps. Even so, out of a sense of duty to his fellow Nisei, he went voluntarily to Camp Number 1 at Poston, Arizona, a sandy wasteland where he stayed for seven months as an internee, designing parks, recreation areas, and a cemetery for the camp. Fuller remembers a train ride he took with Noguchi between Washington and New York after Noguchi was released from the camp on a temporary basis. It was the end of a working day, and the train was crowded with prominent government men. "Isamu was expressing himself very freely to these people in the passageway outside the dining car. He was giving lectures to the whole car, fighting hard and passionately. It was very beautiful."

Since the war, their only disagreements have continued to be political. They respect each other's convictions on many matters, and Fuller admits that Noguchi has taught him "a great deal about the philosophy of the Orient: For example, I once said to Isamu, 'Love is a verb.' He said, 'You can't say "I love you" because you obviously do or you don't. It's not something you protest. You don't talk about it.' " They thrive on testing philosophical ideas on one another in prolonged discourse ("a constant wrestling," Noguchi calls it), but when a political bone is thrown between them, it still gets picked clean, and nearly polished. Shoji Sadao recalls numerous occasions when he alone was present during Fuller and Noguchi's animated talks. The conversation would begin warmly, with reminiscences about common friends and recent situations in various corners of the world. "Then," Sadao reports, "it would always get on to a political discussion and I could see that they were taking opposite tacks. Each would speak out his particular point, and it would seem almost that they were going to get violent with each other, but then, at the end—not."

Their disagreements were resolved, says Fuller, by their practicing a form of benign acceptance. A gradual change of subject would prevent a decisive outcome or victory; neither man was determined to win the argument by converting the other to his side. Fuller cultivated a lenient disposition: "I'd never get very far in a dispute with Isamu because his were not sound arguments. I wouldn't try to overcome it because I could see that he was this way. It was clear he wanted to make a point, and so I let him make his point, and then I'd let it go because I really value our friendship much more than whether or not he wins those points."

The passage of fifty-two years has altered the texture of their dialectic encounters. Noguchi believes that while the particular issues of past disputes seem less significant now, the potential for disagreement is now more pronounced than before. In the early days, Noguchi was less apt to contradict Fuller because, he explains, he didn't have enough ideas of his own. With age has come a sharper critical readiness, a smaller measure of tolerance: "People generally become less tolerant as they get older. They're more fixed in their thoughts. Sometimes I have to listen to Bucky three times until I finally get it through my head what he really means. Bucky may be less tolerant; so might I. But our friendship seems to allow for this. We don't always agree now, but this has in no way detracted from our friendship. And that, I think, is rather wonderful. In fact, our very disagreements also make us better friends. Bucky is so surrounded by people who are only listeners and not contradictors."

As Fuller grows into his late eighties and Noguchi his late seventies, Shoji Sadao senses, too, that in the past decade they have become less tolerant of one another and more critical of the points of view they express individually. For instance, when they argue about an issue such as "the perfectability of mankind," Fuller is the optimist, Noguchi, the pessimist. The changes Sadao has seen in their relationship illustrate one of the reasons for its longevity: "There was a time back in the thirties when they were together in a close and intense kind of way for months on end; they were almost sidekicks. But most recently, it's been chance meetings. There's no obligation on the part of Isamu and Bucky. They're completely free. Their relationship has been very independent, yet both of them have grown in ways that support each other. They've stayed close together by being successful at changing. Each is pure in adhering to a certain sense of his own integrity, and they see, in each other, soul mates—souls who are striving for independence. Each one respects the other one for that. It's that kind of respect that keeps it going."

Endurance and survival have been the hallmark of their relationship since 1929. When Noguchi addressed the National Arts Club during the presentation of its gold medal to Fuller in 1976, he recalled the Depression days of camping out in empty hotel rooms together: "Bucky taught us all how to survive," he told the gathering in New York. "His ideas about survival were based on independence, and I learned from him that there was no need to carry excess baggage." The luggage they have carried between them is now lighter, and for Fuller, less restrictive than in any other friendship: "I've had other long friendships with people I met before I knew Isamu. But none were so philosophically free and so Bohemianly free in the kind of life we were leading." Noguchi attributes the survival of their friendship to "our freedom and lack of dependence, either on each other, or anything else.

"But," he continues, "that may not be the reason for preservation in friendship. There are other kinds of friendships. I don't question that there might be people who are friends because of their great need and dependence. But for Bucky and me, it's a free thing. We've gained freedom. You've perhaps often observed that very old people throw everything overboard and walk out naked. They don't give a goddamn anymore."

With this freedom comes deliverance from expectation. They neither expect to hear from each other at given intervals, nor to be on hand to share crises or celebrations, milestones or cocktails. The idea of being hurt if a birthday were missed is as foreign to them as Montaigne's notion of the perfect friendship in which "each man gives himself so wholly to his friend that he has nothing left to distribute elsewhere." Their belief in one another seeks no results. Fuller says he has assumptions, not expectations, about the way he and Noguchi treat one another: "Expectation is really anticipatory. I assume that Isamu and I—we really—I call it love; it's in love. If there's an occasion when I know he's sick, I'm going to call him up. Yet our lives have grown apart because he has so much to do, and I have increasing responsibilities so that I no longer have time for cocktail parties or even wonderful friendly visits of the past, but this does not lessen our love for one another."

If Noguchi turns up somewhere, Fuller will always make time for a reunion, however brief. In 1969, for instance, when Fuller was first presenting The World Game (a multiscreen strategic forecast and inventory of the earth's resources and its peoples' needs) at the New York Studio School, he uncharacteristically stopped himself in midsentence—Noguchi had entered the hall. Whereupon Fuller completely interrupted the presentation, and went up the aisle to embrace his old friend.

7: The Endurance of Triangles

Since kindergarten, Buckminster Fuller has believed that all nature's structuring and patterning is based on triangles. With the omni-triangulated spherical systems in his geodesic domes, he created the strongest, lightest, largest, most efficient clear-span structures in the history of the world. Even polio viruses were subsequently discovered to be structured by omni-triangulated geodesic patterns. "When I want to build something, and really make it work," Fuller once said, "I've got to use all triangles." Noguchi demonstrates a similar point by extending his arms full-length and clasping his hands together: His shoulders and hands become the points of the triangle; his arms and chest, the sides. "Friendship is a triangulation," he says, "of the shared vision of the world out there"—he indicates his intertwined hands—"and the two people over here"—he nods curtly to both shoulders. "It's not just directly between the two people. When two people can share a vision of the world for as long as Bucky and I have—that accounts for the friendship."

Perhaps their mutual perception of the world as a unified whole is, finally, their strongest, most enduring bond. They get around and they grow old; rapid mobility and old age have given them a perspective from which to see the biggest possible picture. International celebrity has provided a wide variety of intimate friendships for each man without diminishing or diverting their interest in one another. ("Here you have two men who have incredibly rich lives in the sense of the people with whom they've had relationships," says John Dixon. "Both men have known the high and the mighty in their respective lives, yet they've always kept in touch.") Today, episodes, incidents, and adventures they have shared with mutual friends are rarely dwelt upon by either man: Of the 1934 road trip on which the two men drove with Clare Boothe Luce and Dorothy Hale in Fuller's catfish-shaped Dymaxion Car—stopping to see Thornton Wilder in Hamden, Connecticut, before going on to Hartford for the out-of-town opening of Gertrude Stein's opera *Four Saints in Three Acts*—Noguchi recalls only that "it was quite an occasion." Of an entire decade of frequent mutual adventures, Fuller will simply say: "The sixties were seeing each other around the world. In Paris, Isamu brought John Huston to a lecture I was giving; then John and I went over to see Isamu's new garden at UNESCO. We met in Japan, in Italy, in India—we have mutual friends all around the world, such as Indira Gandhi who's very close to both of us."

Fuller and Noguchi depreciate the role of the singular anecdote in their common history because in their friendship, as in their work, they prefer to talk about the whole more than the parts. It is not surprising that Fuller, the first man to own a United States patent for cartography, frequently employs the word element *omni-* (meaning "all" or "everywhere") to describe whole systems such as an omni-crossbred world society or an omni-active friendship. He has been determined to give the world an accurate perception of itself as a unified whole. (He was using the phrase "whole earth" long before a counterculture generation of "Earth Shoe" wearers and dome builders came of age in the early nineteen-seventies with the *Whole Earth Catalog* as their bible and Fuller as their guru emeritus.) His Dymaxion Airocean World Map, patented in 1946, gave the first complete projection of the spherical world on a flat surface without visibly distorting the continental landmasses: Generations of students had previously turned weary eyes to the front of classrooms where Mercator's map was hung. There, they saw a world in which the relationship of landmasses became progressively misproportioned as one moved north or south away from the equator. In Mercator's projection, Antarctica resembled a wad of Kleenex stuck to a shaving cut on the chin of the earth; Greenland was depicted as the Big Sheriff of the North, appearing larger than all of Canada, when, in reality, it would fit into an area the size of Ontario and Quebec; the oceans and their shipping lanes seemed to be partitioned by Eurasia, Africa, and the Americas; the continents were displayed as barriers to the direct passage of ships. One couldn't blame old Mercator though. He was, after all, a Flemish cartographer whose map first appeared in 1569, the era of Dutch maritime empire building. But in 1946, one could finally, with Fuller's map, see a truer overall picture of one continuous world-ocean which surrounds one archipelago of continental masses. It is the map for a world unified by air travel; the straight-line projection of great circle grids demonstrate the shortest routes for global flight. "It is the world of the airplane, of speed—my world," Noguchi once wrote.

Over these migratory lines, Fuller and Noguchi continue to travel incessantly. Fuller has been around the world forty-eight times in this lifetime. During the last two decades, he logged an average of one hundred thousand miles a year, slept in two hundred different beds and airplanes every year, and wore three wristwatches on his arm—one set for the time zone he was in, one for the zone where he would be the next day, one for Philadelphia time. In 1981, his annual migration took him to seven different countries around the globe. Noguchi swept back and forth between the Occident and Orient four times that year. "I was much more a traveler than Bucky in the beginning," says Noguchi. "Now he's more a traveler than me. He is everywhere. I don't go quite that rapidly around, but I do still function in the world outside national boundaries, and so does he, but more so."

Fuller's widespread lecture schedule keeps him in the public eye eleven months of the year; Noguchi's public appearances are fewer and far between. Neither man, however, is an unwilling subject for attention. Reports of their activities appear with reliable regularity in the general news media as well as specialized publications. A mutual friend of theirs, who has observed their individual reactions to worldwide notoriety, says: "They are two of the most internationally publicized men of the century, so there's a comfort for them in that they knew each other before either one was famous, but Isamu doesn't have the hubris that Bucky has. I don't think Isamu takes himself as seriously as Bucky takes himself. Bucky is a completely public figure. Isamu is more private."

Privacy is a complicated word for men who attract publicity just by appearing somewhere for an hour. It is no small matter that their friendship took hold during the days when Fuller was called a crackpot and Noguchi was virtually unknown. A long-standing bond of trust is shared by two men who eagerly accepted and supported one another long before an adverse, skeptical world caught on to the value of their work. Though both men reject the notion that celebrity could ever alter their friendship, Noguchi admits to his preference for a private, one-on-one relationship with Fuller: "It's always been a great delight for me to talk to Bucky without the adulation of the crowd. I don't find Bucky's conversation with the general public always interesting. I've always found his conversation with *me* interesting. Other people whom I've known as friends—well, our interests have diverged. I don't see them so much. When I do see them, we haven't got really very much to talk about. But with Bucky, there's plenty to talk about always. His world, which has become international, happens to be my world. I meet him, suddenly, by circumstance, in strange places. He happens to be there, and I am there, and we continue our conversation. There's no break."

Fuller also talks about meetings in out-of-the-way places. When pressed for the exact year of one particular encounter with Noguchi, Fuller's face goes blank. Before his eyelids shut tightly, the eyes themselves gather intensity, as if this were a necessary provision for a long, solo journey. He is trying to remember. There is silence and contemplation. He is seated at the small kitchen table in his summer home in Deer Isle, Maine. His hands, which have been in his lap, are now raised to the edge of the table, almost in an attitude of reverence for the span of time under consideration. His palms are pressed flat together. His fingers are spread, and they are touching lightly at the tips. An ordered sequence of fingertip touching begins to repeat itself rapidly: First the index fingers come together, then the middle fingers, the fourth fingers, the pinkies, then back up to the index fingers, and so on. Thirty seconds later, he is still counting.

III : CHINAS

Duncan Spencer / George Cadwalader

A foggy night on the North Atlantic Ocean.

The two men aboard the twenty-foot sloop *Nimbus* have been out at sea for two days. The date is Tuesday, June 17, 1969. The sight of land has long since receded astern. The boat beats eastward—or so it seems. Uneasiness and doubt have crept into the cockpit of this small vessel which was designed exclusively for weekend coastline sailing. But here she is—on the first leg of an ocean voyage which her helmsman and navigator hope will take them to 42 North/47 West, and then on a great-circle track across the North Atlantic, destination: Ireland.

At the moment, however, the two men are silently anxious. In the past, they've braved through enough close ones, individually and together, to know that they both perform best (and, in fact, *thrive*) in the kind of tough, survive-by-your-wits spot that pits men against the elements. So they're not about to call this little situation an outright emergency. No reason to turn back now. Really nothing to get alarmed about—it's just that they're about seventy-five miles into their first transatlantic passage, and they're not exactly sure where east is.

The problem is the ship's compass. Before setting sail from Newport, Rhode Island, they inadvertently dropped a hefty steel anvil on the rim of the instrument. Never mind why a cumbersome hunk of steel had been brought aboard such a light, oceangoing vessel in the first place, or which man had done the dropping—the confusion of getting under way had been enough to bamboozle even the finest yachtsman. Curiously, the anvil is still aboard, and the compass itself seems unscarred; its red light is still glowing dimly. Nevertheless, they suspect its accuracy.

One of the men, a self-described amateur navigator, is harboring private doubts about finding Ireland. His confidence in his deviation figures is waning. The other man, the helmsman, seems less concerned about navigational precision. "Hell," he says, staring into the soupy muck, "just head east and we're bound to hit *something!*"

By and by they come abeam of the Nantucket Shoals light-ship. They can barely make out the word NANTUCKET painted above the waterline of the 192-foot vessel. She is the last light-ship on this transatlantic traffic lane—their last chance to swing ship and check the accuracy of the cardinal headings on their compass.

By sailing away from the stern of the lightship on a north-erly course, then reversing direction, sailing back, and repeat-ing this procedure thrice in other directions, they are able to confirm that the compass and their deviation figures are cor-rect. Relieved, they make one farewell circle around the de-serted lightship, then set their course for the longest leg of the passage: "085° true for 1,016 miles," the navigator notes in his log.

The helmsman retires below, leaving the navigator to stand the first watch. The cockpit is chilled with fallen dew. A few hours press by with the fog. Then lights begin to appear several hundred yards off the port side. At first they look like fireflies coming out of a summer gloaming. Then they become a bank of haloed lights, row upon stately row, glowing fuzzily above the water . . . and music? Yes, an ocean liner, en route for New York, is passing nearby, evidently unaware of the small sloop obscured by fog. The liner offers no salutatory whistle, but the sloop's navigator can hear an orchestra playing on her fantail. Peals of laughter and the clinking of glasses carry through the fog. Voices are audible. Soon the sound of these ghostly revels fades into the night, leaving emptiness behind. The navigator begins to worry anew about finding Ireland. Ahead is darkness and dawn and three thousand miles of ocean.

I

The two men had met ten years earlier, on a bright autumn afternoon in 1959 when the Yale University varsity crew team was assembled on the sloping dock beside the Housatonic River in Derby, Connecticut. Sprawled out on the sun-warmed wooden planks, waiting for practice to begin, the oarsmen were telling stories. The conversation was wry and humorous. A premium was placed on barbed wit, and there was one man, a junior, who dominated the proceedings and set the tone for the other oarsmen. He had not earned a seat in the varsity's first boat, nor had he ever advanced above the third boat, but this did not diminish his standing in the team's social pecking order. He was admired for his wit and personality.

His name was George Cadwalader. His background was the Main Line suburbs of Philadelphia, and his particular branch of the Cadwalader family (an old, native clan immortalized in Philip Barry's *The Philadelphia Story* with the quip, "One, my child, is a lot of Cadwalader") featured a long, unbroken line of military officers and genteel ladies. There was about him an aura of martial authority and a suggestion of Lindbergh-like, modest, old-fashioned heroism. He was a tall, handsome man, with bold good looks and an unyielding set to his jaw which seemed to say: "If you're going to do something, then by God, you will do it right and not give up." He was a dogged oarsman. He had strong arms and powerful legs, yet he could not seem to master the fine points of rowing. Nevertheless, he stuck with it. What he lacked in finesse on the river he made up for on the dock. With eyes flashing sardonically, and tongue double-parked in the neighborhood of cheek, he delivered lofty orations, sounding, at times, like an officer in the Grenadier Guards lecturing his cadre about the consequences of moral truancy. To the men on the dock, and one in particular, George's spirit was irresistible.

Duncan Spencer had been raised a gentleman. An excavation of his voice would have revealed a New England boarding school, a Scottish father, a mother whose maiden name was Choate, and the warm, civilized tone of a cello in a vaulted room. Of average height, he was lean and trim; with his high forehead and broad brow, patrician nose, Celtic blue eyes, and courtly manner, he seemed more like a sportsman of the nineteenth century than of the twentieth. He was the kind of man whom women of a romantic nature would be apt to praise as

"gallant" and "chivalrous." Duncan Choate Spencer was, indeed, the knight-errant sort. Yet pressed for self-description,
he himself would be apt to employ humorous self-deprecation.
("Dunderhead," for instance, was a favorite word of Duncan's.)
His earnest convictions about proper conduct and manners
were likely to be exploded at any time by a volatile sense of
the absurd. He had a huge capacity for the kind of lung-
seething laughter that ends with an eyeful of tears and pointil-
listic dots. His customary reserve often gave way to sly humor,
particularly when sharpening wits with George Cadwalader
on the dock.

Duncan, a sophomore, looked up to George. Having already earned a seat in the first boat, Duncan was high above
George in the team's athletic hierarchy, yet he still thought it
was "very much of a big deal" to be included among
George's friends and the fraternal jousting of the older oarsmen. It was, in Duncan's words, "an admiration type of
thing: I tried to trade barbs with George, who was sort of like
the old lag at prison—the old prisoner who knows everything
about the institution except how to finish his sentence and
get on to something else. Underneath his cheerful pessimism
everyone knew how hard he tried at his sport, and how much
he loved it even though he was never able to be a success
himself. In a sense, he was a prisoner of rowing. And that
combination of his cheerful pessimism, his failure to achieve,
and his good humor was immensely attractive to me. It
showed a strength that had nothing to do with the surface,
and I liked that very much."

On this autumn afternoon before practice, Duncan was
avidly listening to George tell the story of a recent run-in with
the crew coach, Mr. Radschmidt—with whom George had
never gotten along. That year, George had started an unofficial
parachuting club at an airfield in Bethany, north of New
Haven. Frustrated by his lack of progress on the crew team,
George enjoyed parachuting because it was, in his view, an
individualist's sport. He was by no means an expert sky-diver
—he'd made only a few jumps the previous summer in Pennsylvania—but he was a quick learner and an intuitive teacher

with a particular talent for instructing people in activities that require technical skill, courage, and derring-do. Following George's lead, a few of the star oarsmen decided that parachuting was the thing to do. Unbeknownst to Coach Radschmidt, the cream of the Yale varsity crew's first boat was soon pouring out of an airplane, plummeting earthward from a height of thirteen thousand feet . . . and *who* was in charge of these harebrained, daredevil stunts?—the coach wanted to know soon as word got back to him—Why, Third-boatsman Cadwalader, sir . . .

There was laughter on the dock now as George recounted how Radschmidt had reprimanded him. "Cadwalader," the coach had declared in an insinuating tone, "it's all right if *you* parachute. In fact, you go right on ahead and parachute as much as you want. But just don't ask anybody from the *first* boat to parachute with you ever again."

DUNCAN: *When it begins, friendship, I think, satisfies some sort of need for an alter ego. I had a feeling that George and I were close and kindred spirits, and everything seemed to work out to reinforce that. We became friends over the choice of a motorcycle.*

GEORGE: *I think we immediately shared a sense of the ridiculous.*

II

Their friendship began when George convinced Duncan that motorcycles were a sublime form of transportation. In the realm of technology, George was reverent, patient, impeccable—a perfectionist. He was the type of person, Duncan later observed, who would take apart a toothbrush and put it back together in pursuit of perfection. In this case, the object of his perfection was a 250-cc German-made Zundapp motorcycle which George called "The Mighty Zundapp." He was rarely seen in transit without his iron horse, so Duncan figured that he should get some kind of bike—mighty or not—just to keep pace with his new comrade. While George advised him on technical matters, Duncan began looking at secondhand imports. He fell under the spell of a Horex-Regina, an old German rattletrap that didn't have any notable features, but it ran, and that was all that mattered. George dubbed it "The Mighty Horex," and they were off. With the discovery of what Duncan later called "the shared romance of motorcycling," they became inseparable.

The Mighty Zundapp and the Mighty Horex took them everywhere. Whenever George and Duncan weren't in the library, they were in motion together. George was the sparkplug of the team, forever proposing plans, inventing procedures, initiating adventures. Duncan was perfectly willing, delighted even, to be in the role of George's follower. He was captivated by the sense of consequence and resolution that George injected into every undertaking. Rather than dawdling around the campus, for instance, George's idea of a great way to spend a day was following a course which would afford the two of them a spectacular venue in nature. It was crucial to have a mission. That was the main thing. To Duncan, it seemed that George was always on a mission. Raised on military and pentathlon sports, such as shooting, fencing, riding, George considered wing shooting one of the great gentlemanly pursuits. He thought Duncan should learn the sport. Roaring out of New Haven on the Mighty Zundapp and Horex, they blasted down to George's grandmother's farm in Norristown, outside of Philadelphia.

On the farm, George taught Duncan the proper way to shoot trap and skeet. Then, for Duncan's waterfowl debut, they went after duck on the marshes near the farm, accompanied by George's father and older brother. Medically retired from the Navy, the elder Cadwalader had been a captain in the Atlantic and Pacific theaters during World War II, and later an ice specialist in the Arctic Ocean. Duncan was impressed by Captain Cadwalader's "Wellingtonian deployment" of the shooters on the marsh. As he had expected, the Cadwaladers were excellent shots, dropping ducks from the sky with efficient regularity. Duncan, for all his efforts, managed to drop but one duck. He felt unfamiliar with the shotgun, and was impervious to whispered instructions because the more he blasted away, the more it seemed as if he had two quivering tuning forks attached to his ears.

It went like that until they came off the marsh after the shoot—a woodcock suddenly flew out of a hardwood stand. Duncan shouldered his gun, followed the low arc of the bird's erratic flight path, and pulled the trigger. A long and terrible silence fell over the Cadwalader cadre after the bird hit the ground. Duncan, meanwhile, was amazed, and not a little proud of himself. His knowledge of upland birds was not extensive, but he knew that the woodcock is a shy and wily bird, and that great prowess is required to drop one cleanly. Nevertheless, as he collected his prize and crowed about his accomplishment, the ominous Cadwalader silence continued.

After they'd gone in and had breakfast, George called Duncan aside, gave him a sympathetic look, and said, in his most solemn voice: "My boy, I hate to tell you this, but my father is a heartbroken man today. That woodcock you shot—that was my father's favorite pet woodcock. Don't be surprised if you are never invited here again. . . ." George continued in this manner for some time, and Duncan felt terrible about the whole episode, and was offering humble apologies until, as Duncan continues it, "I realized that this was a typical trick of his. There could never be such a thing as a *pet* woodcock, but when George puts the heavy confidentiality on you, you'll believe anything."

Likewise, when George's sense of mission and purpose turned to competitive games, a humbling, reprobative tone would come into his voice. According to George, "the competition was fun—it didn't matter who won, but the fellow who won was relentless in reminding the other of his failings and his dismal performance." Because of an ocular imperfection that affected George's depth perception, his skills were handicapped in games that required dexterous use of what he called "the little muscles between the hand and the eye." Duncan, therefore, would try inconspicuously to steer their rivalry toward tennis or golf. George solved the problem of rarely being able to beat Duncan at those games by heaping scorn on the games themselves, calling them (much to Duncan's annoyance) "effete exercises" or "ridiculous playthings of idiots and lounge lizards."

Well then, Duncan wanted to know, if golf and tennis were out, and the guns had been oiled and put away for the night, what were the proper pastimes for gentlemen sportsmen? The answer, of course, was exercises in strength and valor. There were any number of tests (mostly of the sword-in-the-stone variety) and wondrous deeds such as knights-errant of old were wont to perform. And after an evening of grog at Campbell's Oasis, the local bar in Norristown, what better arena was there for the Exercises in Strength and Valor than the barn on Granny Cadwalader's farm? For here they found a large steel anvil, black as coal, a truly mediaeval-looking object from which distinction could surely be acquired by the strength of their arms. After much dispute about the anvil's weight, it was agreed that lifting the thing above one's head would be the true distinguishing feat—the ultimate test of Strength and Valor.

Shirtsleeves were rolled up, biceps were flexed, lungs were inflated. George went first. He managed to lift the anvil to his chest. His brother, John, tried next and did little better. Then Duncan stepped into position, grappled the anvil, and, with his face reddening and veins popping, he hoisted it shoulder level and then over his head. He was quick to proclaim his physical preeminence. "Duncan's delight at having performed this feat was finally," George recalls, "even more remarkable than the feat itself."

When they rowed in separate boats during crew training on the Thames River, there was no outright competition between them. Their rowing styles were as different as their respective performances. While Duncan concentrated on the fine points of technique, achieving quick, clean strokes, George stroked with power, putting more force than was necessary on the blade of the oar. On one occasion when they were both selected to row in a special four-man boat which Coach Radschmidt hoped to send to the 1960 Olympic trials that July, Duncan increased the stroke rating to a high number at the end of a brutal three-mile piece. After the practice, they showered, and sat on the porch of the boathouse, cooling off. Duncan was feeling relaxed and clean after the sweaty workout and the shower. George turned to him, and said, "I just don't understand how you can crank it up to forty-two after a long piece."

"Well, George, has it ever occurred to you that I don't pull as hard as you do?"

George looked astonished, as if Duncan had betrayed some sacred trust not to put everything he had on the end of the blade during each stroke.

"When I'm stroking the boat," Duncan continued, "I have to remind myself that I'm the man with the baton in his hand, not the man with the tuba."

The next morning, they were out on the river again, rowing the four-man shell with Bill Cook and Tom Charlton (who had led the Yale crew team to a gold medal in the 1956 Olympic Games). It was a good combination of personalities, but the speed of the boat wasn't coming up right. They changed positions in the boat, and rowed up and down the river. Nothing worked. Another man was brought in provisionally to replace George. The new man made the boat go faster; there was no doubt about it. But they continued to shift seats until finally it was clear: George would have to go. Duncan and Tom Charlton broke the news to George. Duncan felt lousy about it, but to his surprise and relief, the cut was not a humiliation for George. ("It never would have occurred to him that his inability to make the boat diminished him in any way. It just didn't seem to make a damn bit of difference to George.")

George remembers those days at the crew team's training camp on the Thames River in Gales Ferry, Connecticut, as "good times marred only by my inability to make the first boat." It was considered a great honor to be "invited up to the Ferry," an oarsman's paradise. Reserved exclusively for two weeks of training before the Harvard race in late spring, the camp was a relic of Yale's opulent past. There were terraced gardens, slate-roofed Victorian gingerbread buildings with spacious verandas overlooking the Thames, and wonderful aromas from another century—lacquered wood, Coleo soap, and oiled brass, mixed with the timeless scent of sweat upon hard bodies. From the main sleeping quarters high above the river, the oarsmen had a fine view down to the broad wooden docks of the boathouse and the little stone pier where the launches were moored. Abutting on the main quarters was a well-clipped lawn upon which a course of croquet wickets was traditionally arranged by the crew captain. Croquet was perceived as the proper pastime for oarsmen resting between practices because it was presumably a sport in which injury was unlikely, though, in fact, not a few toes were broken when one player tried too hard to "send" another's ball.

Duncan and George were ardent competitors even on the lawn. Like other games that involved skill of eye, croquet put George at a disadvantage. To overcome his natural difficulties, he decided that one could always find a solution in technology. He located a large log, and fashioned from it a mallet to which he attached a handle. The face of this monstrous implement, which he called "The Super Mallet," was about eight inches in diameter, and with it he hoped to undo the conventions of croquet, or at least put an end to Spencer's victories. To meet the threat, Duncan devised skillful techniques of distraction and deception such as "The Thrown Mallet" and "The Feigned Rage" (while "The Foot" was busy adjusting the position of the ball). "The Dropped Handkerchief" and "The Loud Cough" proved less successful for harassing George while he took his shot than "The Mallet Wiggling Before the Eye." Finally, if all tactics failed, "The Thrown Opponent" (into the hedges beside the lawn) was an efficient method for winning the game.

The oarsmen never rowed in the heat of the day. Their regimen of practices at dawn and dusk allowed them free time to catch up on work or lounge like young lords. Duncan and George played gin rummy in wicker rocking chairs on the veranda overlooking the Thames. The only sight that spoiled the bucolic serenity of the view was the Connecticut Valley Power Company's coal-fired electrical generating plant, a half mile across the river. Duncan and George could see enormous piles of what appeared to be coal heaped up on the far bank beside the power station.

On the playing table between them large piles of vitamin pills were heaped. Obtained from the team trainer, the pills, numbering in the hundreds, were used as monetary tokens to represent their winnings in gin rummy. More exactly, the pills showed which man was the more unprincipled card player. Duncan's pile was the larger of the two. ("Two-handed gin rummy doesn't sound like a particularly interesting game," Duncan explains, "but if the rules include cheating, which they did in this case—we both agreed that cheating was permissible—it becomes much more interesting because it is very hard to cheat on an intimate friend. But it is possible. You have to work extremely hard at cheating on your best friend.")

Duncan's method was simple and brazen. By simply selecting cards as needed from an identical pack in his lap, he consistently produced the winning hand. George couldn't figure out how he was doing it. Whereas Duncan recalls that George attempted "amateurish" counterploys of his own ("He cheated abominably and clumsily from the beginning, doing such things as shortchanging the pot or ginning out with an incomplete hand and then quickly shuffling the cards"), George maintains that he never sank so low ("Being a high-minded man of principles, I refused to cheat, and Duncan took advantage of my high-minded attitude—he cheated like mad"). In any event, the time came when George owed Duncan some five thousand vitamin pills.

"Well, George," said Duncan, dryly, "how are you planning to pay off this debt? You know, fun is fun, but we both worked hard at our game, and you seem to have lost very heavily." Duncan suggested possible forms of remuneration—George's new BMW motorcycle, perhaps? Surely a share of the Cadwalader Trust would squarely settle the debt. . . .

"No," George replied, gazing across the river, squinting with one eye, "if you are willing, we will make one last bet to settle the whole thing."

What the hell, Duncan said to himself. He was sure he could swindle George on this bet, too.

George pointed across the river at the enormous black mounds beside the generating plant. "What do you suppose," he asked, "those piles over there are?" Duncan looked and replied that they were obviously coal. "What do you suppose they *really* are?" George continued—"*Are* they coal? Or are they *ash*?"

"For God's sake, George, of course they're coal."

"No," said George, "I believe they are ash."

"Cadwalader, you fool, you're going to lose more money," Duncan warned, but he was somewhat unnerved by George's confidence, and had to look again across the river before agreeing to the stakes George now proposed: Coal versus Ash; ten thousand vitamin pills; winner take all. They shook on it, and Duncan went to telephone the generating plant.

Over the phone, the plant manager informed Duncan that the piles on the riverbank were a particularly fine type of pulverized-briquette coal. Definitely not ash. So Duncan marched back up to the veranda to deliver the facts and collect on his fortune of vitamin pills.

George was unconvinced. He gave Duncan a sharp look, as if to ask how Duncan could be so naïve. "Well, of course!" George thundered. "The manager *would* say that. It's a disgrace that they've allowed so much ash to accumulate over there. That man has lied to you to save his own skin. It's exactly what I expected! Now that he knows that someone has discovered that it is not coal, but ash, he'll say anything to protect his company and his job."

Duncan was at a loss to respond to George's sophistry. He looked out along the riverbank and said, "All right, Cadwalader. We will row a wherry across after tomorrow morning's practice. We will land, and we will *examine* the piles at close range, and we will *see* whether it is ash or whether it is coal!"

The next morning, as they rowed across the river, George was telling Duncan how sorry Duncan was going to be for having made such a foolish bet; the closer they got to the far bank, the easier it was for *any dunderhead* to see that it was ash!

They landed, and George marched up to the foot of a black mound, thrust his hand into it, and declared: "See! What did I tell you? This is ash!"

"George, you're mad as a hatter! This is coal! *Look* at this stuff—" Duncan picked up a handful of the fine, black briquettes, and shoved them under George's nose.

Neither man could be budged from his position. For about a half hour they argued back and forth, picking more and more samples out of the pile to demonstrate the incontestable scientific properties that proved that the substance was to Duncan, coal, and to George, ash. Duncan's case for coal was based upon the textural compactness of the briquettes, and upon their shading, which could only be called—"Good God, man!"— *coal-black*. Meanwhile, George's line of argument included descriptions of combustion and high-duty electrical generating processes that produced ash of exactly this hue and texture. So beguiling and intricate was George's narrative that soon Duncan began to wonder aloud if this stuff really was coal, after all.

George was magisterial. "Well, my boy," he said as they rowed back to the boathouse, "it's lucky for you that I am a kind and generous man, because I am going to let you off this foolish bet you made, and I shall allow you to get out from under the weight of vitamin pills. You don't even have to confess in writing that you are a fool and a dunderhead for thinking that it was coal when, in fact, it is indisputably ash. . . ."

DUNCAN: *That tone—the lofty bombast and verbal jousting —became an absolute staple of our friendship. And it was his tone. I adapted my own tone to his. When I was with George, I would start talking like him. He was the inventor of the mode.*

GEORGE: *Duncan has a fine way with words, and we both had fun with the language, affecting bombastic tones. We evolved this absurd manner of speaking jointly.*

JOSEPHINE: Friends are mirrors to each other. I think there are times when you want to get to know who you are as well as who your friend is, and Duncan and George's whole dialogue had a way of providing an unobtrusive mirror. . . .

III

Josephine Spencer was home from boarding school for spring vacation in 1960 when she heard the fraternal percussion of two motorcycles roaring up the drive in Bedford Hills, New York. Even at sixteen, Josie's face was fine-boned and strikingly mature; she wore her long blond hair tied back with a silk sash. She was well-mannered, and painfully shy ("the terrified younger sister," she says now). So when her brother Duncan sauntered into the house and introduced her to his best friend from college, George Cadwalader, she said hello in a polite, delicate voice, then retreated. But not for long.

Duncan and George were so charming and mischievous, and such great fun to be around, that within a few hours, Josie was caught up in their activities, if not yet as a participant, then as a bashful listener, just trying to keep her ears tuned to the curious sound of their conversations. "It was wonderful to listen to them because they made up a mythology and a language that was entirely their own. It was a strange mixture of the Old Testament and new chivalric inventions. It was really a language of archetypes, and if you weren't an archetype already, you were elevated to that level as soon as one of them found the wit to do so. Their language resonated with a great sort of agrarian wisdom. They would talk in terms that were definitely Old Testament, often including God. Frequently, George would play the role of God—which seemed to become him more easily than it became Duncan."

On the Morning of the Second Day (for such was the Biblical ring that had been planted in her ear), Josie heard Duncan and George arising very early, and talking about going for a run along the wooded paths. Evidently, they were sallying forth not for a simple jog, but for Pain Before Breakfast. That was the way they phrased it. *Pain Before Breakfast!* So off they sprinted—on a mission to endure physical hardship because (she heard them say) *it was good for the soul. . . .* As the day continued, the terrain of their mythology turned Arthurian. Mundane household tasks became heroic undertakings. Josie was spending her afternoon quietly cutting the overgrown ivy from the facade of the house—a rather dull chore until Duncan and George joined her with ladders and set about chopping the stuff down, with the zeal of knights yanking knaves off a castle wall.

Talk about Galahad and Gawain. "The air was laced with destiny when George was around," Josie remembers. "There was a whole lot of visions of stoic knighthood. They talked all the time about heading off in the pursuit of glory. It was one of their catchphrases: *The Pursuit of Glory!* These great mythic slogans just rolled off their tongues." It seemed to Josie that Duncan and George characterized everything that way. Sometimes she felt as if she were watching a silent movie melodrama full of cliffhangers and title cards: PAIN BEFORE BREAKFAST!, and then she would watch them enact that scene, followed by MEN AGAINST THE ELEMENTS!, and, of course, THE PURSUIT OF GLORY! It was all rather wonderful, she thought. Together, the two of them made life seem full of promise: "They were both filled with a sense that everything was possible, and that the world must have great purpose."

The same was true of Duncan's father. A man of courage and high ideals, he presided over the Round Table at which George and Duncan shared the seat of friendship. Duncan McGlashan Spencer, known as Pat, had been an ace pilot of Sopwith Camels for the Royal Flying Corps in the First World War, and a colonel with the Combined Services Detailed Information Center, gathering intelligence for the Allies in the second. A Scotsman by birth, he was strong-willed, feisty, and outspoken—a distinguished, elderly gentleman whose abhorrence of war was often contradicted by the reverence with which he recounted his own combat experiences. He cherished formal codes of duty, honor, and loyalty; and to his three elder children, and his three younger ones by his second marriage to Louisa Clark, he communicated the importance of resolution in the face of difficulty, firmness of purpose in life, and the goal of perfection in all endeavors. He was chairman of the Fiduciary Trust Company of New York. His pleasure was in sailing, adventure, and family; he combined all three during excursions on his yawl. As a patriarch and seafarer, his demonstrations of pluck and fortitude were touched with humor. He loved to tell stories on, and about, the sea, and in his son's best friend he found an avid audience.

George became a favorite of Duncan's father. Whenever Duncan and George visited from Yale, Duncan The Elder seized the occasion to toast their athletic glories and to herald them both as heroes of his clan. He regarded their friendship with zealous pride. He thoroughly approved of George's strong character, firm principles, and military heritage. Duncan The Younger remembers that later in the decade the old flying ace began to perceive George as the shining hero, the perfect son, compared to whom his own son seemed "a rather seedy fellow." ("George would behave with immense deference, approaching my father as a student would approach a kindly, venerable tutor. 'Mr Spencer, sir,' he'd say, 'I'm doing the best I can with Duncan. I don't know if I am succeeding, but I've tried to steer the boy on the right course. . . .' And my father, being very much older than me, and on the edge of senility, would just lap it up. He adored George. He mythologized him as much as I did.")

"Why can't you be like George?" was Mr. Spencer's constant facetious refrain. Instead of taking the question to heart, Duncan would take George aside for a round of humorous reprobation:

"How can you be so low as to pull the wool over that poor old man's eyes?" Duncan would whisper, feigning horror at George's ability to project the image of a model son. "How much longer is this going to go on, George? When is he going to discover what you're really like, you unprincipled son of a bitch?" To which George would respond: "What do you mean? Are you casting aspersions on my behavior? Your father and I know exactly what kind of man you are. . . ."

And so forth, castigation heaped upon castigation. Listening to them, Josie noticed that there were equal parts of jest and authenticity in their principles about conduct, and in their reprobation of one another's alleged moral transgressions. "It wasn't just toeing a line on morality, but scoffing at it as well. Theirs was brusque, ironic humor, and like most humor, it often told what one couldn't find a way to say otherwise. That mode of theirs was a way of being close and yet private at the same time."

DUNCAN: *I think friendship satisfies everyone's need for unconditional love. In our backgrounds, George and I were quite similar in many ways. Both our mothers died when we were at an early age, and I'm sure I could shrinkologically figure out that both of us are to the other the love which is not conditional. We both make terrific efforts to preserve this friendship because it is an unconditional friendship, and neither one of us could possibly break it.*

IV

In the autumn of 1960 (George's senior year at Yale; Duncan's junior year), neither man was exactly sure what kind of career he would follow after graduation. George had enlisted in the Navy Reserve Officers Training Corps at Yale, later transferring into the Marine Corps training program. He had spent the summer in Platoon Leaders Class. Duncan remembers sitting in George's dormitory room one afternoon when George told him that he believed that the great men in history had been warriors. George didn't pretend that he himself was a great man, but he said that he thought soldiering was a perfectly legitimate occupation—in fact, probably the most important one if you looked at the history books. It was just the fault of the generation of which they happened to be a part that the military was held in such low esteem. But he was fortunate enough to have come from a family in which the virtues of the sword had always been upheld, and he seemed to think that, particularly in these times, the military needed a few capable officers.

Duncan was fascinated, for here was George—hardly a stiff-backed, crew-cut warmonger—a pacifist in fact—making a reasonable argument for soldiering without resort to any moral or political or patriotic fervor. ("It was an extraordinary thing. I had never heard anyone in my generation say this. But, of course, it was quite true. It made a very strong impression on me that this was an unusual and an unpopular choice, but probably a correct one.") To Duncan, it seemed inevitable that George would become a commandant of the Marine Corps, or a general like one of his ancestors. After all, a Cadwalader in every generation had distinguished himself serving God and Country, and the family's military pantheon included several outstanding generals: The earliest was General John Cadwalader, who commanded troops in the American Revolution and who had foiled Inspector General Thomas Conway's plot, the "Conway Cabal" as it was to be remembered—a conspiracy to usurp the power of Cadwalader's close friend George Washington—by wounding the conspirator in a pistol duel. Another was General George Cadwalader who led successful engagements in the Mexican War of 1846. Duncan was not at all surprised when George, using family letters and documents, wrote his senior essay about the exploits of General George.

George graduated in the spring of 1960, and received a second lieutenant's commission in the Marine Corps. ("I didn't go into the Marine Corps with any intention of staying; I went in with some reluctance. It would have been a disappointment to my family had I not gone into the service.") First, however, there was time for one more adventure. By summer's approach, George, as always, had a plan: The two friends would make the Grand Tour of Europe on motorcycles. Duncan began organizing the trip immediately.

Starting in Munich, they traded in their old bikes for a new pair fresh from the Bavarian Motor Works factory. They donned helmets, adjusted their goggles, and sallied forth in Pursuit of Glory. The first campsite they chose, outside of Starnberg in Bavaria, turned out to be a swamp. But the night was not a complete disaster because in the town itself they met an attractive, brunette, Fräulein who was vacationing at a nearby lake resort on the Vorthersee. The girl was by herself —but, says she (in a strange goulash of German and English phrases), the day following she will be meeting a friend of blond hair who will fill out the foursome, *ja*?

Ja! Ja! This seems like a stroke of luck—a friend of blond hair!—and after the brunette bids them *gute Nacht*, Duncan and George are up half the night, encamped in this swampy sump, arguing about which one of them will lavish his affections upon the mystery blond on the morrow. The brunette seems fine, but surely—they are both thinking—the Friend of Blond Hair will be even better. By morning, George has somehow dragooned Duncan into favoring the brunette. And so, their seduction plans laid, they arrive on the sunny shore of the Vorthersee, anticipating a day of *gemütlich* lakeside frolicking, only to find that their little foursome is, indeed, extremely filled out.

Duncan is all of a sudden delighted. George is horrified. The mystery blonde is not merely voluptuous, she is porcine, virtually *wallowing* on her beach towel. In the tire world, this friend of blond hair would be the ideal mate for the tubular-torsoed Michelin Man. However, she is smiling *at George*, and indicating through sign language that she would like him to baste her extravagant rolls of baking flesh with the enormous bottle of suntan lotion she has at her side, *ja*? ("It would have been," George later recalled, "like painting a barn. We parted company with the *schöne Mädchen von Starnberg* shortly thereafter.")

The nights were cool; the days were hot. The motorcycles gleamed in the sun. They covered long distances; four hundred and seventy miles was a good day. But George was not content merely to travel. He insisted that they have a mission. They had to conquer some mountain, visit some site, get somewhere. The mission was fully as important as the place they were going. That was fine with Duncan; he was game for anything. On the road in Northern Italy, they set their itinerary by singing lyrics of a Cole Porter song from *Kiss Me Kate* and following them:

We open in Venice
We next play Verona
Then on to Cremona
Lotsa bars in Cremona
The next jump is Parma
That heartless, tartless menace
Then Mantua, then Padua
Then we open again, where?
In Venice!

Mostly, they found their mission in the mountains. From the Alps to the Dolomites to the Scottish Highlands, George led the way. He persuaded Duncan to climb just for the sheer physical pleasure of getting to the summit. At night, they would set up camp near the tallest mountain in the area that could be tramped without ropes and equipment. They would stretch a tarpaulin between the two motorcycles, creating a shelter they called "The Pleasure Dome," which, when filled with rainwater, sagged within inches of their noses; occasionally it collapsed and drenched them completely. Early in the morning, they would survey the terrain, climb up, climb down, break camp, and move on to the next mission. Life was simple in the mountains.

In the countryside outside Vienna, they saw a storm blowing up from the east. They stopped at the side of the road and got off their motorcycles. George wanted to take a photograph of this dramatic scene. It was early evening. The rising wind carried the rich fragrance of freshly cut wheat. Behind them, the western sky was clear; the setting sun was brilliant. Below them, the checkerboard wheat fields rolled away under the blaze of the sun, contrasting sharply against the darkening sky on the eastern horizon. Facing the oncoming storm, George and Duncan stood side by side with their backs to the sun. When George snapped the shutter, their shadows, joined at the shoulder, were thrown long and purple onto the dazzling, golden field of wheat.

DUNCAN: *That summer was one of the happiest of my life. It was a summer of perfect freedom and simple, straightforward adventure. And I look back now on the summers when he was in one piece as the golden time of our friendship.*

V

When Duncan began his senior year in 1961, there were only 3,200 American military personnel in South Vietnam. Upon graduation in June, he received two documents—a Bachelor of Arts degree from Yale University, and a draft card from the United States Army. He registered with the Selective Services Bureau and was classified 1-A. Like many of his collegiate peers who were 1-A, he debated whether to apply for a deferment to graduate school, or immediately to fulfill the army's required two-year tour of duty. ("It was considered inevitable that one would be called.")

Duncan opted for postgraduate work. He went to Oxford University where for three years he read literature, primarily the work of the poet Spenser. Mainly, he rowed. As the stroke of Oxford's first boat, he led the team to triumph over Cambridge—Oxford's first victory in the regatta rivalry in thirteen years. During the summer of 1963, Duncan married Mary Macnaught, an architecture student at Connecticut College, whom he had met during his last year at Yale. George was unable to get leave to be an usher in the ceremony in Peterborough, New Hampshire.

Since 1962, Lieutenant George Cadwalader had served in a Marine Corps detachment aboard an aircraft carrier stationed in Norfolk, Virginia. He and Duncan corresponded intermittently. Though their letters reverberated with the lofty bombast and humorous reprobation of old, the correspondents found no grounds for philosophical or political argument about their respective attitudes toward the war in Vietnam. "As far as either one of us was concerned, what the other was doing was perfectly proper," Duncan remembers. "We discussed the war endlessly. I saw the war as a place where I would get shot and killed. George saw it, I think, as a means of advancement and a place in history. I think, too, he liked the idea of managing large numbers of men—soldiering was for him an adjunct to teaching. I know that I thought it was perfectly all right for him to think that he could get ahead by going over there, and I know that he thought it was perfectly proper for me to want to resist getting involved in the war."

Having grown up on his father's stories of near-death in two World Wars, Duncan loathed war. He decided that if, after leaving Oxford, he received notice of induction into the army, he would immediately enlist in the navy. (Duncan, after all, was a man who could—with a slug of rum and a few hours beside a set of crackling logs—recount in minute detail the brilliance and courage of Lord Nelson's tactics in the British naval victory at Trafalgar.) For Duncan, the sea held enormous appeal, though United States involvement in Southeast Asia held none; he was, by his own admission, "terrified of the war in a visceral way." When Duncan returned home from England in 1965, a graduate of Christ Church, Oxford University, America's commitment of military personnel to South Vietnam had escalated to 59,900 men. That March, President Lyndon Johnson ordered the first American ground troops into combat.

To Josie Spencer, a junior at Sarah Lawrence College in Bronxville, New York, the war seemed morally wrong but far away that spring. In May she hosted a large costume party at the Spencer household in Bedford Hills. It was a hot evening for costumes that were supposed to evoke the eighteenth century world of Tom Jones. Josie wore velvet. Duncan raided the cedar closet where his father's fox-hunting garb was kept. George, who was on leave from the Marine Corps, barely fit into a pair of Mr. Spencer's hunting pinks. The guests reveled all weekend. George left Bedford Hills on Sunday and reported to Camp Lejeune in the flat, scrub-pine wastes of North Carolina. Several weeks later, Josie drove down to visit him. To Duncan, and to other members of the Spencer clan, it seemed that a romance had begun.

Josie's view of her relationship with George differs markedly in retrospect: "I liked George enormously. There was something very special and atavistic about him. He was always the gentleman—a very loving person, and also someone who was idealistic. I went out with him briefly because he was going off to war, and because he was an old friend of my brother's, and we just saw each other a little bit. It was Duncan who had an overly dramatic view of this thing. He always had a tendency to want to see me marry the friend he was most attached to. Duncan is definitely one of the great romantics."

Indeed, to Duncan, the romance between his sister and his best friend seemed perfect. A protective older brother, Duncan had a fierce sense of territorial prerogatives concerning his sister. He had his own ideas about what kind of man she should marry. (Once, finding objection to a boyfriend whom Josie brought home, Duncan hauled the young man off to a corner for lengthy and intimidating grilling.) But *George and Josephine*—that was Duncan's vision of the ideal couple. "I was trying to matchmake like crazy," Duncan admits. "I thought it would be a very fortunate marriage for both our family and the Cadwaladers. I thought that the Spencers had a great deal to add to the Cadwalader ménage, and ditto the other way around. So I was very much in favor of this match, and in whatever way I could—maybe I made some blunders—I was always pushing my sister in the direction I thought proper."

Duncan also thought that this match would enrich his own friendship with George. Yet during what he perceived to be the delicate stages of a very serious courtship, he felt clumsy about discussing the subject with George. It was the first time he had felt that way. ("George and I had always joked a great deal about women, the way male friends do—'What's she like?' —that sort of thing, but when it's your own sister, it's a little bit different. So for that reason a seriousness precluded my ever talking with him about how things were going with Josephine. I took a very formal and lofty tone regarding their relationship.")

Duncan believed that George and Josephine were going to get married, perhaps when the war in Vietnam was over. It would all turn out, Duncan thought, as it rightfully should. No matter that the glorious destiny they shared in his view was different than Josie's perception of her future with George: "Prior to George's departure for Vietnam, Duncan was more enamored with the idea of George's going out with me than either George or I was. Marriage didn't seem particularly realistic to me, and I think that George went off to Vietnam thinking that he couldn't see his way to entertaining a serious relationship when he was going off to war, especially since my father sat him down and lectured him on this point—lectures my father gave were rarely forgotten by George."

Josie and George corresponded that summer of 1965, and they saw each other in Philadelphia during one of George's last leaves. They avoided talking about the war. Josie was increasingly skeptical of America's involvement in South Vietnam. With George in uniform, it seemed to her that the war was a difficult and sensitive topic to discuss. When either one of them referred to it, George would resort to his characteristic ironic humor. "He talked more about the discipline and process of military life than he did about the right or wrong of the war," Josie remembers. "I think he loved the camaraderie of the military. He had loved boarding school, and I think that the military gave him a sense of possibility of working with a group of peers in a structured environment where he felt comfortable. He talked a lot about his relationship to The Men. I think the military was, in a way, a recapturing of some of the sense of order that he'd had in boarding school, and I don't know that he found that anywhere else."

By now, 132,300 United States military personnel were actively committed to the war. In September 1965, Lieutenant George Cadwalader, USMC, received his orders. He was promoted to the rank of captain shortly after his arrival in Vietnam.

DUNCAN: *I was worried about George getting killed. Because*
he was my alter ego, I thought: God, why isn't he
as worried about getting killed as I am? But, since
he wasn't, I thought: Well, that's his lookout, isn't
it? And I thought he'd be clever enough to stay the
hell out of the way of any cannonballs that came
around.

VI

The news came one night that autumn. Duncan and his wife
were in Bedford Hills, visiting his father and stepmother and
younger siblings. Josie was there too. After supper, the family
gathered in the living room, and engaged in their usual evening activity—animated conversation led by Mr. Spencer. The
telephone rang. Neither Duncan nor Josie remembers who
answered the phone or from whom the call came, but the news
was unforgettable: George had been badly wounded in Vietnam five days before. He had been airlifted from a field hospital in South Vietnam to Japan, then flown to the Philadelphia
Naval Hospital. There was a chance that George would never
walk again.

At first, the Spencers all sat stunned. It had happened so
quickly; it seemed that George had just left yesterday. "Then
we went absolutely bananas," Duncan remembers. "We felt
like the family of a wounded soldier. George was the next
expected member of our family so it was as if a horrible accident had happened to a kinsman."

The next day, Duncan arrived at the Philadelphia Naval
Hospital and was shown to Captain Cadwalader's room.
George looked terrible. ("He had this awful pallor and he
looked literally like a slab of paraffin. They still didn't know if
his legs were going to come off or not.") One of George's uncles
was there at his bedside. The scene seemed extraordinary to
Duncan because George and his uncle were having the kind
of conversation one hears over Thanksgiving dinner between
distant relatives. There were long silences in this stilted col-
loquy; yet even so, Duncan found that he couldn't break into

it. Every time Duncan made a comment, he would get a look of stony disapproval from George's uncle. Then back the conversation would go to polite chat about relatives. ("And, of course, all I wanted was the most intimate possible conversation—to try to get back on base with George. When your best friend has been badly hurt, you immediately want to find out if the center of him, the core, is all right.") So, for Duncan, it was weird being there, listening to these two male Cadwaladers carrying on as if absolutely nothing had happened, as if George hadn't been wounded—as if the man wasn't lying there *looking like a wax candle.*

After a while, Duncan just sat down in a chair by the door. There was no conceivable way to interrupt this palaver. Finally, the uncle departed. Even George seemed relieved; he pantomimed wiping his brow. Then the two friends began to talk.

George seemed dopey from the painkillers he was being given, but he got right down to the bottom of it: "Looks like our motorcycling and mountain-climbing days are over."

Duncan didn't know what to say next. Mostly, he listened. "George told me about his injuries, and how he had been out on patrol with two other men. The man in the middle triggered a land mine. It was an American-made Claymore mine, designed specifically to produce the kind of injury George received. The man in the middle was killed. The charge went right across like a scythe and caught George between the knee and the ankle, and demolished both his legs. When he was taken to the field hospital, he discovered, by coincidence, another Yale oarsman, Jim Elting, who worked in the hospital and recognized George. There had been orders to amputate both George's legs, but George convinced Elting not to remove them. They patched him up, sent him to Japan, and here he was. Right then, I decided to visit him every weekend."

During the next eighteen months, as George underwent surgery and therapy to rehabilitate his legs, Duncan regularly shuttled up to the hospital from Washington, where he had begun work at *The Washington Star.* After several months, George was reviving. Duncan noticed that the color was returning to his face. On several occasions Duncan noticed on his arrival that George was avidly perusing the Sears Roebuck catalogue (tools were a lifelong love of George's) and calling up the ordering division, requesting to see this or that tool.

Though George had become an admired figure on his ward, Duncan worried about the attention George was receiving in this vast and grim veterans' hospital. The cries of men in pain, which Duncan heard in the halls, made a searing impression. But about the time that George's wit resurfaced, a fictive nurse began to appear on the scene—"Nurse Comely" —who George said would come to attend the young warriors every evening after lights-out. Whenever Duncan seemed anxious about George's care, George would tell him about Nurse Comely and how she had been lavishing her attentions on him: All was well, George would report—Duncan should tell Josephine that he wasn't in any need; Nurse Comely's gentle white hand had been taking care of all his wants for she was pleased and proud to attend the young warriors, like himself, who were momentarily inconvenienced by wounds. . . . There seemed to be no end to Nurse Comely's merciful missions, or to George's incredible ability to light up this grim place where real *Pain Before Breakfast* was followed by *Pain Before, During, and After Lunch and Dinner.*

"He had a capacity, that was really awesome, to be filled with this droll humor even when he was in great pain," Josie remembers. She, too, was visiting George frequently. A senior at Sarah Lawrence, Josie had become involved in the peace movement. That winter, she organized, at Sarah Lawrence, a large conference in which representatives from the Department of State, the United Nations, and various organizations discussed international disarmament and the problem of ending the war in Southeast Asia. On weekends, she drove down to Philadelphia to see George in the hospital.

Sometimes she found George alone; sometimes her visits coincided with Duncan's. She remembers it as a difficult time for all three of them. The issues of the war were never discussed. The subject of marriage was just as delicate a topic. "I think I became more of a romantic image to George while he was in the hospital. The idea really blossomed in his mind then, and there was no arguing with somebody who was in great pain, heavily drugged, and very lonely. I think Duncan did more to promote the idea of marriage than I did. I can remember occasionally giving sidelong kicks to Duncan in the hospital because I didn't want that idea encouraged. It took a long time for Duncan to figure out that I didn't always do what he wanted me to do. And it took a long time for Duncan to figure out that *the world* didn't always do what he wanted it to do. For George, that struck him sooner. But for Duncan, it was still all part of that sense of endless possibility and the pursuit of glory."

In time, it became evident that George and Josie were not going to marry. Duncan was disheartened. He didn't discuss the situation with George. Having remained at a distance throughout the romance, Duncan was therefore not privy to what had gone awry. As he later told about it: "Everything had seemed so perfect. When the miscarriage of the marriage took place, I was off balance. I didn't feel like talking about it. I suppose I should have. I divined what had happened and I didn't like it at all. But I got it all wrong. I thought that Josephine had decided that she couldn't put up with this long incarceration in the hospital. Then, only later, I found out that it was he who broke it off—the marriage became impossible for the ridiculous reason that he would not allow himself to marry somebody because they would always be stuck with a cripple. He never said this, but I knew that he felt it would be an imposition on my sister."

Neither George nor Josie would later agree that Duncan's perception of events was accurate. But both would confirm that, in the long run, Duncan's disappointment was the greatest of the three. Indeed, years afterward, Duncan would say: "I suppose the only thing that would make our friendship more perfect is if George had married my sister. That would have been a great thing. I thought it would be the ideal. It was a terrible disappointment to me, though I would never admit that to him." In succeeding years, on the rare occasions when

Duncan brought up the subject, he would always resort to the old lofty tones of humorous bombast so that George could toss it back lightly:

"You were certainly an asshole not to marry my sister," Duncan would say. "That was one of the biggest mistakes you ever made."

"My boy," George would reply, furrowing his brow, "the last time you gave me advice about sex, I was in the hospital for three weeks."

DUNCAN: Our friendship has always progressed along a formal line. The formal line is symbolized by this form of conversation that we fall into, and the way we might approach a serious problem in a light way. There definitely is a code there that has not been broken. And when it is broken—as it once was in the boatyard in Annapolis—it's a calamity.

VII

At first, it was just another of their adventurous ideas—something to dream about during that turbulent summer of 1968. In June, George had bought a sloop at Arnie Gay's shipyard on Spar Creek in Annapolis, Maryland. Promoted to the rank of major, he was now married and teaching at the Naval Academy at Annapolis, where he had met his wife, Yara, a skilled pianist from Brazil, who translated Portugese documents at the academy. On summer weekends, Duncan came out from Washington to sail the Chesapeake Bay in this new boat that George had christened *Nimbus.*

She was a little boat. Twenty feet of length, seven feet of beam, eighteen feet at the waterline, the Cal-20 was a fiberglass, fin-keeled, outboard-rudder sloop designed for simple day sailing. George and Duncan had another idea about her potential. Just for the sake of discussion, they began to wonder aloud about *Nimbus*'s capabilities on, say, the long ocean passage to Ireland. They wondered about design modifications, heavy rigging, and new outfitting. They tried to reckon which dangers would most threaten their lives on a voyage for which the Cal-20 had obviously not been intended.

Yet exciting as it was, all this wondering and reckoning was done very quietly. A transatlantic voyage in a twenty-footer was evidently not a good thing to discuss loudly or casually among friends and acquaintances, for as soon as the inevitable question about the boat's size was answered, polite interest turned to shock followed by what Duncan came to recognize as The Dead Man's Look, "a searching glance that showed the great interest human beings, whose deaths are vague but inevitable, take in those fellow mortals whose deaths are inevitable and nearby."

George and Duncan knew why they wanted to sail a twenty-foot sloop to Ireland and they never had to voice their reasons. They both shared a love of the sea—its arcane history, literature, language, idiosyncrasies, and endless challenges. And—of all the physical pursuits they had engaged in, sailing was the only one they had never shared. Mainly, Duncan recalled, "we began thinking about a transatlantic passage for the simple reason of wanting to have another adventure. The whole spectrum of this friendship had been altered completely by George getting crippled in Vietnam. Before he was wounded, it was a whole different world. And we were so fond of our old adventures, and having seen them come to this abrupt and fatal halt, we had to have some other venue for the physical side of our friendship to survive. That may have never been spoken, but it was clear to both of us: There had to be some other world in which we would both be comfortable, and it obviously was not going to be motorcycling. It was not going to be hiking. It was not going to be wing shooting or mountain climbing or rowing. All those things were suddenly thrown out the window as if they'd never existed. So it was obviously going to be sailing because sailing was something you could do no matter what shape you were in."

At twenty-nine, Duncan was in excellent shape. George, a year older, had made remarkable progress since leaving the hospital in Philadelphia; having undergone a strenuous physical-therapy program, he was able to walk again in a limited capacity—first with crutches, then with a cane, and later with specially molded, high, lace-up boots. Neither man knew much about the mysteries of solar or celestial navigation, but Duncan was a seasoned sailor, and George was determined to master the wealth of technical knowledge that was crucial for their plans. Neither man had crossed the Atlantic in a sailboat, let alone a twenty-footer. Neither man was absolutely confident of his own abilities, but as long as the other was aboard . . . A revival of their old mythology was taking hold—MEN AGAINST THE ELEMENTS!—and soon they were talking in definite terms about Ireland and how they would sail this small boat to its high, bold coast.

By Christmas, their plans were settled and their duties divided: Outfitting of the boat would begin in Annapolis in the spring; because George had bought the boat, Duncan would absorb the additional costs. In June, they would swing ship at Newport and sail on a great circle track across the North Atlantic to Fastnet Rock and the southwest coast of Ireland. George would organize the stores and supplies; Duncan would have control of the interior fittings. George would set their course and navigate at sea; Duncan would cook and have final word on sail trim and other details of helmsmanship. George immediately signed up for a correspondence course in navigation; Duncan went to the dentist to have his teeth cleaned— a mariner's precaution he had inherited from his father—it was never too soon to worry about having a toothache in the middle of the ocean.

It was a tense spring in the boatyard. "Preparation for the voyage became an obsession," George remembers. The problem of equipping *Nimbus* for seas and weather for which she had not been designed often seemed like waterproofing a pair of tennis shoes in preparation for an ascent of Everest. There were delays: Frequently they couldn't obtain the right gear to re-outfit the boat. And there were the beginnings of conflict: Each man had his own idea about how a job should be done. Each man sought his own brand of perfection and was agonized by compromise. And with the start of the voyage now only a month away, pressure was rising.

Progress was slow. Both men were working full time—George teaching French at the Naval Academy; Duncan writing at *The Washington Star*. George was able to put in his share of the work on the boat early in the morning. Duncan regularly drove out to Annapolis in the afternoon rush-hour traffic. From six o'clock to midnight, he labored over the interior fittings of the cabin. He was frustrated and irritable; he just couldn't understand why George was being so obstinate about the bins and shelves.

DUNCAN: *There is nothing more nerve-racking than two close friends preparing a small boat for a long ocean voyage. George and I almost "broke up"...*

VIII

The issue that tested the true character of Duncan and George's friendship was how to store one hundred and eighty cans of juice, vegetables, and soup in the cabin of *Nimbus*.

Duncan knew exactly how he wanted it done. He envisioned four tiers of deep, lightweight shelves on the port side of the cabin. The height of each shelf would correspond precisely with the varying heights of the different kinds of cans—one shelf for the small soup cans, one shelf for the larger juice cans, and so on. Thus, the cans would never fall over. Furthermore, an adjustable belt, pulled taut across the front of each shelf, would hold the cans snug. Therefore, after a can was removed, the belt would be cinched tighter to prevent the remaining cans from sliding out. Duncan thought this was "total brilliance."

George considered the arrangement "impractical." He advocated building bins in which to store the cans. That way, the weight of the cans would be kept low in the boat. "Bins," declared George, "are superior to shelves."

So began the clash—*shelves versus bins*. The divergent mathematics of transport and supply seemed to echo the variant scientific properties of *coal versus ash*, but this time there was no lofty, humorous bombast. They argued furiously. Each man presented the superior logistics of his system, and bitterly tried to win the other to his side. Neither man was willing to concede. Various naval architects from shipyards in Annapolis were called in to consult. They said that it didn't *really* matter which system was used. Stalemate. A terrible week ensued. All work on the boat came to a standstill. It seemed unbelievable; they were deadlocked over shelves and bins. Then, as George later put it, "the Laurel and Hardy performance" began:

Late one night, working alone, unbeknownst to George, Duncan went ahead and built his four tiers of brilliant shelves in the cabin. The next morning, while Duncan was in Washington, George came aboard, took one look at Duncan's shelves, tore them out, and began constructing his own eminently more practical bins before returning to the academy. When Duncan arrived at the boatyard that evening, he discovered the switch. Incensed, he immediately ripped out George's bins ("I *dismembered* them!") and began reconstructing his shelves. . . .

George came aboard as Duncan was hammering away in the cabin. For a moment, they confronted one another pointedly and without saying a word. Then Duncan went back to his hammering and George exploded. He was furious. Duncan was furious that George was furious. He pointed out to George that they had agreed that he, Duncan, was supposed to have control of the interior fittings of the boat.

"Not so," said George, who had been rigging the interior electrical wiring before this bins and shelves business began.

"George," Duncan declared, "I have so much more experience than you at this, you had best stand aside and let me move ahead with my shelves."

There was a long silence. Then more argument. And another flash of silence.

Finally, George said: "All right. If that's what you think, this whole thing is off. I don't think we ought to go together."

Duncan was stunned. ("Those were very heavy sentiments coming from someone who had traveled with me as much as George had. I was sure the voyage was over. I thought we were done for.")

It was a long night. Neither man slept well. Both of them were bewildered by the way they had spoken to one another. After all, they had never before raised their voices to one another in a serious pitch of anger. This was not the old humorous, gentlemanly reprobation. "This was a calamitous event for the two of us," Duncan would later recall. "Both of us have one great quality which has enabled us to do things: We are both very resourceful. So, to have a problem which was without a solution, and to have no resources, and no way around it, was baffling. Neither of us is very subtle in our thinking about human relationships, but we had devised so many ingenious solutions for so many problems that it seemed incredible that we could come a cropper over shelves and bins. That was the worst argument we ever had in our mutual lives. It was like a lovers' quarrel: you had to decide whether the issue was important enough to sacrifice the whole marriage."

The next morning, Duncan was still on edge. From Washington, he telephoned George to make diplomatic overtures. When he heard George's voice, he could tell that all was well again. ("It was like the moment after a thunderstorm—there was a wonderful calm.") During the night, both of them had decided that shelves and bins weren't worth the dissolution of their transatlantic voyage or their ten-year friendship.

It felt good to be talking again in a normal tone of voice. However, a decision about storing those cans still had to be made. Duncan quickly told George that bins would be fine. George was now all for shelves. Duncan pressed for bins, and George said, "Don't worry. After all, bins and shelves, shelves and bins," which somehow seemed to settle the matter.

DUNCAN: *So it was resolved, but not without heavy weaponry which, I think, shocked us both. To compare great things with small, that now seems like the most ridiculous spat in the world, but I think that that experience made us more convinced that formality is the basis of preservation in friendship. Formality is just another way of having good manners. Manners exist for a reason—you can't express*

*yourself without them. Spenser, the poet, said that
the harder the form, the greater the expression. Of
course that's wrong, but it's terribly right, too. It's
correct in an amazing way, and I think that that
may be true of our friendship.*

GEORGE: *I'm still for bins.*

IX

When the *Nimbus* sailed into Newport on the night of Friday,
June 13, 1969, there were four tiers of shelves in her cabin.
(The significance of this fact went unreported in *The Washington Star*'s extravagant two-page spread about the ship's
launching.) The six-day sail up the coast from Annapolis had
been a success except for several humiliating tows they had
received from motor cruisers in the utterly calm Chesapeake
Bay, and except for one night they had spent anchored in the
Chesapeake and Delaware Canal.

It had been a windless day. With no motor aboard, they had
paddled up the canal, the first oceangoing vessel ever to perform that dubious feat, but they had been unable to reach the
open waters of Delaware Bay. At dusk, moored along the dirt
banks of the canal, they were suddenly attacked by a swarm
of ravenous mosquitoes. Pink welts, the size of pencil erasers,
began appearing on their arms and legs. After a frantic search
of the cabin, Duncan discovered that they had no mosquito
netting or repellant on board. Obviously, George, who was in
charge of supply, had not anticipated encountering this peril
on a transatlantic voyage. Duncan saw this as a total screw-up
of supply—*"Cadwalader, you hopeless dunderhead! You
duffer! You fool!"*

Dripping with sweat, and scratching like mad, they passed
the night cramped side by side in the confines of two steamy,
but mosquitoproof, nylon sail bags. Overhead, the mosquitoes
relentlessly awaited the smallest exposure of flesh. Between
the two sail bags, the back-and-forth moaning and groaning
and blaming continued unabated until dawn. All the same, it

was good to know that even in these close quarters the arguments had returned to the old gentlemanly mode of reprobation. "Though neither of us mentioned it," George would later write in an account of the voyage for *Yachting* magazine, "we were not so confident of our ability to get along together for so long a time in so small a space." They need not have worried; all disputes would remain good-natured for the duration of the voyage. A mutual, unspoken understanding defined the limits of friction. As Duncan puts it, "We really had a good time arguing. We argued the whole time, but there was a code. Except for that one time with bins and shelves, the arguments never got out of control. They were always within the realms. It was like two lawyers who knew exactly what the law was—and the law was: the friendship mustn't be affronted."

Duncan had always loved Newport. It was, he thought, an auspicious place to commence a transatlantic voyage. For four days, however, a southeast wind delayed their departure. Meantime, they fretted over Coast Guard reports. They fretted over equipment above and below deck. They fretted even more when they dropped a steel anvil on their compass. And the confusion continued. Plenty of distraction, too. They drank glass after glass of champagne, brought down to the pier by friends. They answered question after question of newspaper reporters—Yes, they were bound for Ireland in a twenty-foot boat with no motor. Yes, they had a life raft. No, they didn't have a two-way radio or a radar set, but they did have a military rescue beacon, a radio direction finder, a compass (slightly injured), fifty gallons of water, forty-eight bottles of wine, six bottles of dark rum, two bottles of champagne, and one bottle of 151-proof rum. No, they weren't particularly worried about falling overboard—they had cockpit safety harnesses. *Drowning?* Well, of course, there was always the possibility of drowning—you could drown in a bathtub if you weren't careful.

On Monday, June 16, a westerly wind was blowing. All was ready. They instructed their wives to honor the seafarer's superstition that says it is bad luck (and probably fatal) to watch a ship sail out of sight. The Spencer clan gathered on the pier for farewells and photographs. Mr. Spencer, the old sea dog himself, came aboard for a final inspection of the vessel. He was more than a little skeptical about *Nimbus*. When he had first seen her out of the water, he had been horrified: "She looks like a skimming dish," he'd roared (which to him was the ultimate insult; he favored deep-keeled, wooden-hulled yachts with big wineglass sections—"a boat with good feet under her.") Mainly, he didn't like the idea of that thin shell of fiberglass being the only thing separating his eldest son and George Cadwalader from five thousand feet of vasty deeps.

He sat down in the small cabin with Duncan and George. After several shots of rum he rose, gravely shook hands, and said, "Well, gentlemen, thank you very much. Of course," he added, "you'll probably drown."

DUNCAN: My understanding of the word china, *which was a term my father used often, is that it was a name for a particular kind of chum, with origins in the golden age of the clipper ships when, on shipboard, friendships would arise in the way that friendships do—not homosexual friendships, but very close friendships on these long ocean voyages, the sixteen-thousand-mile, hundred-day passages around the Cape of Good Hope to the Orient. So that chum would be another person's "china" if they'd been out to Peking together on the clipper-trade route.*

X

Calm. Squall. Calm. Squall. Rolling seas. The dismal slatting of the mainsail. Saturday, June 21, five days out. George is standing the middle watch, and the hours are passing slowly. No wind. Another exasperating seventy-mile day. They are behind schedule. George is disconsolate. He writes in his quartermaster's notebook: "Fog. Our world has shrunk to a radius of fifty yards. Duncan is alseep. *Nimbus* is barely slipping along. I am engaged in holding a tournament on the brim of my sou'wester. Two armies of dewdrops are drawn up on either side of the brim. Every time I shake my head a champion rides forth from each camp and the two rush headlong into battle. They meet in the vicinity of my nose, lock in furious combat, and, as often as not, plunge simultaneously to their doom. . . ."

Midnight. Changing of the watches. Duncan takes the helm. George goes below, makes coffee for Duncan, slides into the quarter berth, and buckles himself in with an automobile seat belt. At the tiller, Duncan grumbles—loudly enough for George to hear: "Jesus Christ, look at this mess. The goddamn foredeck looks like a hellhole. Jib is too tight. Mainsail is too tight. Boat's rolling terribly. No control!" George simulates loud snoring in the cabin to cover the noise. The watch passes. The stars vanish. First light. 0400 hours. Changing of the watches. Duncan goes below and makes coffee for George. Though the sun is hardly over the yardarm, it's time for a foredawn stand-easy: Duncan takes a slug of rum and slides into the quarter berth. On deck, George curses: "God Almighty, this boat is going so slowly. Why can't we get this thing going faster? How many miles did you do, Spencer?—*Spencer!*" Duncan is snoring. With a grin on his face.

June 25. Black clouds advancing from the west. The wind dies. A foreboding lull all around. Then a crash and thunder and rain hard as pellets. Writhing seas. Fresh water fills the cockpit. Duncan scoops up a bucketfull. Thirty minutes later, all is quiet again. George takes up his log, notes "an extraordinary rain squall," but devotes twice as much space to recording the activities of "the Evil Spencer who has preempted the entire bucket of fresh water for his bath, and then affected hurt feelings when I rejected his soapy leftovers."

June 26. Storm out of the northeast. Force Six winds. Towering seas. The storm jib is set. *Nimbus* rises on the white crests, sleds into the gray troughs. Walls of water rear up, then vanish. George and Duncan are now trading two-hour watches. Exhilaration overcomes fatigue. The wind is shrieking through the rigging. Sledding down the troughs, *Nimbus* won't answer to her rudder. She yaws wildly. The crest of a cross-wave swamps the cockpit.

June 29. 0500 hours. The morning star is alone in the sky. George stands watch. He is writing in his log: "Tonight Duncan was cooking dinner and I was daydreaming at the tiller when my woolgathering was interrupted by a very loud and very human sounding 'PURUFF.' I looked over my shoulder and there, not 50 feet away, lay an enormous whale. Whatever I said next was enough to bring Duncan on deck with unprecedented speed. And together we watched this gentleman swim in a leisurely circle around the boat, occasionally rearing up his huge head to cast baleful looks in our direction. He completed his inspection and fell in behind us, puruffing thoughtfully and evidently contemplating what to do next. Now this whale was no doubt a fine fellow, and we were glad to see him. But there was something unsettling about looking at a 60-foot whale from a 20-foot boat, and so, as Duncan put it, we were gladder still when he went away."

July 4. The westerly winds are blowing strong. George frowns over the chart and his navigation figures. Duncan awaits the daily report. He has nicknamed George "Navigator Gump" because of George's profound discontent whenever navigational perfection seems out of reach. It is a bleak morning. Threatening skies. Rising seas. Navigator Gump announces that they are midway across the Atlantic. Their July Fourth celebration begins. One of the two bottles of champagne is opened. The cork arcs overboard. Major George Cadwalader, USMC, struggles to find the appropriate theme for a patriotic speech in these, his nation's troubled times. He seizes the champagne bottle by its neck and stands tall in the cockpit.

Clearing his throat, he addresses Duncan and the passing platoons of waves. "America," the major declares, "is assailed with what I would call gnawing doubt—gnawing doubt is on every hand. There are those who advocate change from within the system. There are those who advocate no change at all. Careful the citizen of our great land who can steer his own ship between the warring influences and arrive at his own individual destination. . . ." With additional champagne, the major and his audience seem hardly to notice the weather now. Gnawing doubt dissolves into "a state of supreme magnificence." *Nimbus* rolls on across the great circle track. Clouds enshroud the moon.

Westerly winds prevail. A thousand miles to go. Then five hundred. *Nimbus* is running fast. The taffrail log ticks off a hundred miles per day. Competing for the most mileage in a single watch, Duncan wins with twenty-four miles in four hours. George can tell by the sound in the cabin that the boat is now almost always sailing at hull-speed. One day, she makes one hundred and thirty-seven miles. Fearing an easterly gale, Duncan prays that the westerlies hold. George frets endlessly over the navigation. The air is cooler now on the northern leg of the great circle. Both men wear heavy woolen sweaters inside foul-weather gear. Shearwaters and petrels swoop and dive around the mast. At night, porpoises crisscross the bow, raising dazzling jet streams of phosphorescent water. Duncan's Zenith Trans-Oceanic radio receives British Broadcasting Company segments of *The Adventures of Sherlock Holmes.* Spencer and Cadwalader listen avidly to the crisp voices of Holmes and Watson. On the same radio, they will soon hear the crackling voices of Armstrong and Aldrin coming from the moon.

July 14. Twenty-eight days out. Their supplies of rum and wine are finished. The westerlies have vanished too. Fog surrounds the boat. She is drifting northward in a new southeast wind.

George is tense. On the radio direction finder, he has picked up a signal from Mizen Head, a navigational beacon. So they are within a hundred miles of the Irish Coast. Maybe closer. But with the wind now shifting to the east, the dense fog, and their uncertainty about the angle of the coastline, doubts are gnawing again. By nightfall, the fog is clearing. Both men try to find a light in the darkness to the east. Nothing is visible. Then, still with no land in sight, an unforgettable aroma reaches their nostrils, carried seaward on a light, easterly land breeze—the voluptuous, summery perfume of peat and freshly cut hayfields. It seems miraculous after twenty-eight days of the rank, cellar smell of the ocean.

July 15. 0200 hours. George sees a flashing yellow light in the east. He hurries below to look at the charts as Duncan counts off fifteen-second intervals between each flash. Duncan estimates that they are about two miles from land. His mood lifts. George, meanwhile, is aggravated, fuming. He has found the light marked on the chart: The Bull Lighthouse, along with Dursey Island, Bantry Bay, Miskish Mountains, Hungry Hill, and Bere Haven. To Duncan, the names and places all sound reassuringly solid. To George, they indicate that *Nimbus* is twenty miles north of her intended landfall at Fastnet Lighthouse. ("True to form," Duncan would later write, "after the first pleasure of knowing where we were had worn off, Navigator Gump began to curse and say he was disappointed. Disappointed! I could have placed a garland of roses on his grimy head, kissed both his bristly cheeks.") But by first light, the scene has changed. The wind has died. The distant shoreline has vanished. A mountainous bank of clouds and haze is all that is visible on the eastern horizon. "World turned to shit," George mutters. No land anywhere. Eyes straining, they both stare at the mirage of mountains and hills. Gradually, as the sun defines the colors of the morning sky, solid shapes and forms begin to appear: High, treeless cliffs; boulders; narrow, steep bays; velvet-green meadows populated by cows; stone farmhouses; chimneys and smoke. The wind is now in the east. A strong tide pulls *Nimbus* toward the coast. Buoys and markers pass abeam. Then, at noon, twenty-nine days and twenty hours after setting sail from Newport, Duncan and George steer their ship past Alderman's Rock and into the narrow harbor at Crookhaven, County Cork, Ireland, setting a speed record for a transatlantic crossing of a twenty-foot boat.

They don't know what to do first or next. Suddenly they are making *Nimbus* fast to the stone quay in this old clipper-ship port. They are gaping at cows, taking down the mainsail, running up the American ensign. The last bottle of champagne is being uncorked. The customs man is hurrying down and putting on his coat and tie. Villagers are gathering on the quay, and the local men in Johnny O'Sullivan's Pub are coming out into the noonday sun to have a look for themselves at the two American "chinas" who have crossed the ocean in the small boat.

XI

These days, when Duncan and George get together, mostly in summer, they like to talk about a voyage they hope to make sometime in the future. It will be another transatlantic crossing, but this time the ship and the crew will be larger. They plan to take along Duncan's two sons and George's two sons. They have not yet discussed how they will store their cans of soup; Duncan anticipates that "all the arguments will be delightful."

Looking back at the voyage of 1969, Duncan insists that it was more than a passage across the ocean. He thinks of it as an important transitional event in his friendship with George: "The voyage rinsed the Vietnam War out of our hair. It was a terrific emotional breakthrough because we had thought that our old little world was over forever because of the war. But then it wasn't—it just took form in another place. And we could see that our friendship would survive old age and other physical calamities. His getting wounded was just a preparation for what happens to everybody. It's what happens to all friendships in old age; everybody gets wounded in the same way: They just can't do what they did when they were younger. It just happened in a rush in our case."

Today, George walks with a slight limp which is not nearly as conspicuous as his drive to get things done, and to do them right. Unable to meet the physical requirements for promotion in the Marine Corps, George left his teaching post at the Naval Academy and moved his family to Woods Hole, Massachusetts, where he went to work at the Oceanographic Institution. He hoped to combine his love of the sea with the order and discipline he had found in the Marine Corps. But, as the assistant to the director, he was swamped with paperwork, and he soon became discouraged by the limited number of positions available to nonscientists on the Oceanographic's seagoing expeditions. In 1973 he struck out on his own.

Starting from scratch, on the lee of Penikese, a treeless, offshore island (southwest of Woods Hole) uninhabited except by squadrons of native herring gulls and migratory birds, George established a school for the rehabilitation of delinquent boys who had been arrested in Massachusetts for crimes ranging from armed robbery to assault and battery. With funding from the Department of Youth Services and private contributions, a small staff, and boys who were more familiar with the skills of thievery than those of carpentry, he constructed a landing pier, a barn, several outbuildings, and a two-story shingled dormitory and work center. He is still director of the Penikese Island School.

"Who would have thought that a bunch of hoodlums could build that beautiful big house?" Duncan wondered when he first sailed to Penikese in the summer of 1974. It seemed to him that George had at last built something his own way, "from the ground up, in typical Cadwalader fashion." George's ability to incite purpose—a mission—was evident everywhere on the remote island. But it was not just the school's facilities, nor its programs in farming, carpentry, boat building, seamanship, and job training on the mainland that impressed Duncan. It was the way George had created a flexible, humanist regime on the island, inspiring confidence in boys who were in trouble; who felt they had no control over their own future; who clearly detested authority but admired George; and some who liked the island so much that they hated to leave when their term was over. Listening to George talk to the students on the pier, Duncan recognized the gruff, funny, but no-nonsense tone he had first heard in George's voice on the dock at Yale, fifteen years before.

"George's school is a terrifically courageous and single-handed achievement," Duncan says now. "You can call it a prison camp if you'd like, but George *founded a goddamn school*, while I've always worked for other people. George doesn't disregard that, and I don't disregard what he's done. I don't think that either one of us would regard conventional success and failure as having anything to do with our friendship. We never get in competition about progress in the world. I feel no discomfort with people describing George as a prison warden. He's never seemed to feel any discomfort about my being just a hack reporter."

Yet Duncan and George easily slip into their old mode of humorous put-downs when they refer to each other's work. Duncan is fond of reminding George that he is "just a turnkey in an island jail," and of saying: "You know, George, you do a wonderful job keeping these recreant youths here, but perhaps the shark-infested waters play their part as well." And when Duncan wrote a Signet paperback original for New American Library in 1981, after his coverage for *The Washington Star* of the Jean Harris/Scarsdale murder trial, George was quick to curl up his lip with mock disdain over the book's commercially suited title: *Love Gone Wrong*.

Duncan frequently wonders why the *modus operandi* of their friendship has not changed for over twenty years. "It's weird," he says. "I often ask myself why our friendship continues to bounce along the way it is, but I'm not going to try to alter it to serve some other god such as 'progress-in-a-relationship' or what one calls 'growth.' This friendship is not trying to produce a family. This is not trying to satisfy the various ego needs of the participants, though it may do that anyway. It simply satisfies some sort of ultimate human regard: That you are highly regarded and that you regard another with the highest esteem. But I don't know if friendships do progress anywhere. I've often wondered: Why do he and I find it perfectly comfortable to continue playing at these roles that have been comfortable for so long. I guess we return to that mode because it seems natural to both of us. I've found it very convenient. I don't think there has ever been any uncomfortable problem that we haven't addressed—our wives being a perfect example. There's no role-playing when we're talking about the wives. Plenty of serious discussions go on. But even those discussions are guided by the same limits. There definitely *are* limits."

Candid criticism of the other man's marriage is, according to Duncan, "within the code." And the enduring, unwritten code continues to be: "The friendship must not be affronted." Duncan has been critical of George's marriage ("George, Jesus Christ, you're such a great guy, but now you've got a wife who doesn't sail") and when Duncan separated from his wife in 1979, George articulated his objections ("Well, Spencer, I saw my duty, but apparently you don't see yours. I think you're doing a bad thing, you're hurting the children," Duncan remembers George telling him). Duncan maintains that their reciprocal frankness does not create friction.

"I suppose," says Duncan, "I should resent terribly George's criticism of my marriage, but I don't. I appreciate his point of view even though we're completely different as black and white on the subject. If I weren't such an intimate of his, I would never dare say the things I do about his marriage. And George would never make the frank comments that he does without the presupposition that I would never put our friendship on the line over issues of marriage. It's one thing for Cadwalader to say that he disapproves of the way I'm handling my marriage and of me getting a divorce. But he knows that I would never put him in the kind of position, were I to say: 'Well, George, if you disapprove of what I'm doing, then you must disapprove of me also—so farewell.' That would never happen because the friendship certainly means much more to me than his opinion of my ex-wife."

Josephine Spencer has not seen her brother and George together in several years. A single woman living in New York City, she is a sculptor and a trustee of the New York Studio School of Art. From a distance, she has noticed changes in their friendship: "Real friendships," she says, "don't have limits. George and Duncan didn't seem to have limits when they were in college, but they did when they each got married. I think that since Duncan's separation from his wife, the friendship has become somewhat a shell of what it used to be. George, I think, felt that if he could stick to his marriage, then Duncan had to stick with his because they share the same morality. George is a real stoic—a Don Quixote version of a stoic. But it may be that for Duncan, more of the past is preserved in the golden light than for George because George has perhaps had more senses of disillusionment in his life than Duncan—"

Josephine hesitates. She is hunting for words, and pinning them down carefully, as if they are butterflies too delicate for display. Then, she laughs. "It's funny talking about Duncan and George because you automatically fall into their old language of archetypes. There was so much expectation in that tone. The world was there to be conquered. It was all in the realm of possibility. And that's not true anymore. They're both in their forties. You write a different mythology when you're forty. That earlier perspective changes. There may be some crystal, beautiful time, suspended in the clear liquid of anticipation, that is perfect for the best of friendship."

Early on a May morning in 1981, a youthful tone can still be heard in Duncan's voice. Dressed in jogging togs for a little Pain Before Breakfast, Duncan has forgotten about the time and is now late for work. Were it not for that fact, he admits that he could happily spend an entire day talking about his friendship with George. "It's so unusual," he says, "to find someone in your own generation who is a close friend and who you realize is a remarkable character. Of course, George may not seem that to everyone, but I feel that so far in his life he has proved to be a most remarkable individual. The things he does are touched with some crazy genius—like that school.

You don't meet too many people in this life who start a school from nothing. And he's one of them—" Duncan's eyes widen, as if he's startled by sudden observation of an obvious fact: "The man is made of gold!" Then, he shakes his head, and quietly says: "I wish like hell he'd married my sister."

IV : MUCKERS

K. LeMoyne Billings / John F. Kennedy

Choate: 1935

This time they were really in trouble.

The twelve boys lined up in the Headmaster's office at the Choate School in Wallingford, Connecticut, awaited, with noiseless sideways glances, the sentencing for their crime. It was Monday, February 11, a glowering, heavy-skied New England winter morning. The most audible sound in the Headmaster's chambers was the rattle and hiss of a radiator. Sitting at his desk, severe as a noose, the Headmaster was systematically silent. Before announcing their punishment, he would wait until every one of the thirteen accused was in his presence. All of them were guilty. One of them was missing.

The tallest boy in the lineup, K. LeMoyne Billings, a bespectacled six-foot-two-inch, 175-pound Sixth Former, knew exactly where the missing boy was at that moment. The twelve of them had just been summoned during the middle of a class from which the thirteenth had been absent. Billings was worried that the boy's truancy would further complicate the proceedings here in the office. He felt the particular and physiologically intricate kind of adrenal anxiety which only an eighteen-year-old schoolboy can experience when he and his best friend are in trouble, and the best friend is, by whatever means, only making it worse.

At this moment, Billings was mostly concerned about the face he himself presented as he stood before the Headmaster. Billings had difficulty with his face. That is to say, the natural expression of his emotions upon his more prominent features was usually about half under control. His eyes, for instance, consistently revealed the whole truth. Friendly, blue, and guileless, they were nearly incapable of bluffing. If the demands of loyalty to a friend in crisis were sufficiently intense, Billings could, with the aid of his vocal chords, produce a lavish lie. But anyone who knew him well could detect the supreme effort of trying to keep the rest of his face, not to mention his story, straight.

Billings possessed another trait that was inauspicious for a schoolboy on trial: His forehead and colorful cheeks were set high; his chin was bold; his torso and arms were stocky and powerful; but no single feature conveyed so well the gigantic dimensions of his sense of humor as the size and shape of his mouth when he laughed. The better part of a six-inch ruler would have been required to measure the distance between his upper and lower lip during a peak of hilarity. And if his best friend had activated his funny bone, a baseball could probably have been pitched into that exultant cavity and still have left Billings room to breathe.

In any circumstance, but especially one such as this, the lowest aperture of Billings's smiling mouth could dominate his physiognomy, getting him into even more trouble. Little could be expressed without the consent of his smile. It was the landlord of his face. The rest of his features, and his better judgment, had to rent space from that smile. It was inclined to officiate recklessly. Sometimes, and especially when Billings's best friend was nearby, it simply, and without warning, evicted a laugh, or—worse—threw a whole family of untidy guffaws out into the cold, unappreciative environment of mandatory daily Chapel, mathematics classes, and, even, the Headmaster's office.

So, for the moment, it was probably better that Billings's best friend and roommate, John F. Kennedy, was missing. If there was a single offense that would surely and swiftly bring the end of all things to a Choate boy, it was laughter in the face of the angry Headmaster.

Mr. George C. St. John was among the American pantheon of boys' preparatory school headmasters (a legendary group including Frank L. Boyden of Deerfield; Endicott Peabody of Groton; Father Sill of Kent; Rev. William Greenough Thayer of St. Marks) who ruled their institutions with absolute despotic authority and shaped the lives of three generations of boys. St. John had been the inscrutable monarch of Choate since 1908. A conspicuous, omnipotent, silver-haired presence among his staff and the five hundred thirty boys now enrolled, he personally sought to cultivate academic discipline and strict moral boundaries.

To his students in general, and LeMoyne Billings in particular, George St. John was scary. He didn't seem to understand, much less tolerate, behavior that might have been considered normal or harmless (albeit mischievous) among boys living on a stately, elm-lined campus where high academic standards and rigid rules and regulations conspired to make anything hinting at happiness illegal. The Headmaster's enforcement of rules, and his punishment of renegades, was harsh, inflexible, and final.

"Ten percent of the boys at Choate are *muckers,*" St. John had thundered during his sermon in evening Chapel last month. He had gone on to portray the typical "mucker" as a "bad apple in the basket," a boy who cut up in class, behaved impiously in Chapel, and made a general nuisance of himself in the eyes of the school and God above.

In the new term ahead, St. John warned, muckers would not be tolerated. If their identity was discovered, they would be expelled. Surveying his congregation with a menacing eye, he wound up his sermon with the endlessly fascinating information that, at present, he did not know the name of a single mucker. But, for that matter, neither did any of the students in the chapel. They had never heard of a mucker, at least not until Mr. St. John had brought such a bewitchingly bad citizen to their attention.

That evening after Chapel, during the half hour before the bell rang for dinner, Billings and Kennedy reflected on the Headmaster's sermon. Life for Sixth Formers (seniors) was deregulated to a small degree; they were allowed to play records on Victrolas in their rooms. Because Billings and Kennedy roomed near the dining hall, and because Kennedy possessed an excellent Victrola, which attracted the flow of students shuffling to dinner, the popularity of the room at that hour was epidemic. Sometimes, the doorway was so jammed that they had difficulty getting into their own room. Action had to be taken to restore privacy.

Billings and Kennedy founded a club that night, and offered membership to eleven of their closest friends who would share the exclusive privilege of listening to Kennedy's Victrola between Chapel and dinner. A wildly democratic resolution was unanimously carried, naming each member of the club president. Later on, each member purchased a gold, charm-sized shovel upon which were engraved the individual's initials; the abbreviated title, "Pres."; and the initials of the newly established institution, "C.M.C.": Choate Muckers Club.

The thirteen members of the Muckers Club gathered nightly in Billings and Kennedy's room. The club had no official rules, dues, or bylaws (except the enforced exclusion of non-Muckers from the Victrola). And neither did the club break any of Choate's cardinal rules during its brief and risky existence. Its membership roster showed a majority of outstanding athletes (including four varsity captains), none of whom drank or smoked or sneaked into Wallingford after lights.

The Muckers, however, were not without peccadilloes when confronted with the restrictive force of Choate's minor, quotidian regulations. The appearance of their rooms, for example, was below school standards. Personal neatness, in most cases, was on the careless side of casual. Occasionally, when they were supposed to be in class, a collective and chronic recurrence of "sore throats" permitted them to have their throats sprayed at the infirmary where they were issued a "tardy" slip which they were then required to place on a clipboard in the Headmaster's office before returning immediately to class. When it was discovered that the tardy slips themselves could be doctored with a pencil and crinkled with a fist before presentation as an "absent" slip, a few Muckers were not merely tardy but altogether absent from a class or two.

Now, on this grim Monday morning, John F. Kennedy was carrying a well-crinkled absent slip to the clipboard in the Headmaster's office, unaware that the balance of the Muckers Club membership was assembled within. If he was startled when he entered the office, he did not show it.

He looked extremely inquisitive, his best friend, LeMoyne Billings, noticed. His eyes were candid and steady, examining the situation with an interested gaze which suggested, but did not reveal, amusement. He seemed to want to know all that could possibly be known by a seventeen-year-old who stood five feet eleven inches, and weighed 155 pounds. The upturning corners of his slightly opened mouth, in combination with the protuberance of his ears and the jaunty tilt at the end of his nose, gave his face a droll and charming, though distinctly irreverent, expression. It was a face that naturally urged a smile on the world.

Kennedy was not smiling now. Still, there flowed from him a continuum of controlled and irreducible energy. He carried himself with hopeful confidence, as though he would retreat from nothing. Quietly, he joined his friends and faced the Headmaster.

Mr. St. John briefly summarized his knowledge and opinion of the group's immature behavior. Then, he declared that the punishment for establishing an illegal club—indeed, deliberately giving it a mocking name which he did not care to repeat —was expulsion. He advised them to pack their trunks immediately and make arrangements to leave Choate by the end of the day. Their parents, he added, would be notified by the school. Then, with stunning suddenness, they were dismissed.

Billings and Kennedy called each other Billy and Johnny, or any of a dozen nicknames which included, respectively, Lem, Lemmer, Leem, or Moynie; Jack, Ken, or Kenadosus. A 1935 yearbook photograph of the two of them roughhousing in a snowdrift was captioned "Leem and Rat-Face." To their families, close friends, and a few genial masters, they were known as Lem and Jack. Now, in the school at large, they were identified with a dual nickname: Public Enemies Number One and Two. (Kennedy had somehow earned preeminent status.)

Both Public Enemy Number One and Number Two agreed that the Headmaster's punishment did not fit their crime. They decided that probably it was a personal matter after all. Mr. St. John had been specifically irritated by the two of them ever since they had begun rooming together in the West Wing dormitory in the fall. More than once he had considered separating them by reassignment to two different houses where supervision was stricter than in the dorms. St. John had even recommended to Kennedy's father that the source of their childish and immature behavior might be isolated if Jack and Lem were sent to a gland specialist. Billings, for one, did not share Mr. St. John's diagnosis. The problem, Lem knew, had never been caused by the secretions of their glands, but by the fusion of their wits.

He and Jack had first met in the spring of 1933 when Jack was elected to the business board of *The Brief,* the school yearbook, which Lem had joined the previous year. From the outset, they were as inseparable as they were irrepressible. In part, they were bound together by their mutual dislike of Choate. For Lem, Jack was the best thing about life at school. Jack knew how to create the kind of fun that lightened the mood of everyone around him. His innate gaiety and zest for living challenged even the most caustic, passive members of their class. His high spirits were contagious. For Kennedy, Billings was more than just a partner in schoolboy crime. He was the first intimate friend Kennedy had found outside his own family. And he was more fun to be with than anyone Kennedy had ever known. Lem's passionate readiness to experience the world enhanced Kennedy's cool curiousity. Lem's unfailing loyalty matched his own. In Billings, Kennedy had a unique ally.

The making of a best friend in preparatory school was no easy matter. Adolescence itself was ruled by codes that were as restrictive as those that Choate drilled into its students. In academics, an imaginative mind had to be forcibly restrained because it drew excessive attention to itself. Originality and sincerity were scorned. In athletics, rivalry was the highest form of complementary affection. Emotional candor was suicidal. Digging for any level of intimacy deeper than laconic sarcasm was tantamount to digging a grave. Yet, in their friendship, Billings and Kennedy discovered that neither one of them was afraid of having the ability or the imagination to enjoy each other without rivalry.

It was an important discovery for each of them. Both were second sons. Both had older brothers who had gone to Choate, amassing an outstanding number of athletic and scholastic glories. F. Tremaine "Josh" Billings, Jr., '29, had been captain of the varsity football team, a letterman in three sports, president of his class, editor-in-chief of *The Brief.* Joseph P. Kennedy, Jr., '33, had been vice-president of the St. Andrews Society (a charity organization), a letterman on the undefeated football team of 1933, the winner of the Harvard Football Trophy ("awarded to that member of the Choate football squad who best combines scholarship and sportsmanship").

Lem and Jack were made acutely aware of the Headmaster's admiration of their fraternal predecessors and his inability to fathom how the next boys from the same families "could be so different." "Both of them had elder brothers who were very successful, who were prodigies in their own ways, and for whom there was great expectation," said Robert F. Kennedy, Jr., who became Lem's closest friend in the next generation. "Both Lem and Jack were almost runts of the litter. Lem's father was always displeased with him. Lem was practically blind, he grew up scrawny, and he could never match his older brother. Jack's older brother was really the hope of the family. So when Lem and Jack got together, it was almost as if they were thumbing their noses at the world, at all those expectations, particularly the way people underestimated the two of them. But, together, they really had everything. They loved each other and they got satisfaction out of the successes that each of them enjoyed."

Instead of completing, Billings and Kennedy relied on one another. By amiable challenges, they advanced each other's best abilities. Each was equipped with a restless optimism which was intensified by the sensibilities and interests they had in common. Both of them were exceptionally bright. Though not yet superior students, both shared a genuine respect for books and a passion for detail, especially the fine points of history. Both were animated storytellers; invariably, one was the hero of the other's favorite anecdotes. Both were outgoing, charming, curious. (". . . P.S. Gertrude Stein lectured here," Jack reported home to his parents. "LeMoyne + Moi rushed up and got her autograph and had a rare old conversation!") Both took pleasure seriously, as if it were among the fine arts. Both were disposed to mischief.

During their first year as roommates they discovered that when they were younger, they had both loved a set of old-fashioned boys' books about a frolicsome, mischievous goat named Billy Whiskers (whence came Jack's favorite nickname for Lem: "Billy Billings"). The Billy Whiskers Series (twenty-six volumes by Frances Trego Montgomery, including *Billy Whiskers at the Circus, Billy Whiskers on the Mississippi,* and *Billy Whiskers in France*) characterized its hero as "a true friend," and "a leader," who was not always "a model of good behavior." Billings and Kennedy brought to bear on the Choate School the same "love of excitement, adventure and mischief" that had drawn Billy Whiskers into antics around the world. And like the plucky ruminant whom they had both admired during boyhood, Lem and Jack "got into serious trouble more than once."

The medium of their friendship was fun. Wit was its instrument, laughter its melody. Their cadence was exhilarating and fugal. Jack's wit was the quicker of the two, the more piping, cerebral, and eye-sparkling; Lem's was a roll on the kettle drums and a heart-stopping lunge for the gong. Jack had the self-assurance of a sharp, lyrical tongue; Lem had a Chaplinesque sense of situation, and how, coupled with his own foibles, it promoted comedy. Lem's vast appreciation of the abstract elements of fun was turned to immediate realistic effect by Jack's willingness to color almost any predicament with humor. Once, upon returning to Choate from summer vacation, Lem was helping Jack store his steamer trunk in the dormitory basement. The dorm master, J. J. Maher, was angered by the commotion during the quiet study hour. Harshly reprimanding them, Maher sent Lem and Jack back to their room with the decisive, but unspecific, instructions that the proper time for trunk storage was "in the morning." Inspired to obey, Jack and Lem were up at 5 A.M., hauling the trunk as quietly as it is possible, at that hour, to drag a heavy steamer trunk down three flights of stairs. Lem was delighted when the master's door opened, and a groggy, bathrobe-clad figure emerged to hear Jack's explanation: "But Mr. Maher, you told us to take it down in the morning."

Though it annoyed the more brittle masters, their fun sparkled most when it simply made light of each other's differences: Lem's devout service as a baritone in the choir, Jack's inability to carry a tune; Lem's fastidiousness about possessions, Jack's absentmindedness: JUST ARRIVED HOME, Jack wired Lem on July 5, 1934, I HAVE YOUR SHAVING BRUSH SO PLEASE QUIT BEEFING. . . . ; Lem's fraternal charm with girls, Jack's "smoothness"; Lem's zealous pride in his family's distinguished genealogy, Jack's astonishment whenever *another* Billings ancestor was discovered to have crossed on the *Mayflower.* "They made fun out of Lem's having a great-great-great-grandfather who was in the Society of the Cincinnati, whereas the Irish had come over to America more recently. So Lem always felt that the Billings family was historically more important than the Kennedys and the Fitzgeralds," recalled Eunice Kennedy Shriver. "But Jack came right back at him about the kings of Ireland, and how the House of Parliament in Dublin had originally been the home of the Fitzgeralds. And Lem would talk of how he had never met any smart Catholics in Pittsburgh."

Their differences complemented each other. Physically, Lem was the stronger of the two. Jack was quicker, more graceful. Lean, lightweight, Kennedy possessed the kind of natural coordination and rhythm that enabled him to adapt readily to any sport. He could, for instance, pick up a tennis racket, not having played in a few seasons, and perform respectably. Without much training, he could stroke a golf ball and make that complex series of motions look slow and easy. His long spiral passes were unhurried, glamorous. His timing, in most sports, was Zenlike. He was a serene athlete; he took his time. Lacking superiority of physique, Kennedy athletic weapons were patience, confidence, control.

Billings had an arsenal of explosive muscles. He played sports subjectively; his style was dogged, grinding, sometimes emotional. With minimal effort, he could work up a sweat. Usually, the effort was maximum; Billings had to work for athletic achievement. He was not a natural. Myopic since birth, Lem had difficulty catching Jack's poetic passes. "Can't throw a ball, can't catch a ball," Lem would later admit with characteristic self-acceptance. "Any sport with strength— great! Anything with a ball—*forget it.*" Twenty pounds heavier than Jack, bigger than most of their classmates, Lem was captain of the varsity crew; he also earned letters in wrestling and football (as a lineman). Jack, due to poor health in his junior and senior years, was not on a varsity team. "When Jack brought Lem home to a family where Jack was probably dominated by a much larger and healthier older brother," said Robert Kennedy, Jr., "he was bringing Lem home as his champion."

There were other differences. Lem's strength kept him in good health. Jack's health was precarious. During their years at Choate, Jack was chronically ill, susceptible to a variety of viral ailments, vulnerable to infection. A knee skinned on the tennis court, later infected, kept him in the infirmary for several weeks. A blood condition led to hospitalization during his Fifth Form year. It was serious; Lem was among the students who prayed for him during evening Chapel. Jack recovered and returned. Golf became his only official sport. Discontented with orders to avoid strenuous physical activity, he learned how to live vigorously with pain. His brother Robert would later write: "At least one half of the days that he spent on this earth were days of intense physical pain. He had scarlet fever when he was very young and serious back trouble when he was older. In between he had almost every other conceivable ailment."

Throughout all, Lem and Jack concocted cures in kidding. Typically, they found irony in their differences in health. They speculated about the number of illnesses, if any, which Lem had had that Jack *hadn't* had. One joke, which would recur over the next twenty-eight years, went that if Lem ever wrote Jack's biography, they would call it *John F. Kennedy: A Medical History*. In fact, Lem rarely, if ever, heard Jack complain about his medical misfortunes. Lem usually knew nothing more about the diagnosis of an illness than that "a blood condition" was "serious." Devoid of self-pity, Jack was either stoical about his afflictions or humorous. His letters to Lem from various hospitals were wry and sardonic. Often, he repeated a joke started by his brother Robert who had once expressed pity for any mosquito that took "the great risk in biting Jack Kennedy," for surely one drop of Jack's blood would poison the insect.

The kidding aside, Lem privately worried about his best friend's health. Lem's father, who had died in 1933, had been a prominent physician in Pittsburgh. Though healthy himself, Lem was accustomed to medical concerns. However, his empathetic impulses were deflected not only by Jack's stoicism but also by Jack's remarkable ability, whether he was ill or well, to detach himself from his surroundings. Lem soon learned that no amount of fun or kidding could divert Jack when Jack was reading a book—or *The New York Times* (Kennedy was the only boy Billings knew at Choate who had a daily subscription). To some extent, his roommate's capacity for preoccupation annoyed Lem. Because Jack's power of concentration was absolute, it momentarily rendered Lem obsolete.

They shared other moments of individual privacy. They never talked about their religions. But every night of their Sixth Form year, Lem, a Protestant, observed Jack saying his prayers, beside his bed, on his knees.

Public Enemies Number One and Two both prayed a lot during that perilous week in February. After being expelled on Monday morning, Lem and Jack learned that one of the more compassionate assistant headmasters had persuaded George

St. John to downgrade the sentence to strict probation. Despite the reprieve, there was still trouble ahead.

Mr. St. John sent cables to Mr. Kennedy and Mrs. Billings, requesting that both come up to Choate for private conferences on Saturday. On Friday, Joseph P. Kennedy, chairman of the newly created Securities and Exchange Commission, sent a wire from Washington, stating that the earliest he could arrive in Wallingford was twelve-fifteen on Sunday. Mrs. Romaine LeMoyne Billings, widowed, living under extremely modest financial circumstances since the death of her husband, would nevertheless make the journey from Pittsburgh.

More prayers were uttered. Complications ensued. A telegram, addressed to Jack and Lem from Jack's 15-year-old sister Kathleen and her roommate at the Convent of the Sacred Heart in Noroton, arrived on Saturday at the school office: DEAR PUBLIC ENEMIES ONE AND TWO ALL OUR PRAYERS ARE UNITED WITH YOU AND THE ELEVEN OTHER MUCKS. WHEN THE OLD MEN ARRIVE SORRY WE WONT BE THERE FOR THE BURIAL.

Intercepted, opened, and read by the Headmaster, the message further enraged George St. John. He had had just about enough of this indecorous "muckers" business. Lem and Jack were not given the telegram until after it had been shown to Mr. Kennedy. The private conferences, lasting most of Sunday afternoon, were held in the Headmaster's study. Jack and Lem were contrite. Promises for better behavior were made; parental displeasure was expressed. Mr. Kennedy slipped from stern disapproval into momentary blazes of steely Irish wit. "My mother's reaction was 'much ado about nothing,'" Lem would later recall. "So I was not terribly worried because, after all, we had done nothing overtly illegal. But, God, if my father had been alive, I wouldn't have had a behind to sit on."

Their promises were kept until one dark, moonless night in May. It was Festivities Weekend. Sixth Formers were permitted to invite a girl up for two days of organized activities which featured a production of Gilbert and Sullivan's *Patience,* fol-

lowed by a dance in the dining hall. Attendance at the musical
was mandatory, but Lem and Jack, having already seen the
production several times during the school year, were loath to
subject their dates, Pussy Brooks and Olive Cawley, to the
amateur jollity of Lanquid Maidens and Fleshly Poets. Lem's
former roommate, Pete Caesar, now a freshman at Princeton,
had returned for the weekend. He had a car. Driving off campus was strictly forbidden. They would risk expulsion. Graduation was three weeks away. But it was a convertible coupe, and
the top was down, and it was a deepening blue spring night
with promises sailing on a whim.

The five of them went for a drive in the countryside. They
intended to return just in time to slip unnoticed into the post-
theater, pre-dance, crowd filing into the dining hall. Lem and
Jack were wearing white tie and tails; the girls wore formal
evening dresses and high heels. It was an exhilarating drive,
past open fields, along conifer-veiled lanes; on the return
sweep up Main Street in the village of Wallingford, one of
them noticed that a car seemed to be following them. Actually,
someone else suggested, the car was *pursuing* them. It was the
school proctors.

Pete Caesar accelerated, speeding past the school grounds
and out into the countryside again. Lem and Jack and the girls
ducked out of sight. Lem was nervous; this time they *really*
were in trouble. If they were caught, Lem felt sure that Mr.
St. John would not allow them to graduate. The night sky
rotated wildly above them as Caesar slammed around stone-
fenced corners, eluded the beams of the proctor car, roared
down a country lane, swerved again, then braked suddenly.
Certain they had been followed, Caesar doused the headlights
and told them to jump out and hide. Lem smelled the rich
redolence of manure.

They landed in the barnyard of a farm. Lem and Jack and
Olive scattered into separate corners of the darkened barn,
leaving Pussy with Pete (who was immune from punishment)
in a well-staged tableau of smooching in the car. Lem hid
himself in the deepest bales of hay he could find. In the darkness, he couldn't see where Jack or Olive was concealed, but

he could *hear* farm animals rustling close by. Lem didn't like the sounds of them—possibly goats, maybe geese. He wondered if the animals were safely ensconced in stalls, or whether they would begin freely hoofing and honking around, putting up a big fuss over the intrusion. Lem darkly pondered the behavior of a perturbed goose if Jack decided to be funny at a time like this.

Fortunately, all was silent and somber until the headlights of the proctor car swerved into the barnyard, garishly lighting up Pete and Pussy's amorous, but perfectly legal, clinch. Lem heard the two proctors get out of their car. There was a brief, inaudible conversation followed by the sound of someone clomping *around* the barn. A few minutes went by. Then, a car door shut; one of the cars drove away fast; the other one followed the first; then darkness and silence. If there were geese in the barn, Lem concluded, they were nesting far enough away from Kennedy to maintain composure.

The silence was ominous. Lem was sure that one of the proctors had been left behind to force their capture. He didn't dare try to locate Jack or Olive. Simply *breathing* was loud enough. So he lay under the hay, in his white tie and tails, trying to decide if this whole situation was actually as funny as Jack probably thought it was.

After a while, a car zoomed into the barnyard and stopped. Pete Caesar identified himself; Lem rushed out, followed by Olive. Jack did not appear. They waited a few moments. Lem was in favor of *quietly* calling to Jack; Pete was reluctant. If one of the proctors was somewhere nearby he would hear Jack's name. Pete opened the lid of the trunk; Lem hid himself inside. Olive lay down on the floor of the backseat with a coat over her. Off they sped, leaving Jack with the goats and the geese.

Lem had a rough ride. The trunk was small, Lem was large, and with all the careening and honking it felt as though Caesar had driven in reverse *through* the barn. In fact, the proctor car was again chasing them on the road and Caesar was doing his best to lose them in the small streets of downtown Wallingford. Finally, they came to a sharp halt behind the shrubbery near the dining hall. Pete opened the trunk, said the coast was clear, and Lem and Olive danced into the packed hall, trailing loose stalks of hay. Apparently, their absence had not been noticed by the dance chaperones. Thirty minutes later, Jack appeared. He mixed in with the crowd, picking up the beat of the rhumba. Smiling, he cut in on Billings because, after all, Jack reminded Lem, plucking a piece of hay from Lem's hair, Olive was Jack's date.

Jack, Lem learned later that night, had walked back to school through two miles of pitch-dark woods.

They graduated in June. Kennedy was voted "Most Likely to Succeed," outpolling the two runners-up with the largest plurality (thirty-seven votes) in the class elections. Billings was elected "Best Natured" with a plurality of twelve votes. They exchanged copies of their senior pictures; Kennedy signed his: "To Lemmer—the gayest soul I know. In memory of two tense years and in hopes of many more. Your old pal and supporter! Ken." The picture that Lem gave to Jack was notable because, in fact, it was the second senior picture of Lem that had appeared in the Choate yearbook in two successive years.

It has been said that a man will never again be so sure of himself, never as old and wise as he is the day he graduates from secondary school. Where age was concerned in Lem's case, this was literally true. He would never again be as old as he was in 1935. Beginning then, and for the rest of his life, he subtracted a year from his actual age.

"In 1934, at the end of Lem's *first* senior year, he decided that he wanted to spend a *second* senior year at Choate because he and Jack were having such a fantastic time and he had found his first real friend," said Peter W. Kaplan, who, a generation later, was one of Lem's closest friends and the only person, outside Lem's family, to whom Lem acknowledged his actual age. "Lem asked permission to stay the extra year, and he got it. It was hard to believe; he was on scholarship, and this was the Depression, and it was an awful time for Lem. His father had died. His mother was having a tough time. But he wanted to stay at Choate, which he disliked intensely, to be with Jack, and he consciously adjusted the year of his birth to be the same age as his best friend. It made sense that he would want to attune himself to Jack. Lem was the kind of man who got his emotional rewards from the fact that a friend gave to him and cared about him, and he gave so much back."

Hyannis Port: 1934

Taking off his glasses, Lem opened the glass door of the shower stall in the bathroom adjoining Jack's room. It was his first visit to Jack's parents' summer home, a roomy, white, green-shuttered house abutting on a broad, unfenced sward of lawn facing a low dune-grass bluff beside Nantucket Sound. Out the window there was a view of the austere Wianno Senior sailboats on the yacht club moorings. Everywhere, there was the smell of salt and the newness of summer and the extraordinary mixture of sounds from nine children, their parents, governesses, maids, visiting cousins, and pets.

The daily schedule here was more rigorous than at Choate. Lem had swum; run; played tennis; played softball; sailed (as Jack's crew), learned that a jib was necessary (to win a race—"Lemmie never quite caught on to how a jib worked," Eunice Kennedy Shriver recalled. "Jack would say, 'Who's going to pull up the jib, Billy? I've got the mainsail and the race starts in two minutes, so who's going to pull up *the jib*, Billy?' "); learned that winning was necessary (to be invited back); played touch football; dropped passes (Jack's); rushed in too fast on the enemy quarterback (Jack's older brother, Joe); run some more (faster this time: away from Joe); been teased (by Jack's sister Kathleen); joked about (by Jack's nine-year-old brother, Robert); teased again (by Jack's thirteen-year-old sister, Eunice); teased some more (by Jack's ten-year-old sister, Patricia); pawed over (by a variety of more or less friendly dogs); and finally, allowed to take a shower.

It was the first time he'd been alone all day. He was hot, exhausted, ready for a shower. He stepped into the stall, shut the door behind him (it opened inward), and turned on the cold-water faucet.

In May, Joseph P. Kennedy had been thrown from a horse

in Bronxville, New York, breaking his right leg and his left ankle. Because Mr. Kennedy did not wish to have the restraint of two plaster casts, his doctor had prescribed scalding hot baths four times a day to heal the leg and the ankle. His house on Cape Cod did not have sufficiently hot water, so Joseph Kennedy installed special boilers in the cellar, providing therapeutically hot water to any bathroom in the house. During installation of the new pipes, the plumbers had apparently reversed the faucets indicating Hot and Cold.

A jet of scalding water shot out of the nozzle, hitting Lem on the chest. Struggling to open the inwardly hinged door, he slipped and fell on his back. The boiling water poured forth. Lem felt as though he were melting. He yelled for help. He couldn't get up. He writhed and kicked and caved in the shower wall. The metal soap dish cut a deep gash from his right ankle to his knee. Finally, Mrs. Kennedy got him out. An ambulance took him to Cape Cod Hospital in Hyannis where he remained for three weeks. Years later, Lem would refer to his first summer visit with Jack's family as "Mother's bad summer."

All three of Mrs. Billings's children were in hospitals that summer. Lem's older brother, Tremaine, a Rhodes Scholar, had contracted polio while swimming in a pond in England; returning to America, the former Princeton football star was wheeled off the ocean liner on a stretcher and whisked to Johns Hopkins Hospital in Baltimore. Lem's older sister, Lucretia, was suffering mild complications after the birth of her daughter, Sally. And now Lem was in Cape Cod Hospital with second- and third-degree burns. His mother visited him there. She was a warm and generous woman, devoted to Lem.

It was not an unhappy time for the patient. He received sympathetic letters, telegrams, and other visitors, too. Mrs. Kennedy and Jack's sisters came regularly to Lem's hospital room, bringing games and flowers and gentle joshing. Robert Kennedy, encouraged by his mother, made a daily visit. Bob was shy and good-humored; Lem liked him enormously. They got along well, but, years later, Bob would kiddingly confess to Lem that although he had been genuinely concerned about

Lem's burns, one of the worst sensory memories he had of his childhood was the stench of scalded flesh he had had to endure every day in Lem's room.

It was also the first time that Lem and Jack had convalesced simultaneously. Both had come up to Cape Cod from Choate. Then, because of an intestinal disorder, Jack had been sent to the Mayo Clinic in Rochester, Minnesota. They exchanged humorous letters from their respective hospital beds. "I feel very sorry for my family being burdened with you for 2 or 3 weeks," Jack wrote Lem, "but I am burdened with you for *9 mo.*"

Far from a burden, Lem was embraced by Jack's family as if he were kinsman. During that summer and the summers that followed before war broke out in Europe, Lem became a kind of ancillary brother in the Kennedy family. He was first and foremost Jack's best friend, but he grew close to all the other children—"So close," Patricia Kennedy Lawford later recalled, "that he was almost raised with us. (Mother thinks he was!)"

Lem had enormous affection for Jack's family, as they did for him. He took pleasure in watching the younger children grow up (Edward, the youngest, was two years old when Lem first met him) and paid special attention to the concerns of each family member. While he would ever after hesitate before turning a Kennedy hot-water faucet, he himself became a fixture in the household. He participated enthusiastically in all family events. He was not a timid visitor during the legendary current-affairs discussions led by Mr. Kennedy at family meals. "Of all the things you can say about Lem—that he was sweet and good and kind," said Eunice Kennedy Shriver, "one quality that has to be remembered is that he was very bright. He had a great sense of history, he absorbed the world in all its dimensions, and he made everybody else look amusing. A lot of people would come in and be funny and make everyone laugh, and the manner in which they were funny had to do with their own ego. But Lem had the ability to make *you* feel funny and clever." He throve in the atmosphere of spirited competition and close-knit family love engendered by Mr. and Mrs. Kennedy. He was trusted.

Though Lem received his share of Mr. Kennedy's infamous icy looks of disapproval, he never met with the kind of coldness or disinterest that outsiders and a few of Jack's other friends would later report about encounters with Mr. Kennedy. Lem and Jack had become such fast friends, and Lem's involvement with the brothers and sisters was so immediate and comprehensive that the duration of Lem's experience as an outsider in Mr. Kennedy's domain was relatively brief. The qualities that Mr. Kennedy revealed to Lem were those of a loving man whose greatest emotional consideration was his children. Lem admired Mr. Kennedy's ability to love his children without spoiling them and to direct them toward intellectual independence without policing whichever path they chose. Probably Mr. Kennedy perceived that Lem's dedication to Jack and the other children was as strong and enduring as that which any father could hope for his children to have from a friend. A few years later, Lem received a letter from Mr. Kennedy:

Dear Lem,

This is as good a time to tell you that the Kennedy Children from young Joe down should be very proud to be your friends, because year in and year out you have given them what few people really enjoy. True Friendship. I'm glad we *all* know you.

J.P.K.

Princeton: 1935

MADE IT BY GOD HOW ABOUT YOU, Jack wired to Lem from Hyannis Port on July 23. Lem was extremely anxious. He hadn't heard anything from the Princeton admissions committee. Another telegram arrived. IN. NO WORD FROM YOU YET. VERY NERVOUS. WIRE IMMEDIATELY—RIP. Rip was Ralph D. Horton, Jr., a close friend of Lem's and Jack's who had been nicknamed Public Enemy Number Three during the Muckers Club episode at Choate. All three of them wanted to go to

Princeton together. Two days later, Lem was at his mother's new home in Baltimore when his acceptance to the Class of 1939 finally arrived; it had been sent first to the old address in Pittsburgh.

In September, though, Jack announced that he was going to take a year off. His father had encouraged him to broaden his education by studying with the Socialist professor, Harold J. Laski, at the London School of Economics. He cabled Lem: SEND GRAY HAT IMMEDIATELY. SAILING 1045 WEDNESDAY MORNING. . . . In England, Kennedy became sick with jaundice and decided that Princeton's Indian summer climate was a better place in which to recuperate than the dampness of London. Lem was in high spirits after receiving a wire from Jack on October 21: ARRIVING PRINCETON THURSDAY AFTERNOON. HOPE YOU CAN ARRANGE ROOMING—KEN.

In the mid-thirties, undergraduates rented dormitory rooms on the basis of their individual financial capabilities. Wealthy students obtained the choicest suites. Lem, who was on scholarship, could afford his share of only one of the cheaper suites on campus. It was a two-bedroom-and-a-living-room arrangement on the fourth—and top—floor of South Reunion Hall. It had one closet, one radiator, and it cost $169 a year. Seventy-two steps separated their bedrooms from the bathroom in the cellar.

At first sight, Rip Horton agreed with Lem that the room was "terrible." Horton, the son of a brewery owner, could have afforded a better suite, but he didn't mind the place. And Kennedy, when he arrived, didn't mind either. Living with Billings, they said, was more luxury than anyone could stand. Besides, the view of Nassau Hall across the treetops was magnificent. They made a joke of loudly counting off each step whenever they ascended from the bathroom.

It was a happy, but brief, autumn for the roommates of 9 South Reunion. By the time they had sent out a Christmas card, parodying lyrics from Fred Astaire's current hit movie *Top Hat* and depicting the three of them in pajamas with a top hat (Rip), enormous white tie (Lem), and tailcoat (Jack), Jack's jaundice had forced him to withdraw from the university.

". . . I will always have a very tender spot in my heart for Old Nassau," Jack later wrote to the class secretary.

The two friends began a feisty correspondence of telegrams. They sent so many wires back and forth that they became friendly with the Postal Telegraph manager in Princeton, an elderly woman named Mrs. Warren. HELLO MRS. WARREN . . . began Jack's seventy-four-word message inviting Lem to Palm Beach for Christmas. ISN'T HE SWEET GIVE HIM MY LOVE was the message Mrs. Warren appended at the bottom of Jack's telegram before delivering it to Lem. A volley of wires was exchanged, discussing Lem's financial uncertainty about the round-trip bus fare. A compromise was negotiated. Jack cabled: WILL PAY HALF OF BUS TICKET COMMA MY SHARE THUS AMOUNTING TO FIFTEEN SMACKEROOS . . . LET ME KNOW WHEN YOU ARRIVE HELLO MRS. WARREN STOP—SWEET ESSENCE OF BUTTERMILK MERCY. Lem wrote to his mother about Christmas plans. She wired back: GO TO JACK I APPROVE —MOTHER.

The Kennedys' house in Palm Beach was a large, elegant, white-stucco villa facing the ocean. There was a well-tended lawn bordered by a seawall planted with tall royal palms; a series of frond-shaded patios; a Grecian swimming pool. Beside the pool was a sundeck surrounded on all sides by tall, adobe walls. Inside this open-air solarium, known as "the Bullpen," were cushioned benches, wicker furniture, and a telephone. It was here that Joseph Kennedy took the sun and conducted his business affairs by telephone, in privacy, and, sometimes, the Altogether.

Despite his continual bus-fare difficulties, Lem was a veteran of enough Palm Beach visits to know that no one, repeat, *no one*, was even allowed to *look* into the Bullpen when J.P.K. was working and sunbathing. If one of the children had to talk to his or her father, he or she knew to call him on the telephone, using the local line. During working hours, the door to the Bullpen was kept locked, and there was to be no noise in the pool area. So it was with not a little horror that Lem listened one sunny day to a proposition of Jack's.

Lem had an excellent singing voice, and he knew a song

which had become a favorite of Jack's. It was not a Christmas carol. Jack especially liked the song when Lem sang it, which was often, because Jack would persuade Lem to sing it whenever they were having fun, which was most of the time. Billings probably sang more renditions of "I'm No Angel" than Mae West, who had made the honky-tonk tune famous:

Aw, come on let me cling to you like a vine
Make that low-down music trickle up your spine
Baby, I can warm you with this love of mine—
I'm no an-gel!

Aw, let me feel your fingers running through my hair
I can give you kisses 'till you walk on air
Love me, honey, love me 'till I just don't care—
I'm no an-gel!

I'll take your blues, stomp down your troubles,
Bank you with a steady roll
Here's your connection, take my affection,
You're my new ace in the hole.

Aw, let me have you now before the night is gone
Come on let's flag this joint so we can carry on
I can make it heaven where the shades are drawn—
I'm no an-gel!

Lem's performances were full of deliberate slurring. "He couldn't sing those lyrics without getting embarrassed," said Peter Kaplan. "In that thirties way, those lyrics were dirty, and there was something delicate about Lem's moral sensibility. He had a Victorian embarrassment about sex which made the Rabelaisian side of him seem so vivid. He saw boundaries, and when he crossed them, he could do anything he wanted. But when he was on the delicate side, there was that old Billings morality he had grown up with."

Usually, Kennedy was able to coerce Billings into crossing the boundary, with the first stanza at least. Now Jack was making an astonishing offer. "In those days," said Robert Kennedy,

Jr., "a hundred dollars was a lot of money and Lem was very poor. Jack offered him a hundred dollars to go into the Bullpen and sing 'I'm No Angel' to my grandfather. What Lem was supposed to do was knock at the Bullpen door, and when my grandfather opened it, naked, and probably already mad, Lem, who was wearing only a towel, was supposed to step in, drop the towel, and fling it to one side so that they would be facing each other absolutely naked. Then, Lem was supposed to say—'Hi, Dad. I've always known you've wanted me to call you Dad. And these are words I've always wanted to tell you' —and then he was supposed to burst forth with 'Aw, come on let me cling to you like a vine . . .' "

This was one of the few occasions on which Lem did not yield. (Lem finally did sing "I'm No Angel" to Mr. Kennedy— both fully clothed—at the ambassador's birthday party on Cape Cod in 1961. Afterward, he recounted the President's earlier proposal, and the ambassador replied that Jack should have offered to pay *him* five hundred dollars to listen.) "Whenever they went to a party," Eunice Kennedy Shriver recalled, "Jack would get Lem to sing that song. Jack would never do that, never sing in public that way, but Lem would. So they complemented each other and made each other laugh. They laughed about everything."

After Christmas and Easter at Palm Beach, Kennedy spent the remainder of that school year recuperating on a ranch in Arizona. His health improved. Encouraged by his father, Jack enrolled as a freshman at Harvard in the autumn of 1936. Lem, now a sophomore, continued on at Princeton. They regularly met in New York on weekends. By Thursdays, the telegrams would begin flying back and forth, sometimes as many as seven in one day, enlisting one another to meet trains, arrange dates, obtain invitations for each other: WILL BE IN TOWN AROUND NINE FORTY FIVE DRESSED WIRE ME IN BRONXVILLE ADDRESS TO MEET YOU WILL HAVE ROLLS OR CHRYSLER . . . HAVE YOU GOT ME A DATE BEST—KEN

. . . HAVE WIRED OLIVE ABOUT A DATE FOR YOU—KENNEDY THE EFFICIENT.

WITHOUT TOO MANY GRUNTS AND GROANS WHAT WOULD

YOU THINK OF GINGER WHITES PARTY AND RUSS CLAIMS
HE CAN GET ME IN AND YOU ALREADY HAVE AN INVITE . . .
BRING YOUR GIRL LEAVE YOUR PHONE NUMBER AND I WILL
PHONE YOU IF I CANNOT COME REGARDS—KENADOS THE DE-
PENDABLE.

The telegrams were notable not only for their frequency
but for, as Lem would later remark, their dramatic "complications." There were enough last-minute wires concerning refus-
als by regular dates, standby dates, and blind dates on big
college weekends to keep a Cole Porter musical running into
six or seven acts before a satisfying denouement. Between
scheduling plans, Kennedy never missed an opportunity to rib
Billings: (TUESDAY NIGHT STOP BILLINGS IF YOU HAD AN-
OTHER BRAIN YOU WOULD HAVE ONE—JACK). Kennedy also
sought every opportunity for Billings's company; many of the
wires from Jack were invitations for trips, a source of economic
complication for Lem. Regarding one invitation, Lem would
later note: "I didn't go—I wish I had—I suppose it was money
again." And later, another notation: "Again, money problems
to get to Palm Beach for Easter vacation. I had to ask Jack if
I could bring Spankie Baker—a rather unattractive Choate
friend—but he had a car!!"

On one weekend, Kennedy wired Billings from Palm
Beach with information about the handsomeness of his suntan,
the hour of his arrival in Pennsylvania Station, New York, and
plans for a night on the town. The ribbing about the Palm
Beach tan—or Lem's lack of one—provoked Lem to rummage
through his medicine chest for a bottle of iodine. ("As you
know," Lem would later write to Jack's sister Kathleen, "there
is nothing more irritating than Kennedy with a sunburn when
everyone else is pale.") Although Lem had not been in Palm
Beach, he nevertheless had a becoming, deep-bronze tan
when he met the 1:50 train from Florida. He spent the rest of
the evening in the men's room at the Stork Club, trying to
scrub the iodine stain off his face.

In its heyday, during the thirties, the Stork Club at 3 East
Fifty-third Street was more than the most fashionable nightclub in Manhattan; it was a way of life. Kennedy would fly

down from Boston; Billings would hitchhike into town from Princeton; they would meet (often at the Roosevelt Bar), pick up their dates (sometimes with one of Jack's father's cars), and go to "the Stoke" for a night of dancing. Lem was self-conscious about his lack of spending money. Kennedy matter-of-factly solved the problem by spending on an equal basis with Billings. They created their own ritual to avoid the embarrassment of a large bill: They would each order only one drink. (At the Stork Club, pretty girls in general, and their dates in particular, were usually given champagne on the house.) Then, during a lull in the dancing, Billings and Kennedy would exit to a less-expensive pub-style bar around the corner where they would have a few glasses of beer before returning to their single, extravagant Stoke cocktail.

While Kennedy naturally accommodated himself to Billings's spending limits, Billings, for his part, had to adjust his own cash flow to the slightly annoying paradox of Kennedy's financial situation. It was, Lem believed, one of the great mysteries of life: Jack never had any cash in his pockets. Sometimes, Jack didn't even have pockets—or pants: His finely tailored evening clothes, suits, sports jackets, and trousers were in a perpetual state of being lost. It was the damndest thing. Lem, who took possessions very seriously and couldn't bear to lose a single one, was bewildered. Eventually, he came to realize that although Jack provisionally had a room of his own in each of his parents' houses, Jack had never grown up with just *one* room with *one* closet, or for that matter, *one* tuxedo, *one* dress suit, and so on. Money was not spent lavishly by Jack or his family, but where clothing was concerned, there were certainly multiple items, perhaps too many to keep track of.

So Lem, with some amusement (because he had grown used to this phenomenon since their Choate days) kept tabs on Jack's wardrobe. "Dear LeMoyne, Many thanks for sending Jack's tuxedo and the three blankets," a Kennedy governess wrote from Bronxville on January 28, 1936. "Jack had wired me about the tuxedo, intimating I had given it away in the charity box, but, I wasn't a bit scared, as I thought it would arrive in the mail from somewhere. A package arrives for him almost daily containing various articles of wearing apparel he has dropped somewhere. . . ."

Good-natured about Kennedy's absentmindedness, Billings was humorously competitive about Kennedy's popularity with girls. They each had a more or less steady girl friend throughout college (Billings dated Katharine Duncan Hartwell, a striking brunette from Stamford, Connecticut; Kennedy continued to date Olive Field Cawley) and were successful with casual party dates. Jack was the more sought after of the two. Corresponding with Jack's sister Kathleen, Lem described a wedding reception at which "brother John was right in his element as he found Dotty Burns & Missy Geer there—all anxious to hear about how Marlene Dietrich thinks he's one of the most fascinating & attractive young men she's ever met." Lem constantly needled Jack about Jack's success with girls, insisting that it could only be attributed to his father's wealth and fame. Kennedy disputed this theory, and because Billings continued to espouse it so persistently, Kennedy decided to put it to the ultimate test.

They agreed to switch names for one night. Ralph Horton arranged blind dates for them. Jack became LeMoyne Billings and turned over his father's chauffeur-driven Rolls-Royce to Lem who was introduced to his date as John F. Kennedy. The matter was settled to Jack's satisfaction, Lem's chagrin. All things being equal, "LeMoyne Billings" enjoyed a memorable date that night, while "John Kennedy" had only a fair evening with his girl.

Most weekends ended with Billings hitchhiking back to Princeton and Kennedy training up to Boston. Gradually, their studies began to occupy more and more of their time: (Kennedy to Billings: HAVE THREE EXAMS NEXT WEEK TWO ON TUESDAY SO WILL HAVE TO BE WORKING THIS WEEKEND. . . .) Kennedy began devoting serious concentration to economics and history, and later, his political science courses. Billings decided to major in Princeton's Art and Archaeology Department; he developed what would become a lifelong passion for painting, sculpture, and architecture.

Increasingly, their attention was drawn to the news from Europe. Nazi Berlin and Fascist Rome proclaimed a political Axis that year. Ethiopia fell to the Italian dictator, Mussolini, and the demilitarized zone of the Rhineland was suddenly occupied by the Nazi Führer. Germany and Italy aided Franco's forces in Spain's civil war. In May, a short item appeared in a Pittsburgh newspaper: "Though all American passports legibly state, 'Not good in Spain,' ex-Pittsburgher K. Le Moyne Billings, son of Mrs. Frederic T. Billings who moved to Baltimore last year, and John Kennedy, son of Joseph P. Kennedy of Washington, will visit that war-torn country this summer for three weeks. They sail June 30 on the *George Washington,* will attempt to study war conditions."

Not to mention cathedrals and girls.

Europe: 1937

Lem and Jack were on their own. The two-month grand tour began in Le Havre when Jack's convertible Ford sedan was hauled off the boat. Kennedy had hopes of getting to Paris quickly, but before reaching the capital, Billings insisted on visiting every single cathedral town, from Rouen to Beauvais to the bomb-blasted ruins of Rheims. Billings had taken his first architecture course at Princeton, and was now reaching a high pitch of excitement over the actual choir vaults and naves themselves. Kennedy, usually a rapid motorist, became content to drive at cathedral-pace while listening to Billings's trenchant commentary on Gothic architecture. In fact, he didn't have much choice.

It was characteristic of Lem to awaken Jack's interest in the cultural aspects of their tour. Lem was the sort of traveling companion whose enthusiasm made everything—even things he loathed, such as toupees, the sight of blood, or cantankerous maîtres d'hôtel—seem fascinating. He had an eye for detail. Jack's traveling techniques got Lem involved in political discussions, night life, and events that were closed to the average tourist. Discovering a huge crowd swarming around Notre Dame in Paris, Jack led the way past police barricades, and discovered that Cardinal Pacelli, the secretary of state of the Vatican (later Pope Pius XII), was celebrating Mass for the president of the Republic and numerous foreign dignitaries. Special passes were required for admission. Kennedy, with Billings in tow, marched straight up to the VIP portal and automatically entered the cathedral without offering so much as a single word of his atrocious French. Billings was stopped, then pushed back into the crowd despite his protests in slightly less atrocious French. Lem was annoyed, but finally chalked it up to not having the *savoir-faire* Kennedy possessed. Afterward, back at their walk-up room in the Hotel Montana, a modest establishment near the Gare du Nord (their room cost 80 cents per night), Jack described the Mass. He had sat six seats away from Albert Lebrun, the French president.

Throughout their travels, Kennedy was determined to gauge the heated political temperature on the continent. He kept a diary of observations, asked questions of everyone they met (especially those who spoke English), and wrote letters to his father, reporting, for example, that the French were confident of the security of the Maginot Line against any Nazi threat. Billings dispatched to his mother long letters containing vivid descriptions of chateaux. By day, they were model travelers; by night, they were *bon vivants,* eager for educational experiences at any hour. Sallying south through the Loire Valley, they pointed the convertible toward the Iberian Peninsula.

At the border, they discovered that in contrast to Notre Dame, there was no VIP entrance to Spain. Heavily armed border guards turned them back. They stayed instead at nearby Saint-Jean-de-Luz with Kennedy's Harvard classmate Alex de Portalis, whose family had a house on the Gulf of Gascogne. There, they met Loyalist refugees who had been high-ranking officials in the former republican government of Spain before the civil war. Billings and Kennedy listened to horrifying firsthand stories of Franco's bloody persecution of the Loyalists. Somewhat less deplorable, but more immediately offensive to them was a bullfight they attended in Biarritz. Sitting next to an ecstatic French woman and her unwitting young son, Billings and Kennedy realized that they were alone in their disgust at the cruelty of the bull's slaughter. The people of this part of the world seemed, to the travelers, positively bloodthirsty. When one of the picadors' horses was gored and led from the arena with its guts dragging in the dirt, Kennedy elbowed Billings to make sure Lem noticed how intense was the mother's eagerness for her child to witness this impressive spectacle.

Visiting Lourdes, the holy town to which a million pilgrims flocked annually seeking miraculous cures, a rare thing happened: Billings got sick. Next stop, Carcassonne, of which Kennedy remarked in his diary: "An old medieval town in perfect condition—which is more than can be said for Billings." Despite Kennedy's small winnings at the tables in Monte Carlo, they continued to stay in the cheapest hotels; throughout their journey, Kennedy cheerfully accommodated himself to Billings's low budget. In Italy they attended a Mussolini rally and had a private audience with Cardinal Pacelli at the Vatican. Billings did impersonations of Mussolini all the way up to Germany. Munich was their first exposure to the arrogance of the Nazis.

Years later, Lem would recount his impressions of prewar Germany to Robert Kennedy, Jr.: "Lem said that he and Jack didn't like the self-confidence of the Germans, the contempt. They saw contempt for Americans everywhere. For instance, instead of shaking hands, the Germans would salute and say, 'Heil Hitler!' And Lem and Jack were expected to return this salute. Instead, they got it down so that they just casually threw back their hands and waved, saying, 'Hi ya, Hitler.' " On the top floor of a beer house in Munich, they drank with a group of Black Shirt Nazi troopers, one of whom was Oxford educated, chubby, and friendly. Confirming that Billings and Kennedy could take a couple of large beer mugs as souvenirs, he helpfully directed them to a door through which they were assured an undetected passage. No sooner had they followed his instructions than a waiter brusquely confiscated the mugs, detained them, and asked for their passports. Meanwhile, they saw that the Black Shirt trooper's pudgy face was gaping with laughter. They had no regrets about leaving Germany, with the one exception of having missed, by three days, seeing Hitler at a Nuremberg rally. For years afterward, they would talk ruefully about their untimely departure from Nuremberg.

After Amsterdam, Brussels, and London, they finished their tour in Scotland with a visit to the country estate of Sir James Calder, an acquaintance of Jack's father. Sir James's manor house, though it had more than twenty-five bedrooms, featured only one operative bathroom which happened to be a great distance from Billings's and Kennedy's rooms. Furthermore, their host, an elderly Scotsman, had the peculiar habit of shutting off, with a master circuit breaker, every light in the manor at precisely nine-thirty every night. Billings and Kennedy were often caught by the blackout. Hunting in the dark for the bathroom, they grew fond of counting off blackened rooms, as they had once done with the seventy-two stairs leading to the bathroom in South Reunion Hall. Sir James also encouraged them to try their luck with grouse shooting; he remarked that they were a trifle tardy for the season, though.

On a damp, drizzly day, Billings and Kennedy were sent out across the moors accompanied by Sir James's gamekeeper. Neither Lem nor Jack had any experience with shotguns. The gamekeeper had positively no experience with two unskilled, yet highly competitive young Americans. Both were wretched shots. Nevertheless, Kennedy declared his resolve to bag more grouse than Billings who was already complaining about a handicap: With the fog and drizzle on his glasses, Lem shot at angles that would have startled Pythagoras. He maneuvered awkwardly with his weapon, filling the air with scattered shot and oaths. Jack persevered. The gamekeeper successfully concealed whatever surprise he might have had when Kennedy hit the first of two birds. Billings did nothing to conceal his own fury. Finally, with his last shell, Lem managed to fell one spindly-looking grouse. For a long and loud few minutes, he expressed his pleasure at his achievement. Jack, however, claimed victory. Among all creatures on Sir James's heath, the gamekeeper was more silent even than the dead game.

A week later, Billings and Kennedy were still carrying their now pungent grouse when they boarded the ship for the passage home. For Lem, it was an unforgettable crossing. On the second day out, unbeknownst to Lem, Jack struck up a friendly conversation with a man in the ship's gymnasium, a Dutch wrestler who claimed to have recently won the world title of professional wrestling in South Africa. He was on his way to a title bout in New York City. The Dutchman admitted to Kennedy that he was having problems maintaining his normal level of prebout training. There was no one aboard who could give him even a decent warm-up. He had wrestled the ship's cook, but apparently the cook was no match for the world champion.

Kennedy offered a solution. He informed the Dutchman that his best friend was a highly touted, though strictly amateur, wrestler. Kennedy then proceeded to give the champion a rather expansive profile of LeMoyne Billings's wrestling career at Choate and Princeton. He spontaneously conferred on Lem four or five interscholastic tournament trophies, not to mention a half dozen of the greatest wrestling feats in Ivy League history. By the time Kennedy had captured the champion's interest, Billings had fallen just short of turning professional. Promising the champion a challenging opponent, Kennedy made arrangements for a preliminary match the next day.

"Jack was always trying to test Lem by entering him into competition, almost as his second," said Robert Kennedy, Jr. "Both of them got, I think, vicarious satisfaction out of each other's achievements. They were able to get as much pleasure out of the other person's success as they did out of their own. Later on, Lem certainly enjoyed Jack's political successes as much as Jack Kennedy did. And I think that Jack probably enjoyed it when Lem won a wrestling match as much as Lem enjoyed it. He enjoyed Lem's strength and physical abilities probably even more than Lem because Lem never really put that much stock in his own enormous strength. It was almost as if all the times Lem demonstrated his physical prowess he did it for Jack as a return, as part of a sort of reciprocal arrangement in which each of them would show off the best of their abilities so that the other one could take enjoyment out of something that he couldn't do himself."

In the ship's salon that evening, Jack broke the news of the match to Lem. He mentioned that a wrestler whom he had met needed some good competition. Lem was receptive to the idea, and also curious about what sort of opponent would *need* him for competition. Jack replied offhandedly that Lem's opponent was just "some guy" in the gymnasium.

The next day, 175-pound LeMoyne Billings found himself facing a man who outflanked him by at least 100 pounds. It was too late to back out. Acting as bout promoter and referee, Kennedy was already discussing the rules with his fighters. Billings hotly contested a few minor regulations, hoping that his opponent would get bored and call off the whole match. The Dutchman began taking off his warm-up togs. Lem noticed that he didn't have a merely impressive build; he had a whole Olympic stadium of muscles, multiple tiers with box seats and a grandstand.

The champion regarded Billings with high interest. Lem felt helpless as a lamb, and just as sacrificial. He removed his glasses, and grimly positioned himself over the bulk of the Dutchman who, following Kennedy's urging, began on the bottom in referee's position.

Lem vaguely saw Jack begin the match with a wave and a grin. Lem couldn't budge the Dutchman who did a quick sit-out, bucked, and immediately held Lem in a half nelson. Lem's face was squashed into the mat. The soft mat had a familiar feel to it, but that, and the recollection of a few improbable moves, were the only reminders of a sport that Lem had once known as wrestling. As far as Lem was concerned, the matches, which continued every day, had nothing at all to do with wrestling, even less with *sport.* They had more to do with Jack's unquenchable laughter and Lem's body being simply *moved,* at will, from one part of the mat to another. Yet Lem was not entirely discontent.

Years later, Lem would tell Peter Kaplan about Jack's huge enjoyment of the contests: "Lem used to say that nothing in the world gave Jack more pleasure than watching Lem being hauled all over that gym, day after day, by this monster. It was that whole idea of torturing somebody as a show of friendship. And I mean *torture.*"

The following summer, Lem made tentative plans for an even more arduous crossing.

Transatlantic: 1938

In March, Joseph P. Kennedy, now the ambassador to the Court of St. James's, moved part of his family (Jack and Joe remained at Harvard) to the ambassadorial residence in London. From Princeton, Lem kept up the correspondence he had begun in 1934 with Jack's sister Kathleen.

Known as "Kick," she was witty and high-spirited. Lem adored her. She had become part of Lem and Jack's collegiate social life; Lem frequently invited her to football games, parties, and once to a museum: BET MAH BOOTS YOU'VE NEVER BEEN TO METROPOLITAN, he cabled to Bronxville, New York, in February 1938, GOING THERE WILL GIVE YOU SOMETHING TO DISCUSS WITH EUROPE'S CROWNED HEADS AROUND THE TEA TABLE. Replied Kick: THERE IS NO ONE I'D RATHER SEE METROPOLITAN WITH THAN YOU. . . .

Their cables and letters—a kind of continuous epistolary romance that would sustain one another through times of happiness and tragedy until Kathleen's death in a plane crash in 1948—were full of deep affection and gentle kidding. "I really hated to see you go," Lem wrote from the Ivy Club library on March 13 after Kick's departure to England on the *Manhattan.* "I can't figure out why—but I did—maybe it's because that for 6 months I won't have anyone to gaily go to the Stoke with & scrutinize critically all the meatballs & their sweeties there— I had such a good time that night that it gives me a pain in the neck to realize that I would have to go all the way over to England to repeat it." He then added: "I'm really very fond of your picture—you ironically enough almost look like an angel in it. There's one thing that I am certain of & that is that I won't possibly forget an angle of your face. . . ."

Kathleen, preparing to be presented at Court in Buckingham Palace on May 11 and for her debut on June 2, wrote of the latter: "Wish you could be here for it. I so often think of you when I meet a guy who thinks he is absolutely the tops and is just a big ham. What laughs you and Jack would get. Very few of them can take any kidding at all. . . . Anyway you are still the mystery man in my life. . . ."

Eager to join Jack and Kick at the ambassadorial residence that summer, yet not wanting to go into debt and unable to afford passage on the transatlantic liners, Lem inquired at merchant shipping companies about the least expensive way to make the crossing. He discovered that the Manchester Line in Montreal had a cattle boat that sailed for Europe on the morning of June 29. Lem notified the company of his intention to sign on in Montreal on the twenty-eighth. But when he learned the details of the passage ("You had to pay a twenty-dollar fee," Lem recalled years later, "and then water the cattle the whole way over"), he declined. Instead, he spent part of the summer canoeing with a Choate friend four hundred miles north of Quebec.

In September, when Jack returned from London and descended the gangplank of the *Bremen,* Lem stood on the pier in New York, happily expecting to see Kathleen appear behind her brother. He was chagrined to hear Jack tell the surrounding group of reporters that she had decided to remain in London. "Have heard the *bad* news," Lem immediately wrote to Kick. "I had no idea you were even considering staying over there for a year—it's really a large pain in the neck. If I'd known this I'd really have swum across this summer. . . ."

Interlude: 1941–1945

Contemplating his future two months before graduation from Princeton in 1939, Lem wrote to Kathleen: "None of us are worrying too much about jobs—this country is getting more and more war conscious—and we all expect to be over there at least by fall. . . . Last night at the movies they showed the newsreel pictures of our Air Force and Army maneuvers and everyone hysterically got up and cheered—even brother John's flat feet and bad stomach won't keep him out of this one."

As old classmates began to enlist after graduation, Lem grew increasingly anxious about his own medical defects. Poor eyesight would keep him out of any service if and when America entered the war in Europe. By September 1941, Jack had enlisted. After rejection by the army and the navy because of his bad back, Kennedy was granted a commission as an ensign in the Naval Reserve and went to work for the Office of Naval Intelligence in Washington. Lem, trying desperately to get into the navy, made frequent exploratory trips to Washington. He stayed with Jack at his apartment in the Dorchester Hotel on Sixteenth Street. Both of them were frustrated that autumn: Jack by his inactive desk job, which entailed writing and editing naval intelligence bulletins; Lem by his inability to get any kind of military job. Rejections from the army, the navy, the air force—even the Coast Guard—put Lem in low spirits. There were constant reminders, too, of his lowly 4-F status. When he and Jack went out to parties in Washington, Jack looked particularly dashing in his navy uniform; Lem appeared the same as ever in his Brooks Brothers uniform.

One Sunday, after Lem accompanied Jack to eleven o'clock Mass, they began the afternoon with their usual disagreement about touch football. It was the one issue that consistently disunited them throughout their friendship. In this instance, Jack loved to go down to the sweeping greensward around the Washington Monument where a serious game of touch could always be found on a Sunday afternoon. Lem, because of his myopic clumsiness when throwing or catching a ball, hated touch football, especially when it was played with total strangers in pickup games. It was bad enough playing with, say, Jack's brothers and his Harvard varsity friends; but dropping the passes of competitive, unfamiliar people was more embarrassment than Lem cared for. Always, it was the same: Lem would capitulate to Jack's wish to play, and Jack would find the most challenging game on the Mall. Then he and Jack would be picked by separate teams, and before long, Lem's teammates would realize the terrible mistake they had made. Eventually, it would become a test of Lem's endurance simply to appear in the huddle.

This particular Sunday was no different, except that the date was December 7, 1941. After the game was over, the two of them were driving back to Kennedy's apartment when suddenly a broadcast crackled over the car radio: Japanese bombers had launched a surprise attack on Pearl Harbor. America would at last enter the war. In the excitement of the moment Lem felt disappointed and extremely civilian. Unlike touch football, this was not a conflict he wanted to watch from the sidelines.

Kennedy was soon transferred to Naval Intelligence in Charleston, South Carolina; his duties were no less dull there than in Washington. Billings returned to his job as a junior executive at the Coca-Cola Bottling Company in Bridgeport, Connecticut. Each man was restless. They corresponded frequently—Jack expressing his annoyance at the inefficiency of the navy, Lem relating his difficulties with a second unsuccessful round of military optics examinations. In February, after his brother's wedding in Nashville, Lem visited Jack in Charleston for a week. There he saw Jack give his first public speech.

Before the workers of an armaments factory, twenty-four-year-old John Kennedy lectured about two different kinds of incendiary bombs. At first, Lem was nervous for Jack; the technical details of the assignment seemed hazardous, particularly for an inexperienced public speaker. In fact, Kennedy knew very little about any kind of incendiary bomb. Nevertheless, he carried off the presentation with flair. Lem was impressed. Jack was, too. The speech went so well that Ensign Kennedy was emboldened enough to call for questions—a dreadful mistake, Lem thought. The first question came from a man who wanted to know precisely how to distinguish one kind of incendiary bomb from the other. Lem held his breath. The ensign appeared unfazed: "I'm glad you asked that question," replied Kennedy, pausing for a moment. "Because in two weeks, a specialist will be coming down here and that is exactly what he wants to talk about."

By the summer of 1942, both Billings and Kennedy were a few steps closer to the war. Curiously, Lem was the first to see action. While Jack was engaged in the officers' training program at Northwestern University, Private LeMoyne Billings was bound for Cairo aboard a ship sailing in a secret convoy out of New York Harbor. He had been accepted by the American Field Service, a paramilitary ambulance corps which soon went into the front lines of desert fighting against Rommel's forces in Egypt. Meanwhile, a few letters arrived from Jack. Although he had applied to the PT boat training unit in Melville, Rhode Island, he was still champing at the bit of stateside rules and regulations. Comparing officers' training to their days at Choate and his commanding officer with their dorm master, Jack heartily endorsed the more autonomous freedom of Lem's active duty as an ambulance driver. Unlike Lem, he felt that in his present position he was not the master of his own destiny. He was itching to get his hands on the wheel of a PT boat in the combat zone. While enduring the wait for sea duty, Jack told Lem, he often reminded himself of President Roosevelt's famous words: "This war is bigger than you and me." In February 1943, Kennedy finally received orders to the South Pacific as a replacement officer for Motor Torpedo Boat Squadron 2.

For Lem, the war was German machine-gun bullets making Swiss cheese of his ambulance. German butterfly bombs were "damn disconcerting," he noted in his diary. By early April 1943, Lem recorded that "Rommel's Afrika Korps has been bashed again. More than 10 prisoners have been taken. Germans in full retreat." He wrote Jack long, graphic descriptions of the fighting and of his continuing struggle to get a naval commission. In May, Jack wrote back from his hut on the Solomon Islands. Lieutenant Kennedy was now skipper of his own boat, PT 109. He advised Lem to get home safely and soon, but added that he wished Lem were part of his crew.

During the summer, their correspondence abated. The three month silence was worrisome. Then in September, Lem received a *New York Times* clipping from his mother: Jack's bravery had saved the crew of PT 109 after a Japanese destroyer had cut his boat in two in the Blackett Strait. A few weeks later, a long letter arrived from Jack, but the news was mostly about the large percentage of Jack's old girl friends who had recently gotten married, and about his desire to spend a month in Palm Beach with his family and Lem. He alluded to the PT 109 episode only briefly, laconically mentioning that he had lost his boat and some of his men.

By November, after receiving minor shrapnel wounds during General Montgomery's decisive victory at El Alamein, Lem was home. Jack, who was now executive officer of his squadron and commander of a new motor gunboat (PT 59), advised Lem to stay put, settle for 4-F, and wait for his return, which he hoped would be soon. He felt confident of getting home in one piece.

Out of uniform, Lem was restless again. With the help of Ambassador Kennedy and Congressman John W. McCormack, he received a commission as an ensign in the U.S. Naval Reserve. Jack sent congratulations in his last letter from the South Pacific. He advised Lem to report to Palm Beach for a special head-start tutoring program from his old pal, the lieutenant. Kennedy, the twice-decorated war hero, returned home in January. Billings, the desert veteran and raw ensign, arrived in Palm Beach dressed in uniform. He had orders for sea duty aboard the attack transport U.S.S. *Cecil,* soon to depart for the South Pacific "for the duration." Their reunion lasted until Easter. Kathleen, stationed with the Red Cross in England, wrote to Lem, wondering if he and Jack were "lounging on the beaches of Palm Beach. I'd just like to see you two recounting your war experiences to each other."

In fact, Billings and Kennedy did not spend much time during or after the war swapping combat stories. They took pride in each other's military careers (Lem began a small archive with the newspaper clippings about Jack's leadership and gallantry aboard PT 109; Jack wrote to Mrs. Billings, expressing his admiration for the job Lem had done voluntarily in North Africa), but each man downplayed his own wartime experiences. Getting home in one piece was the best story each man knew. They both looked thinner and a bit more owlishly intense around the eyes, but they were whole. Their friendship, too, was intact. Despite the losses that the war brought to them as individuals, and the sudden personal growth evoked by rapidly encountering decisive change, their relationship continued as youthful and exuberant as ever.

Two weeks after the Japanese surrendered in August 1945, Kennedy received word from Billings that he would remain aboard the *Cecil* in the South Pacific until February or March of 1946. "As I was still getting over V-J Day," Jack replied from Hyannis Port, "your letter set me to thinking and wondering if it wasn't time you came home for a long rest. I have been figuring out your points and it comes to nine as close as I can figure it, which leaves you forty more to go which indicates eighty months more in; which comes to about seven years. Frankly Billings are you happy in the service?"

Kennedy had just returned from Europe where he had spent a month in England, covering the British elections for the Hearst newspapers, and several weeks in Germany, accompanying Secretary of the Navy James V. Forrestal in Forrestal's private plane. ("I tried to get in a few licks for you," he told Billings, who was now a lieutenant jg, "but it just so happened that your name never came up and I thought it might prejudice my standing if I brought it up.") He reported that the trip had been "extremely interesting," but didn't want to "bore [Lem] with the details," which included, Lem later learned, a visit with Forrestal to the summit conference of the Big Three—Truman, Stalin, and Churchill—in Potsdam, Germany, where Lieutenant John F. Kennedy first met General Dwight D. Eisenhower.

"As to my present plans," the young war hero continued, "I am making some speeches around—one is going to be at the Waldorf-Astoria in NY on Oct. 4th—the other speakers being Baruch, Dewey, and Byrnes—I suppose I'll speak after Baruch and Dewey and just before Byrnes." He had also been made assistant to the chairman of the Boston Community Fund. "As you can see," he told Lem, "I'm getting ready to throw my slightly frayed belt into the political arena any time now. I'm expecting you back to vote early and often. Would you suggest a question period after my speeches? It went so well the last time I tried it in the deep South. . . ."

By December, Kathleen reported to Lem, "Jack never stops thinking and talking about his political career and is really interested in it. So you'd better prepare yourself to listen."

Stateside: 1958

During the past thirteen years, Lem had listened and watched and remained closely involved as Jack had grown almost annually into new roles: as the congressional candidate in the Eleventh District of Massachusetts; the freshman congressman; the junior senator; the husband of Jacqueline Bouvier; the patient of a nearly fatal spinal operation; the Pulitzer Prize-winning author of *Profiles in Courage;* the vice-presidential contender at the Democratic Convention in 1956; the father of a baby daughter, born in November 1957, whose sparkling eyes were revealed to the nation four months later in *Life* magazine, peeping at her father over the edge of her bassinet.

Meanwhile, by 1958, Lem had introduced a different kind of effervescence into the national consciousness. After graduating from the Harvard School of Business Administration in 1948, Billings had gone on to become a vice-president of Emerson Drug Company in Baltimore. Since the eighteen-nineties, Emerson Drug had been manufacturing Bromo Seltzer, the nation's favorite remedy for hangovers and pain due to upset stomach. Yet by 1953, Emerson Drug's main competitor, Miles Laboratories, had won a larger share of the national effervescent market with their product Alka Seltzer. Unlike Bromo Seltzer (a granular compound of bicarbonate of soda, citric acid, and caffeine), Alka Seltzer included aspirin and was sold in tablet form. So in 1954 Emerson Drug installed approximately $75,000 worth of new tableting and packaging machinery in its Baltimore plant. The result was Bromo Seltzer tablets, the first batches of which were immediately shipped for test-marketing in Cuba.

Meantime, the tableting machinery in Baltimore lay idle.

Billings had an idea: Since people had always complained about the salty aftertaste of Bromo Seltzer (bicarbonate of soda and citric acid when introduced to water produce a salt called sodium citrate), why not add flavoring—grape, orange, perhaps even root beer—to mask the taste of sodium citrate? Moreover, why not make immediate use of the new tableting machinery while the shelf life of the Bromo Seltzer tablets was being tested in Cuba's tropical climate? Billings then took the idea a step further: He proposed that the company manufacture an altogether new effervescent tablet which would be introduced to water, producing a flavored soft drink.

The other Emerson Drug executives were skeptical. "A lot of us weren't sold that it was a good product," recalled Francis McAdoo, who was then the company president and also a close friend of Billings's from Princeton days. "LeMoyne was the most enthusiastic, and he worked very closely with the laboratory technicians. When the product was made, none of our marketing people knew how to handle it: It wasn't a medicine; it wasn't exactly a food; and even with the flavoring, it left a salty aftertaste. But LeMoyne was very bullish on the idea of the product as a soft drink." Billings even had a name for the new tablets.

Before the July Fourth weekend of 1953, the product was shipped to selected grocery stores and supermarkets in Harrisburg, Pennsylvania. Billings drove up from Baltimore on Thursday, July 2. He spent all of Friday in a supermarket aisle, monitoring the shelf where the new product was displayed. The thirty-seven-year-old man in the Brooks Brothers summer suit was amazed by what he saw. "It was incredible," McAdoo remembered. "We sold hundreds that day. Children were wild about it. LeMoyne himself was jumping up and down with excitement."

By Monday evening, the entire first shipment of the product was sold out. By Tuesday, the tablets were being asked for by name. "After Harrisburg," said McAdoo, "we realized that we didn't have to advertise the product very hard because the kids just asked their mothers to buy 'Fizzies.'"

Billings's Fizzies confounded the drug company executives

and parents everywhere. It was hard for adults to understand how a beverage that tasted so unpleasant could be so popular. Billings had cannily foreseen the secret: Despite its salty aftertaste, the product was incredibly fun to drink. To children, the tablets seemed magical. In 1956, the first year of nationwide marketing in eight different flavors, Fizzies became a craze among children between the ages of six and twelve, earning $10 million in net sales. "We didn't ever lose money on it, which is a very unusual thing for a new product," McAdoo recalled. "But during the early sixties we began losing sales volume and it became apparent that the product wasn't here to stay, so the company decided to phase it out."

For a time, Billings considered trying to buy the rights to market Fizzies himself. He asked McAdoo to become his partner, but McAdoo, who "didn't have confidence in the longevity of the product," declined. Lem turned to other friends, but as McAdoo said ironically: "Jack Kennedy was pretty busy with other things by that time so I don't think LeMoyne ever asked him to go in on it." There was, however, talk of Lem's borrowing investment capital from Ambassador Kennedy, but Lem finally decided that he would prefer to remain financially independent from his best friend's family.

In 1958, Billings was made vice-president of Lennen & Newell, a New York advertising firm; Kennedy was reelected to the Senate. Individually, their lives had become full of important new relationships; between them there continued to be a bond of loyalty and easygoing affection. "Sometimes," said Eunice Kennedy Shriver, "friendships have to have an equal level of respect to continue on. If you're always pulling someone along, it's a different kind of relationship. But you never pulled Lemmie anywhere because he had so much talent of his own. Lem was always an equal to Jack. In friendship you must have an equal amount of affection and respect for one another, and they had that. Jack was a better politician than Lem, but Jack never looked down on Lem because he wasn't a better politician."

One night in 1958, Lem made a light joke about Jack during a private dinner with Ambassador Kennedy at the Pavilion restaurant in New York. Jack was not present. Joseph P. Kennedy was not amused. Lem listened with some incredulity as the ambassador sharply upbraided him, then explained that now was the time to learn that he should never again talk that way about Jack in public. "LeMoyne," he said, "you are one of the people who must understand this. You can never know who might be listening. From here on, you must think of Jack less as a friend and more as a potential candidate for President of the United States." Lem just sat there, speechless, totally unprepared for the ambassador's final remark: "I will tell you right now that the day is going to come when you will not call Jack, 'Jack.' You will call him 'Mr. President.'"

Hyannis Port: 1960

On November 8, Election Night, Lem sat listening to the nationwide returns in Robert Kennedy's house which had been turned into a communications command center, wired with webs of telex machines, televisions, and telephones connected directly to distant cities across the land and to Ambassador Kennedy's house next door and the candidate's house across the lawn.

Lem was confident that Jack was going to win. He had seen only Kennedy victories on such nights as this, first in 1946 in the Eleventh District of Massachusetts where he had headed up the Cambridge headquarters, later in the statewide senatorial primaries and elections, and this year in the decisive primaries of Wisconsin and West Virginia. Now, with the early returns showing a strong Kennedy lead over Nixon in the East and parts of the South, Lem joined in the small, cheerful clusters of family and friends who were surrounded in the living room and on the sun porch by the upper-echelon campaign staff led by the candidate's brother Robert. Ambassador Kennedy's prediction to Lem seemed to be coming true, at least partly so.

During the long campaign, Lem had occasionally wondered what salutation he would use if Jack was elected President. They had continued to call each other Billy and Johnny during their adult lives, though more often it was simply Lem and Jack. Lem, of course, had used "Congressman" and "Senator" in conversations *about* Jack, but never *to* Jack in a private setting. So the thought of greeting the closest friend he had had for twenty-seven years with a hearty "Good morning, Mr. President" seemed, to Lem, unutterably awkward. He had enormous respect for the dignity of the office of the President and resolved never to call Jack by his nickname in front of anyone except the family. But in private, casually? He wondered... *Please pass the salt, Mr. President?... Jack?...* You couldn't call the President of the United States *Johnny.* It was definitely a problem. And now, such thoughts seemed no longer premature. Lem felt certain that it was only a matter of time before he would be right in the middle of that situation.

As the long night wore on, Kennedy's early lead shrank. Unexpected losses in Ohio and Wisconsin and early returns in the crucial states of California, Illinois, and Michigan were now signaling danger. The traffic in the command post and on the lawns between the three houses swelled and ebbed, carrying bad news, then good news, then more bad news. Lem, who had been shuttling among the houses through the evening, was one of those who did not go to bed until the outcome looked favorable, though still uncertain.

Before turning in at the Joseph Kennedys', he decided to make one last visit to Jack's house. Cutting through the gap in the shrubbery and then across the lawn, Lem was approaching the front porch when several men dressed in dark suits suddenly closed in on him and demanded identification. He had none. Naturally, he hadn't figured on needing his wallet on Election Night in Hyannis Port. He explained who he was, but they would not allow him to enter the house. Lem was furious. He tried explaining again. He pointed out that he had just been in the house only an hour or so before, at 3 A.M., and wondered why they hadn't taken notice of him then. They stood unmoved and it occurred to Lem that he had not been aware of the Secret Service's presence up until this very moment. The change had come.

Jean Kennedy Smith happened to be passing by at that

moment. The Secret Service men asked her to verify Lem's identity. "Never seen him before in my life," she replied and continued into the house. A few moments later, Jean returned, laughing, and Lem was permitted to enter the house of the next President of the United States.

Miami: 1960

After his victory, the President-elect stole a few days rest in Palm Beach before building the new administration. He asked Lem to accompany him on the trip south. They would fly down to Miami on the *Caroline.* Sitting beside the President-elect in the first car of the motorcade winding through the streets of Hyannis to the small airfield, Lem looked out at the clusters of people waving in the bleached November Cape Cod sunlight. The crowds were not as large as some he had seen during the campaign, but they had a completely different quality. Instead of the blurry excitement of a campaign mob, these people contained a kind of thrilling clarity; they knew at last on whom to focus all their energy and hopes.

The solid throng waiting for the new President's arrival at the Miami airport was as focused as a compass needle. Following Jack out of the airplane, Lem had the impression of standing behind the magnetic center of the Northern Hemisphere.

Another motorcade was waiting on the tarmac. The President-elect smiled and waved to the crowd. The fatigue of the campaign was not visible in his clear gray eyes or in the color that suffused his skin with an Alpine luster. Long gone from his face was the mischievous expression of schooldays; the rakish, debonair, collegiate handsomeness; the wan, gaunt look of the congressional days. With each passing change of his appearance, he had above all retained his youthful essence. His face and physique had reached a fullness that was perhaps commensurate with the office he had aspired to and won. His weight of 172 pounds was now nearly equal to Lem's. The size and power of his smile, if not actually larger than Lem's enormous smile, surely surpassed Lem's in dental wattage. Now that both men were in their early forties, there was more physical similarity between them than there had ever been before. Yet of the two, Lem looked older—not just because he was, in fact, a year older but because Kennedy appeared unimaginably young to be the most powerful man in the free world.

The motorcade was waiting. There were more greetings from the mayor of Miami and other local officials. Then a general move was made toward the limousines. Lem automatically followed the President-elect into the first car. He thought nothing of it. After all, he had been traveling beside Jack since they left the house in Hyannis Port, and for that matter, in similar situations all his life. But the dissimilarity of this situation, the new requirements of protocol, and the very difference in his role as the President-elect's oldest friend, escaped Lem.

There was a pause. Lem sensed that something was not quite right. The President-elect looked sideways at Lem. "Well," he said, grinning, "where do you want the mayor of Miami to sit?"

The White House: 1961

"Can you imagine"—Lem would later exclaim—"my best friend becomes President of the United States and I spend his presidency *in Denmark*?"

Such a fate was unimaginable. Lem wasn't going anywhere. Although the President-elect had offered Lem three positions in his administration—director of the Peace Corps, director of the proposed U.S. Travel Service, ambassador to Denmark— Lem had respectfully declined. He carefully considered each post and came to the conclusion that working for the President in an official capacity would mean becoming an employee of his best friend. He was sure that having an official role in the government would change their relationship. Besides, what role could be better than the one he had had for twenty-eight years? "Of the nine or ten men who were close to the President, I would say that Lem was Number One," Eunice Shriver explained.

Two hours after John F. Kennedy took the presidential

oath in the brilliant winter sun and frosty air on Capitol Plaza, Lem walked into the White House for the first time in his life. It was an experience he would always remember. The Executive Mansion seemed, to Lem, the final, tangible evidence that Jack was President. Up until now, the greatness of the mansion had been more symbolic than actual. But here it was—and they were in—the greatest living museum of American history. Lem considered it the perfect house for Jack; it contained privilege without ostentation, dignity and elegance without affectation, grandeur without pretensions, unlimited opportunity. It was amazingly white. Entering the mansion with Eunice Shriver, Lem had a sudden flash of *Gone With the Wind:* the scene in which Mammy and Prissy accompany Scarlett into her new mansion in Atlanta—their struggles are over; Prissy looks around wide-eyed and declares: "Lawzy, we's rich now!"

Before the inaugural balls that evening, they had a chance to look around upstairs. "We laughed a lot," Eunice Shriver recalled. "And we scooted up to the Lincoln Room." Lem, an American antiques nut, was drawn to the Lincoln Room, a high-ceilinged bedroom and sitting-room suite on the south side of the White House. Here was Abraham Lincoln's dark, austere furniture arranged as it had been during his presidency. The bed was massive and high. Lem and Eunice jumped up on it and had their picture taken. They had a view of the Washington Monument surrounded by snow, ablaze with light across the South Lawn. All of Washington seemed to be aglow that night.

Lem's mother was also in town for the inauguration. The President, despite the formidable demands on his time, had ordered that a memorandum be sent to the inaugural garage concerning Mrs. Billings's arrangements for the Armory ball: *This comes from the President-elect: Please have a special car take care of Mrs. F. T. Billings (78 years old). . . .* Lem's pleasure at Jack's thoughtfulness was enormous. "That is one of the astounding parts of the relationship between Lem and the President," said Peter Kaplan. "It puts a stamp on it that says, this is a lifelong friendship. Their mothers actually mattered to both of them equally. When they were boys, Jack had stayed at Lem's house in Baltimore, and he knew Lem's mother well. You've got to remember what childhood friends are like: When you go to stay at your friend's house, you have to check with your mother, and their mother has to check with your mother, and that's exactly how it was done when they were boys. Jack knew Mrs. Billings as his best friend's mother, and you know how much you care about your best friend's mother. So, of course the President would take care of her."

As the new administration got under way, the White House became, of course, less a museum, more a home for the President and his family. For Lem, it was like a home away from home. Living in New York, working for Lennen & Newell, he often came to Washington and stayed in the mansion as a houseguest. Later, when the President appointed him a founding trustee of the National Cultural Center (which finally became the Kennedy Center for the Performing Arts), Lem's visits were even more frequent. The White House guards knew him well. The Secret Service gave him a code name. A guest room on the third floor became more or less Lem's room. He was able to leave his things in the closet there. His presence was not necessarily required at official functions. Whenever the President and the First Lady were otherwise engaged, Lem took care of himself. He came and went without any special formality.

Although the burdens of the presidency dramatically changed Kennedy's life, his enjoyment of companionship was as strong as ever. Not since Franklin D. Roosevelt had there been a President who was able to preserve the continuity of a long friendship while in office. "The presidency is not a very good place to make new friends," Kennedy observed at a news conference. "I'm going to keep my old friends." Friendship was important to him. It momentarily released him from the pressures of his job. "Some people like to go on long walks alone; Jack liked to be with a friend like Lem," said Eunice Kennedy Shriver. "Just because he got into the White House didn't mean he was going to stop having a friend like Lemmie.

If someone has always had friends, they keep them up, and Jack was that way. It was just a natural part of his personal life. He had a great capacity for this friendship. Well, it's hard to describe it just as friendship; it was a complete liberation of the spirit. I think that's what Lem did for President Kennedy. President Kennedy was a completely liberated man when he was with Lem."

The President's wry sense of humor, an integral part of his friendships, also became a hallmark of his presidency. In the White House, the President kidded Lem more than ever, especially at official ceremonies. The President never failed to introduce Lem formally to visiting heads-of-state, dignitaries, and celebrities, but the introduction was never simply a matter of . . . *I would like you to meet my friend, LeMoyne Billings.* When Alan Shepard came to the White House to receive the Distinguished Service Medal after his historic space flight in May, the President presented Lem to the astronaut as "Congressman Billings." He made the introduction with an absolutely straight face. The idea was to see how Lem would hold up, in office.

"He was always doing this," Lem would later recall. "He'd introduce me as Congressman Billings or Senator Billings, and even *General* Billings. The person, whoever it happened to be, would of course take him quite seriously, which was awfully funny until the President turned away to someone else, and I'd be left alone, standing there with this terrifically important individual. And then they would *always* turn to me and say, 'Well, Senator, which state are you from?' And I'd move away as fast as I could. What was I going to say?—'Oh, the President was only *kidding.*'"

The title "General Billings" posed the most trouble for Lem. He would have rather had a sudden promotion to admiral because his knowledge of the army was nil, compared to his slightly greater familiarity with top-level naval procedures— on account of his final status in the Naval Reserve as a lieutenant junior grade (one rank above the lowly ensign). The worst of it was that Lem never knew what rank to expect from the President. Once, when the President convened a high-level meeting aboard the presidential yacht *Honey Fitz,* moored in Newport, the President stood at the head of the gangway, presenting all those coming aboard to the officer of the deck, a navy captain in dress blues: "This is the Secretary of State, Mr. Rusk; the Secretary of Defense, Mr. McNamara; General Taylor, the Chairman of the Joint Chiefs of Staff—" and so on down the line until, at last, the President announced without a change in tone of voice: "This is Lieutenant Junior Grade Billings." The captain's eyes swiveled dubiously from the lieutenant junior grade to the Commander in Chief (whose expression indicated that no error had been made) and back again to this bespectacled, forty-five-year-old junior officer in mufti. Meanwhile, General Taylor had stopped abruptly, and was looking back over his shoulder to see what kind of lowly lieutenant was coming aboard the presidential yacht with members of the Cabinet.

The President also enjoyed practical jokes with longer fuses. One weekend in Newport in November 1961, the President hosted a luncheon at Hammersmith Farm for the visiting prime minister of India, Jawaharlal Nehru. The President and Nehru and the Indian ambassador, B. K. Nehru, ate in the dining room, discussing matters of state, including American policy in Vietnam. Jacqueline Kennedy and Nehru's daughter, Indira Gandhi, and Lem lunched in another room. Lem got along especially well with Madame Gandhi, a fact that Jacqueline mentioned to the President when they returned to Washington that evening for a state dinner at the White House. The following weekend, Lem was in Washington, staying with the President's sister and brother-in-law, Jean and Stephen Smith. Almost from the moment Lem arrived, a series of messages began coming from Blair House where the prime minister's daughter was staying. The messages were invitations from Madame Gandhi, requesting the pleasure of Lem's company. Each one was more compelling than the last: Would Lem join her for luncheon? For tea? For dinner? For a drink after dinner? And so on, throughout the weekend. Lem was dumbfounded. And a little pleased with himself. Repeatedly, he returned the calls to Blair House, and each time was told that

Madame Gandhi was out—she would, however, be back shortly, and was expecting his call. It wasn't until late Sunday evening that Lem discovered that Madame Gandhi's passion for his company had been concocted by the President with the help of the White House switchboard.

The White House: 1962

Lem came back from France that spring with some pretty hot news. He had become very friendly with Greta Garbo. He had been introduced to her by a mutual friend on the Riviera. They had hit it off immediately. Garbo thought Lem had a wonderful sense of humor, and Lem thought Garbo was, well . . . *Garbo.* She was the most hypnotically beautiful woman he had ever met. They had a lot of laughs together. Lem told the President *all* about it, and the President listened with great interest.

That summer, Lem saw Garbo again in Europe. They took a rambling tour by car along the Italian Riviera. They had more laughs. Back at the White House, Lem again told the President about all the blithe and enchanting adventures he had had with his great new friend, Greta Garbo. The President's curiosity was aroused; it was time to hear Garbo's side of these stories.

The President and the First Lady invited Garbo to dinner at the White House. She would be the guest of honor; Lem would be the only other guest. The evening was planned so that Garbo would arrive shortly before Lem, giving the President an opportunity to chat with the actress, and to make special arrangements with her for Lem's arrival.

Lem was sure that it was going to be a perfect evening. He arrived at the White House, glowing with anticipation, and was greeted by the President in the family dining room on the second floor. Then Jacqueline came in with Garbo at her side. The President ushered Lem over to say hello to their guest, saying, in effect, how happy he was to have them both to dinner since they were already so well acquainted. With a spring in his step, Lem greeted her: "Greta!"

There was a ghastly pause. Garbo looked at Lem blankly. She turned, puzzled, to the President.

"I have never seen this man before," said Greta Garbo.

Thereupon followed the most disorienting half hour Lem had endured since World War II. The foursome sat down to dinner. Lem was unable to eat. He was in shock. He could not fathom the inexplicable amnesia that had overcome Greta Garbo. She repeated that she was quite certain she had never met Mr. Billings before this evening. *(Mr. Billings!)* Directing his full confusion on Garbo, Lem rattled off the names of places they had been together, the people they had seen, the approximate *dates,* for crying out loud. . . . Nothing seemed to refresh Greta Garbo's memory about the enchanting times they had shared on the Italian Riviera.

The President was full of earnest curiosity about how such a mix-up could have occurred. Perhaps Lem had become friends with someone who *looked* like Garbo. Lem testily declared that that was impossible. But for a wild moment he wondered if indeed he had spent those enchanting evenings with someone who had actually *impersonated* the actress. Such people did exist, living falsely off the notoriety of those celebrities who avoided the public. Lem did not know what to think. He was mystified. In his befuddlement, the one possibility he did not consider was that Garbo's amnesia had been recently contrived by the President of the United States.

The actress kept up the ruse until the second course. It was, Lem later recalled, "one of the worst things I ever went through in my life. I was dying . . . *dying.*"

Glen Ora: 1962

For Lem, the best of times during the Kennedy presidency were the weekends at the President's Virginia retreat estate, Glen Ora. The President firmly believed in separating work and relaxation; part of each weekend—when no official business kept him in Washington—was devoted to relaxing with his family in the country. His service as a congressman had demanded frequent trips to Massachusetts and long hours on

Capitol Hill away from his family, but now the President, for the first time in his married life, was able to be at home with his family not only for breakfast and dinner but for lunch and weekends, too.

The President also maintained a strict distinction between business friends and private friends. His moments of genuine relaxation, especially during weekends, were guarded for family and old friends. Members of his staff and official visitors were rarely invited to Glen Ora for the weekend. "Oftentimes when Jack wanted to relax," Eunice Shriver recalled, "he would call Lem on the phone, or they would go out to the country—just the three of them: Jack, Jackie, and Lem. Jack liked to have Lem around. With Lem he didn't have to talk politics all weekend long."

The weekend would begin on Saturday morning. Lem would accompany the President on the trip by helicopter from the White House to Glen Ora, arriving in time for lunch. After the meal, Jacqueline, an avid equestrienne would go riding, leaving Jack and Lem to stroll around the grounds. "They'd just be talking," said Eunice Shriver, "just going on as if nothing had changed. Jack was a Jeffersonian man. He and Lem would talk, for example, about the restoration of the important buildings from the Federal period in Lafayette Square across from the White House. They could talk about everything. Jack trusted Lem completely. Lem never used Jack for anything. His loyalty to Jack was always absolute. He never wrote about him. He was never disloyal because he didn't want to use what President Kennedy had said to him for any ego-building for himself."

On some weekends during their walks, the President would discuss the political events of the week. During the weekend immediately before the Bay of Pigs invasion in 1961, and especially during the weekend after, the President talked extensively with Lem about his reactions to the situation in Cuba. But usually their conversations were about people and events removed from the presidency. Sometimes after lunch they would play an abbreviated golf game on the lawn. The President, having strained his back during a tree-planting ceremony in Canada in 1961, chipped his shots lightly, but still with much greater accuracy than Lem, whose coordination was as poor as ever. The President enjoyed showing Lem how to improve his game.

In the afternoon they rested. The President would take a long nap, sometimes easing the pain in his back with a heating pad. Lem could tell when the pain was intense only by looking at the President's face because he never heard the President discuss it, except for one occasion which Lem later recounted to Robert Kennedy, Jr., who recalled: "In 1962, when the President was in really bad pain, they were talking about this one day, and Jack told Lem, in all sincerity, that he would trade all of his political successes and all of his money for Lem's health just to be out of pain."

Before dinner, they would play a spirited game of backgammon, betting at low stakes, accumulating debts they never paid to one another. Dinner was served early; these were quiet evenings of conversation and laughter. The President and his wife would retire early, and Lem would go upstairs with a book, and the day would be over.

Lem took special pleasure in those days at Glen Ora because there, during certain moments of relaxation, his friendship with the President seemed to continue as it always had— or as much as it was possible for a friendship to endure between two men whose responsibilities had become so varied. ("I don't know if the President of the United States can have a friendship like the one Jack and I had," Lem would later say, referring to the increasing number of relationships that divide any President's time and attention. "It may be impossible.") On the other hand, he would also say that because of their common history, and because they had known each other for so many years, a few moments during a country weekend, a few infusions of the old humor, were all that was necessary to preserve their long friendship.

It didn't seem to matter that there were, of course, huge differences in their lives now. The President was a married man and a father. Lem was a bachelor. Billings was seeing various women—a well-known movie and television actress;

an Italian baroness; a society lady in Nashville—yet, to Lem, friendship had remained such a powerful, emotionally sustaining force that for himself marriage seemed superfluous. "Jack made a big difference in my life," he would say years later. "Because of him, I was never lonely. He may have been the reason I never got married. I mean, I could have had a wife and a family, but what the hell— Do you think I would have had a better life having been Jack Kennedy's best friend, having been with him during so many moments of his presidency, having had my own room at the White House, having had the best friend anybody ever had, or having been married, and settled down, and living somewhere?"

Lem enjoyed his independence and his bachelorhood. "His need for personal mobility and for adventure and new experiences, and his sense of fun and of life and of friendship had more to do with aspects of his own personality than with the need to tie himself to anyone else," Lem's niece, Sally Carpenter, recalled. "He never liked to plan far ahead and thrived on being able to do whatever appealed to him at the last minute." A spontaneous departure with a half-full suitcase was a Billings trademark. His appointment calendar for 1963 shows a busy social schedule—engagements with Mrs. Albert D. Lasker in January; skiing weekends with the Attorney General and his family in February; lunch with Rip Horton in March; two visits to Camp David in April; trips to Hyannis Port in July and August, sandwiching a visit to Mrs. Lasker's Villa Florentina in Saint-Jean-Cap-Ferrat; an engagement in September listed simply "F Sinatra"; and a meeting with the President at the White House in October. The following appeared written in his datebook for November on the twenty-second: "2:30-S. Smith 3021 Park," after which was later added a single word —*canceled.*

New York: November 22, 1963

It was just before two in the afternoon. Lem had eaten lunch, and was now walking back to his office building on Madison Avenue. His stride, as usual, was brisk—all his weight bouncing forward off the balls of his feet. Passing through the lobby doors and into the building, he slowed down, and then came to a halt.

Something was happening. Office workers were exiting the elevators and the lobby, en masse. Some were stumbling. Some were staring. Some were standing stock-still, tears streaming down their faces. Everything was in slow motion. An acquaintance of Lem's recognized him and, assuming that Lem already knew, came over to say: "I'm so sorry . . . about the President . . ."

Lem didn't want to know any more.

Wheeling around, he dashed back out to the avenue, and began walking north, blindly. He saw nothing and heard nothing, yet everything around him was projecting the most cruel, dazzling, unnatural clarity he had ever known. He had no idea where he was going or if he was going to make it there. When he looked up, he found himself on Fifth Avenue at Fifty-first Street, standing in front of St. Patrick's Cathedral.

He entered and sat in the cool darkness, perspiring heavily and breathing deeply. He was unable to move. Some time passed. Then he was aware that the cathedral was quickly filling up around him, and he began to cry.

There is a photograph that was taken of Lem five or six months after that day. Outwardly, it shows him enjoying a spring morning with neither lamentation nor grief—though instead of dominating his physiognomy, his smile seems to be propping up his face. Inwardly, the picture shows a forty-seven-year-old man who has devoted himself so wholly to a friendship that its loss will forever shape his future, and divide his life. "In many ways," said Robert Kennedy, Jr., "Lem thought of his life as being over after Jack died. For one thing, he stopped being physical. He refused to play sports or touch football after Jack died—almost as if he'd done those sports and physical activities for Jack and for Jack's enjoyment, as part of the trade-off which allowed them both to take enjoyment out of the other's best strengths. Lem always said that the one good thing he got out of Jack's death was that he never had to play a sport again."

And he didn't. At least not until a new generation had grown up around him.

East Eighty-eighth Street: 1981

Into his sixty-fifth year, Lem lived in a beaux-arts style townhouse adjacent to the Guggenheim Museum. A visit to 5 East Eighty-eighth Street was like touring a museum beside a museum. Every room was crammed full of carefully preserved treasures, overlapping collections of art and antiquities and early American furniture and personal mementoes—all reminders that men in history had actually been alive. But the place had a quality that was unlike any museum. In the vestibule, after pressing the buzzer marked BILLINGS, you felt that you were about to be absorbed into a world that contained the secret of regeneration and of youth that seemed somehow endless.

Lem lived alone, but he had become a friend to a new generation. "To one generation of Kennedys he was a friend and gifted counselor," wrote Robert Kennedy, Jr. "To my generation he gave an even greater gift. The stories he told and the examples he set gave us all a link to our dead fathers and to the generation before us. The titans became men whom we should not fear to emulate." Lem became a kind of folk hero to the younger generation. "It was like the Landmarks Commission," said Peter Kaplan. "We just declared Lem." He continued to live as intensely in the present as he had in the past. His apartment was the focal point of ceaseless activity. It often had the spirit of a collegiate fraternity where anything might happen. Upon arrival, you might suddenly be pulled into a chorus, singing off-color limericks in the hallway, or you might encounter one of Bobby Kennedy's reptiles—a twelve-foot boa constrictor, for instance—somewhat under control in the hall closet. As in any fraternity, there were rituals that governed the evening.

Lem would dispense dozens of stories, each one a masterpiece of storytelling. Like a curator, he would illustrate them with primary source material. He would jump up, returning from his library with one of thirty large scrapbooks which he kept on a double-tiered, five-foot-long shelf, like a multi-volumed encyclopedia of life and friendships that spanned six decades. There was always a new scrapbook in progress. The items in each one were organized nonchronologically. This arrangement gave you a startling perception of the passage of time: A photograph of Lem and Jack in Palm Beach in 1933 would be pasted right beside a photograph of Lem and the President in the Oval Office in 1963.

Opening one of the books, Lem would point to a photograph or artifact and continue his story. Once the background details were filled in, you would begin to feel the funny part of the story coming on; excitement would build; Lem would clench his fists and spread his arms in front of him. When he saw that you were laughing, that you truly understood how *really terribly awfully funny this situation had been,* his fingers would explode from his fists, and he would shout triumphantly:

"Hey, *maaaaaaaan!*"

There were long stories, too, about people and situations that had made him mad. When these were told, his large fingers would huddle up in his fists, the knuckles resembling white helmets. At the climax of the story, one squad of fingers would break from the huddle, like five huge offensive linemen fanning out, ready to die for their quarterback. Invariably the villain of these stories was a mulish traffic cop or a condescending headwaiter or an uncooperative member of his cooperative townhouse. But sometimes it was someone closer to him —a friend—and then the look of exasperation and disappointment in his eyes was profound.

The villain's transgression might have been some minor incivility or, in the case of a friend, a major breach of trust. Whatever the case, you learned quickly that it was dangerous to express support for the villain, even when the villain had been "right" and Lem had been "wrong." If you did not take Lem's side in the matter, he would become hurt and furious.

You would try to reason with him—endlessly—sometimes until the window turned blue with dawn. But ultimately, if sides had to be taken, he expected that your allegiance to him, as a friend, would be inviolate.

The reason for this was simple. In Lem's emotional landscape, friendship was the highest form of devotion. He was committed to friendship as to a covenant, the most important precept of which was ferocious loyalty: You stood by your friend in any circumstance. You defended him against his detractors. You were sympathetic to his opinions. You fought his battles with him. You loved the people he loved, hated those he disliked. You were never away when needed. You covered his weaknesses with your strengths. You accepted his flaws. You did not sit in judgment against him. You suffered no embarrassment from being completely honest. By adhering to such guidelines, you were able to share continuous emotional fidelity and absolute trust. "It was like having a wonderful map to life," said Peter Kaplan. "And it made an awful lot of things better when you shared the same boundaries. You both always knew exactly what you were looking at and talking about. That was Lem's geography."

During the evening, Lem enjoyed looking at and talking about the things he had collected in his apartment. Like Mole in *The Wind in the Willows,* there was nothing he liked quite as much as the sharing of sensitivity about a valued object with a friend. If, for instance, a piece of scrimshaw was important to Lem, it was crucial for him to know how you felt about it. Sharing similar tastes was an important matter (like co-signing a treaty that divided the boundaries on the friendship map). It was vital that you cared about scrimshaw as much as he did, or that you at least *appreciated* the particular piece of scrimshaw he had put into your hand. If you were indifferent, Lem would suddenly say, "Okay, if you could choose *one* thing in this whole house for your own, what would you pick?"

The decision seemed impossible. And, at first, it made you feel uneasy. It was hard to escape the feeling that you were casing the joint. Lem urged you to take as much time as you needed to make your decision. He watched closely for your reactions to certain objects.

Examining the room, you saw the following: a large Audubon folio print of a great-footed hawk; a collection of antique muskets; signed lithographs by Picasso and Miró and Dufy and Chagall; a large stuffed Gila monster; a framed series of twenty-four small, amusement-park-sized black-and-white photographs of Lem and Jack taken during summer vacation from Choate; a collection of antique weathervanes: a cow, two horses, a rooster; dozens of presidential medallions and coins set in Lucite; a framed series of three black-and-white photographs of Lem and Jack, each taken with the subjects sitting on the same outdoor chaise in Palm Beach, dated 1934, 1944, 1954; Lem's small sixteen-year-old dog, Tolly, a pedigreed Basenji who was the great-grandson of a dog named Fulafire of the Congo; a collection of swan decoys; framed eighteenth-century silhouettes of Lem's maternal ancestors, the Le-Moynes; dozens more photographs—Lem's favorite niece, Sally Carpenter; his college roommate, Gus Stroud; Bobby Kennedy, Jr., handling a hawk; Senator John Kennedy and his bride, Jacqueline, on their wedding day; Ambassador Joseph P. Kennedy posing formally with his family in the American Embassy in London; Kathleen Kennedy in a Red Cross uniform; President Kennedy on a lawn in Hyannis Port with the entire Kennedy family and Lem; Lem and Jack beside the pool in Palm Beach in 1934, suavely holding aloft Jack's wriggling younger brother Teddy—a collection of glass pigs; a bust of Charles Lindbergh; a Chippendale highboy upon which was displayed another host of photographs and two framed pencil sketches of John and Robert Kennedy, one of which was inscribed to Lem from Ethel Kennedy: "For Lem—Jack's best friend . . ."

Another sweeping glance at the room revealed that you had missed about nine tenths of its contents, prompting Lem to remark, "Hey, you're really observant, man." You protested that the whole idea of selecting one favorite object was ludicrous, but he was determined to know your taste. He hustled you off to the hallway where the density of things on the ceiling-high shelves was proportional to your inability to arrive at the decision he wanted you to make. Lem pointed out Picasso plates; a collection of Fitzhugh Chinese export china; porcelain miniatures, mostly dogs; a piece of scrimshaw, which had resided on President Kennedy's desk in the Oval Office beside the PT 109 coconut shell; a commission from the Society of the Cincinnati to Lem's great-great-great grandfather; a two-sided canvas by Miró; a print of Mount Auburn Cemetery.

If you happened to pause before a particular 8½" by 11½" painting—depicting a tree-lined Provençal street—Lem immediately clapped his hand over a small identifying plaque on the gold frame. He challenged you to identify the painter who was, Lem claimed, "*very* important." His eyes were playful, as though he knew a double-edged secret which you, too, might understand if you were clever enough. Finally, though, the secret was too much to conceal, and he uncovered the plaque: STREET SCENE *after* UTRILLO by PRESIDENT JOHN F. KENNEDY.

After a lengthy tour of the library, and the back hallway (covered from floor to ceiling with a collection of presidential commissions), and the bedrooms, and the bathrooms, you returned to the living room, dazed. You wondered how he had ever managed to get all that stuff into the apartment.

"Okay, man. You've seen my *whole* house—what're you going to pick?"

You pointed to the framed series of twenty-four small photographs taken during Lem and Jack's summer vacation from Choate. Lem gave you a look that said you were out of your mind. He was sincerely dumbfounded.

"You mean you wouldn't want—" Then he listed on his fingers the most expensive works of art in his collection.

"Nope."

"*Gaaaad,* man." Lem was shaking his head. He looked confused, pained. You had let him down. There was no hope for you. "Why would you want those *little* pictures? I mean, I don't understand you. . . . You've got to say why you'd want those little pictures."

Privately, you were thinking that photographs of two friends in youth often evoke a particular kind of poetic glamour: The camera has caught a time when all of life is just beginning, when there are bright, debonair smiles and arms thrown cavalierly over shoulders. There is an intensity of emotion which is undiluted and invincible. The two young men seem invulnerable to defeat or sorrow or even to change. Life has not yet measured them. Their happiness seems eternal. Yet looking at the faded image, you realize, of course, that now it's all over.

"I don't know, Lem," one finally mumbled, feeling corny and massively inarticulate. "The two of you just look like you were having an awful lot of fun together."

Lem regarded the photographs in a sudden wistful mood. For a moment his youthful demeanor vanished. He looked like a sixty-five-year-old man. The youth he had in him had stayed past its welcome. His eyes revealed that perhaps he was in favor of one's choice after all; they were rimmed with red, and the blue irises contained love and pain deeper than the words he quietly spoke: "Oh, man, we just had the best fun. The best fun—ever . . ."

He trailed off into some irrevisitable place: wherever the best fun had gone. Then, returning, as if it were always within reach, he brightened, spread his arms wide, and exploded his fingers from his fists.

Pittsburgh: June 1, 1981

The trees near the grave in the Allegheny Cemetery were the sort of stoop-shouldered, patriarchal conifers that made one feel very young because they were so old. Kirk LeMoyne Billings's coffin rested on a scaffold over the open grave. The new damp earth was soft and fragrant. It seemed cruel, or somehow unfair, for anyone to die at the beginning of the summer. Lem had had a heart attack on May 28, a day before the sixty-fourth anniversary of John F. Kennedy's birthday.

The mourners, many of them in their twenties, gathered around Lem's family plot where he was going to rest beside his mother. Lem had wanted his casket carried to the grave by ten young friends. This ritual had been very important to him; it was the final act of friendship: to bear the weight of the dead friend's body to its resting place. But, now, the coffin had already been set in place by professionals. There was a muted discussion about what to do. Finally, the pallbearers, led by Robert Kennedy, Jr., lifted the coffin and carried it in a ceremonial march around the grave in the hot sunshine.

They held the coffin aloft throughout the service, sweat dripping from their faces. The minister recited the Protestant burial, adding a eulogy that celebrated Lem as "a prince of friendship." A few women knelt to say the rosary, and then kissed the casket before it was lowered. A bowlful of gardenias teetered on the top of the coffin. Handfuls of dirt and roses were tossed into the grave. The rest was silence, interrupted only by birdsong and weeping and a few quiet farewells: "... Good-bye, Lemmie ... Good-bye, Geez ..." For a while, no one looked too long into anyone else's eyes.

Slowly the group disbanded, moving away from the grave, and down the wooded hillside to a sylvan pond where they opened bottles of champagne for a final toast. Eunice Kennedy Shriver was talking to a reporter from a Pittsburgh newspaper. She was nodding her head briskly. A question had been asked of her. "Yes," she told the reporter, "Lem was President Kennedy's best friend." She paused, and then added: "And it is my impression that the feeling was mutual."

V : ICE-TIGERS

Dave Knowles / Rob Taylor

R ob Taylor was waiting for rescue at 16,000 feet.
The twenty-three-year-old American lay alone in his
bivouac sack on a snow-covered ledge below the Breach Wall
on the southwest face of Mount Kilimanjaro, the highest mountain in Africa. It was a Wednesday, January 18, 1978. Four days
had passed since Taylor had fractured his left leg in a 22-foot
fall up on the Breach Icicle—a 300-foot vertical cylinder of ice
leading directly to the top of the Breach Wall and the great,
white, domed summit of Kilimanjaro at 19,340 feet. Two full
days had passed since Taylor's climbing partner, Henry Barber, had left him on the mountain to summon the nearest
medical help—more than seventy-five miles away, over alpine
terrain and volcanic rock, through rain forest and dense jungle
and the surrounding plains of Tanzania.

Taylor's left ankle was broken; the fracture was compound,
involving both the ankle and the fibula. After the fall, several
inches of Taylor's fibula had been sticking out from the bloody,
ruptured flesh above his ankle. Taylor had reset the bone and
splinted it with the shaft of an ice hammer. More than once in
the last four days, he had smelled the odor of infection. He had
seen yellow pus ooze from the wound. He knew that his
chances for survival were diminishing every hour that a rescue
party did not come. Taylor was a professional ice climber and
a seasoned alpinist with experience in the treatment of catas-
trophic mountain injuries. By his own estimation he was close
to death.

On the morning of his third day of waiting for help, a thick
curtain of snow fell, covering his bivouac sack and the lifeless
glacial moraines sweeping away below the ledge. A dark haze
clouded Taylor's vision. Though feverish, he was awake. And

now, he felt the presence of another human being. He looked up from where he lay, and this is what he saw: his best friend, David Knowles, standing at the foot of his bivouac sack.

Knowles was dressed in a floppy, GI-green, jungle hat; a red neoprene anorak; wool breeches; short red socks; and a pair of climbing boots which, as always, had holes in the toes. As he stood there on the snow, Dave didn't say anything. He simply gestured to Taylor with his arm—a signal to come and follow.

Six years earlier, at dusk of a winter day, Rob Taylor had first met Dave Knowles in the western Highlands of Scotland, the birthplace of modern alpine mountain climbing. Taylor had just arrived by bus and was standing in a desolate spot on a roadway several miles from the village of Glencoe. Setting down his pack, Taylor wondered if the bus driver had left him off at the right place. Sweeping away from him in every direction was a bleak and barren landscape—the Moor of Rannoch. The wind, whipping through the moorland heather, made a sound that was neither a whine nor a howl, but a low incessant moan.

Taylor felt lost. He had expected to be met here by one of the Scottish mountaineers with whom he had corresponded from his home in Sudbury, Massachusetts. On the other hand, it was already a Tuesday evening, and he had been due in Glencoe on Monday morning. He had gotten lost several times during the 120-mile journey north from Glasgow. Nothing he had seen en route, nothing he had read in the romantic, mountain-inspired works of Sir Walter Scott and Robert Louis Stevenson, and nothing in his own atavistic sense of the Scots clan Taylor (to which his ancestors belonged) had prepared him for his first exposure to the utter inhospitality of this place. The moaning of the moors was more than eerie; it was positively hostile.

Night was falling fast. In spite of the gloaming, Taylor could see for miles across the flat moorland (there being neither trees nor manmade shelters), and in the distance, like a monument to silence, stood a mountain, the Buachaille Etive Mor (the

Great Shepherd) whose prowlike shadow spread itself across the Rannoch Moor. Taylor saw two figures approaching from some two miles off, advancing quickly from the heart of the shadow.

One of the figures was lean and medium-sized; the other was large and bulky. Both were equipped with weathered mountaineering gear; each carried a brace of ice axes in their belts. The two men came upon Taylor, and for a few moments looked him over, silent as the mountains from which they had come. The lean one had a thick, drooping moustache which formed a parenthesis around the corners of his mouth.

"You've certainly taken your time getting here—Robbie, isn't it?" the lean one said in a voice as musical as it was snide. The accent was not Scottish. "I hope this isn't an indication of your performance on the hill. We'll see tomorrow. Be ready half seven." Turning to his companion, he muttered gruffly, "Come on, Ian, time for a pint"; then he strode off up the roadway.

The larger one, whose name was Ian Nicholson, smiled sympathetically at Taylor. "Don't mind Dave," he advised. "He got stuck with some real puntas today—from Cornwall. Never saw snow before." With that, he too was gone.

In all, the American had not offered a word—just a nod of his head to indicate that he was, in fact, Rob Taylor.

The next morning at half past seven, in a climate that was as harsh and dour as Dave Knowles's matutinal mood, Taylor and Knowles hiked together across the moors. Taylor, who at five feet eleven inches was slightly taller and skinnier than Knowles, moved with the supple, wary grace of a cat. He kept his thoughts to himself. He was shy by nature, and though he usually came out of himself in the mountains, here he said nothing, mainly because Knowles seemed opposed to conversation. Evidently, Knowles was suspicious of him—skeptical that a seventeen-year-old American could possibly be a worthy alpinist. Taylor had encountered seasoned mountaineers who were sometimes brusque and abrasive in the company of less experienced climbers, but none quite like this crusty twenty-four-year-old man of the moors.

They continued to hike, growing warmer with each mile, though the silence between them remained chilled. The grade of the terrain increased as they neared their objective: a rugged mountain cliff whose summit was three thousand feet high, and whose Gaelic name was Sgor Na h'Ulaidh. Their line of approach to the base of the cliff now took them directly to the edge of a large wooden-fenced sheep pen in which was huddled a fold of Highland Blackface sheep, each weighing some two hundred pounds.

They climbed the fence at separate spots. Taylor went over easily, jumped into the pen, and glanced at the sheep to check their reaction to this intrusion. A moment later, looking back at the fence, Taylor saw Knowles slipping off the top rail, out of control. Knowles fell headfirst into a large, soft, moist pile of sheep dung. He was covered from head to waist. Big clumps of the stuff clung to his shoulders, chest, elbows, and hands. His face was lathered with it; his eyelashes were heavily mascaraed. The fecal matter had even embedded itself in his moustache, beneath which his lips were now firmly pursed for the protection of his teeth and tongue.

The moaning of the moors was interrupted at last by Rob Taylor's uncontrollable, full-throated laughter, accompanied by the strangely appropriate baa-ing sounds of the sheep. Taylor could not help himself. Here was a world-class alpine climber, who had to his credit a complete, solo circumvention of the rim of Mount Kilimanjaro, a successful ascent of the Eiger North Face (the largest, most difficult, and dangerous mountain wall in the Swiss Alps), dozens of summer and winter first ascents of Highland peaks—in short, a mountaineer in the forefront of international alpinism, who was now picking himself up from a fall into a shearing pen. To Taylor's relief, Knowles joined his laughter. "The sheep's pen broke the ice between us," Taylor recalls. "Dave lightened up, but only briefly."

When they reached the base of the cliff, Dave's mood turned brusque again. Looming above them was a diagonal slit, a long fissure in the eight-hundred-foot-high face of the cliff. The conditions along the route of the fissure were evenly mixed between rock and ice. It appeared to be climbable. In any event, the face, which had never been climbed before, was sure to offer a challenge. "It was wonderful," says Taylor, "to go onto new ground together. It was one of the first positive bonding things we shared—going into the unknown, facing it together. The pressures in that kind of situation are extreme. There are no route descriptions in a guidebook. You have to make your own way. And, literally, if you make the wrong decision, you may die. So there's a closeness that's forced there. And that's what actually started the whole thing for us together. When we began to climb, there was something like a truce between us."

As they started up the first pitch, or rope length, of the climb, Knowles and Taylor were linked by a three-hundred-foot Perlon climbing rope with which Knowles had climbed for at least four years. It was fuzzy as a caterpillar. Knowles took the lead, climbing upward with his hands and feet, establishing the line of the route and the safety system that they would use for the duration of the steep ascent, with variations only for the changing surfaces of rock and ice: At intervals of thirty feet, Knowles stopped, and drove a ring-topped piton into a small crack in the rock wall. To these he clipped a carabiner, a D-shaped linking device with a spring-loaded gate, through which the climbing rope was threaded as he moved upward and beyond this safety point. Tied around Knowles's waist, knotted in front, running back through the secured carabiner, the rope trailed down to Taylor. In a fixed position below, Taylor paid out the remainder of the coil, inch by inch, from around his waist, belaying Knowles. Taylor carefully watched the upward progress of his partner, whose life he now held in his hands. If Knowles slipped off the rock face, the most recently installed piton and carabiner would theoretically hold his weight if, and only if, Taylor's weight at the lower end of the rope was acting as a counterbalance. A slack rope, a roving eye, or any lack of concentration on the part of the lower man could easily result in a wildly spinning rope and the rapid, uncontrolled descent of the falling man, whose body would probably be mashed to pulp somewhere along the rock face.

Unparalleled in any other sport, the safety system used by alpinists climbing in "ropes" of two (or more) was thus one of absolute interdependence and absolute mutual trust and faith. In a rope of two, the responsibility of each man to the other was particularly enormous. When the rope grew taut between Knowles and Taylor at the end of the first pitch, the role of belaying was reversed: Knowles now stopped at a ledge and drew in slack, paying close attention as Taylor followed up along the route to join him. Taylor then took over the lead for the next pitch.

As the course varied rapidly from steep rock to steep ice, each climber began to sense the other's respective strengths and weaknesses. Where Taylor struggled over ice-glazed rock sections, Knowles was at ease; and though Knowles had become a master of mixed media climbing, he tended to have more difficulty on ice, where Taylor was at ease. In the Presidential Range of the White Mountains of New Hampshire, Taylor had become an outstanding ice climber on Mount Washington, the highest peak in New England (6,288 feet), which, in winter, offered some of the harshest ice-climbing conditions anywhere in North America. Here in Scotland, he discovered that the ice was softer. That meant easier climbing, so he was feeling at home on even the steepest, most slippery, sections. A certain amount of elegance and efficiency began to mark the flow of his movements as he led the second pitch. Knowles was surprised and impressed by Taylor's ability, but he remained laconic as ever. "Beautiful pitch," was all he said as he joined Taylor on a ledge. ("You would never hear Dave giving anyone a direct compliment," Taylor recalls. "He would always say that *the pitch* was well done—never that *you* had done a good job leading it.")

High up on the crag, they came to a chimney of rock, a vertical cave in the cliff's face. Wedged in the chimney, perched side by side on a ledge the size of a breadbox, they anticipated their next move—a traverse to the left, a sideways maneuver from the mouth of the rock chimney out onto a bulge of extremely steep blue ice. The transition from one medium to another gave the maneuver additional challenge and difficulty.

Knowles was leading this section. He banged in a piton, threaded the rope through a carabiner, and edged over to his left. The moment he reached the ice, he began to struggle. The old-fashioned Grivel crampons strapped to his boots had short front points that were effective on the dimpled surface of rock, but on hard blue ice they offered little with which to dig in. Knowles was simultaneously maintaining balance, hanging on, and executing the traverse by driving first one, then another, ice axe into the brittle bulge. His arms and shoulders were doing the work; his crampons were giving almost no support. His breathing was heavy. Taylor noticed that his legs were shaking. Then he observed small holes in the toes of Knowles's climbing boots.

Holding the rope tightly, Taylor knew that if Knowles slipped, Knowles would swing off the ice into space, and drop in a great thirty-foot air-fall pendulum swing. "That section," remembers Taylor, "broke down any type of barriers between us because he was in difficulty, and of course he was relying on me with his life. So he couldn't keep up his brusque facade in the stress of that situation. Confronting the unknown allowed things to surface that would never have come out on a normal route where he had everything under control. And that was a wonderful thing—it created a strong bond between us. We were coming closer."

For the first time, Knowles was asking for Taylor's advice: "How does it look, Robbie? Do you think it's all right?"

Knowles had ten more feet to traverse before reaching a slab of rock where the membrane of ice was thinner. "Looks good," Taylor told him from the vantage point of his belay station. "You're moving fine—just a bit further."

Then, with Knowles belaying him, Taylor quickly negotiated the traverse, easily digging into the ice with his claw-like, long-pointed, chrome-moly Chouinard crampons, and they began the final pitch leading to the summit ridge. For

Taylor, this last part of the ascent was no more a break-through than every step leading up to it, yet he felt some-thing passing between himself and Knowles—a sense of acceptance, of respect, of communion. As they reached the summit itself, they exchanged a few excited words, and then lowered their voices, like two men entering the narthex of an ancient cathedral.

The sublime elation of standing on a snowbound summit be-side the friend with whom you had just risked your life and overcome danger on a route that no men had ever climbed before—the intensity of this feeling that was now shared just by the two of you was, according to Taylor, "a hard thing to put into words." The phrases that came to mind seemed to lack in descriptive power the force of the experience itself. Some-times one would hear climbers talking about "the kinship of the rope," or about "two becoming one," or about "the mutual dependency, the lifeline of the rope"—and somehow that didn't begin to convey the actual importance, the depth of the bond one could share when one climbed with a close friend.

In mountain-climbing circles, though, there are some who contend that the sport—in and of itself—does not create true and lasting friendships. "There is a well-established fallacy among climbers that climbing automatically leads partners on the rope to form close friendships," maintains mountaineer Peter Donnelly, who claims that "such 'friendships' are by no means automatic, and frequently superficial and/or pragmatic in nature, particularly among competitive climbers. In other words, while climbing does not preclude the formation of close friendships, it is not necessarily the cause of those friendships." To make his case, Donnelly points to: the decline of the "gen-tleman amateur" whose mountaineering aspirations were rooted in the Romantic movement of the nineteenth century and the pure and simple joys of male companionship on or off the precipice; the limitations placed on mountaineering friendships nowadays by the rising professionalism, commer-cialism, competitiveness, and meretriciousness of the sport;

the necessity of forming not a friendship with a rope-mate, but a pragmatic partnership in order to achieve ambitious mountaineering goals that might lead to increased income and fame in the form of product sponsorship and lucrative book, film, and television contracts; and the small number of "perfect partnerships" or famous friendships of the mountains that had actually survived and endured at lower altitudes.

For Taylor and Knowles there was no question on these issues. David Ambrose Knowles, a graduate of the London School of Economics, was born in Preston, an industrial town in northern England's Lancashire County. At the age of twenty-one, he settled in Glencoe where he became a popular local figure, developing a vocation as a winter climbing instructor and year-round guide. In other seasons he doubled as a Highland shepherd and pub barman. He also worked as an apprentice to Hamish MacInnes, an internationally renowned mountaineer who was one of the foremost experts in mountain safety and rescue techniques.

MacInnes's Glencoe-based Mountain Rescue School and Laboratory sent dozens of year-round missions to rescue climbers on the Highland crags and peaks. His eclectic interests as an adventurer, inventor, writer, wine maker, and opera lover had given him the status of legend among the locals and had earned him several sobriquets, among them, "The Fox of Glencoe" and "The Sorcerer." Thus, when Rob Taylor came from America to work for MacInnes, Taylor became known as "The Sorcerer's Apprentice," as Knowles had been known before him. Like Knowles, Taylor had made Glencoe his second home and mountaineering his vocation. He soon found himself earning a living as an instructor, a guide, a photographer (his work soon appeared on the cover of *The New York Times Magazine*), and as a cinematographic consultant for film crews from the British Broadcasting Company and *National Geographic.*

For Knowles and Taylor, the reason for scaling peaks was not the conquest of the summit but the challenge presented on the route upward. "In our case," says Taylor, "we began spending a lot of time together simply walking in the hills, doing things on weekends, going to the pub. Dave was special in that respect because he grew to mean more to me than just climbing. Climbing was just the way for both of us to be closer to the realities of the mountain world. We had no interest in this conquest of mountains as things of nature being beaten into submission."

Theirs was a kind of mountains-for-mountains' sake credo based on the traditional, prevailing belief in Scotland that mountains may be won, but never conquered. They belonged to a particular breed of winter climbers known in Scotland as "ice-tigers"—men for whom there was more pure joy in the hours spent digging the claws of their crampons into steep slabs of blue ice than in the final attainment of the summit itself. There were surely joys atop wind-smacked summits, but none compared to the fight upward in mist and rain and blizzards and gales while boldly facing the uncertainty of a new route with a loyal and trusted friend.

Over the next two years, Knowles and Taylor enjoyed a period of intense friendship in the Highlands. They were inseparable. They climbed together so often that if a local observer looked through binoculars at the northeast precipice of Ben Nevis (at 4,406 feet, the highest peak in Great Britain), and saw Knowles at one end of a rope length, he knew, without a second look, that Taylor was on the other end. They lived in cottages near one another. They developed a relationship that was free of competition, both on and off the hill. "In all the time we spent together, seeing each other every day, seven days a week, he made me look better, not worse," Taylor recalls. "I felt total acceptance from him, which is something you don't always find among climbers who are out there for their own selfish motives—whether it be fame or fortune or whatever. In his eyes, I was accepted for my full worth as a human being, and as a climber also. In all ways, he allowed me to develop into a fuller being. Saint-Exupéry wrote something which I thought about for years in connection with Dave, and that was—in loving and in friendship, a person leads you back to yourself.

He doesn't draw out of you, he doesn't bleed you. And that's basically what Dave did—he reflected me like a mirror."

In winter, their days began before sunrise. They breakfasted on tea and toast, organized their gear, met on the roadway, and went off to collect the students who were enrolled in Hamish MacInnes's Mountain Rescue School. After a day in the mountains with the students, they would return in the dusk of midafternoon and spend the rest of the evening in the Clachaig, a seventeenth-century pub near Glencoe. There, as part of the shoulder-to-shoulder camaraderie around a pub fire, they drank and talked, but rarely about climbing. ("There was so much else to talk about: girls, women friends, relationships.") And they kidded each other a lot: Dave, who drank great quantities of Laphroig whiskey, teased Rob about his preference for hard cider, which Dave considered a woman's drink. (Rob was also partial to Macvitte's Digestive Wheat Biscuits, a favorite snack of grandmothers.) Rob kidded Dave about his reckless driving in his gray Austin Mini (Dave frequently came close to colliding with sheep along the roadways) and about his periodic forgetfulness. More than once, they had hiked out eight miles, arrived at the base of a mountain, only to discover that Dave had forgotten his crampons. Once they both forgot to bring the rope.

Taylor came to know an entirely different Dave Knowles from the crusty, suspicious mountaineer whom he had first met on the Rannoch Moor. "I had been taken aback by Dave's brusqueness in the beginning, but then I got to enjoy it," says Taylor. "Emotionally, we were quite different. For example, if Dave had something on his mind, he let me know about it immediately. Whereas I tended to be a bit less assertive, and not come straight out with things. But as our relationship grew, he became much more sensitive to the way I was, and I to the way he was. He was such a booger—such a difficult character in dealing with people, and he put on a show of being a hard man, but then he would soften and you'd see a warmth and kindness underneath his crustiness. He was a very sincere, caring person, but he wasn't going to let anyone know that."

Taylor especially noticed Knowles's compassion when they

performed rescue missions in the mountains as a team. The spring was the most popular time of the year for hikers, or Highland "ramblers," some of whom came ill prepared for the sudden changes in weather at high altitudes. Avalanches were frequent then. Call-outs, as the rescue missions were known, would occur at a rate of eight or nine in a single week. On one mission, Knowles and Taylor went to save a girl who had been hiking on an icy ridge and had fallen twelve hundred feet. She was about seven miles in from the roadway, and she was still alive when they arrived with a mountain-rescue stretcher. Taylor remembers: "She was in a terrible condition—broken up completely, head gashed—but alive. She weighed about two hundred pounds, so the amount of energy required to get her off the mountain quickly was extreme. You never saw a person more caring and loving than Dave when he was working to save that girl's life." They managed to carry her to the roadside. Her pulse kept weakening. Taylor saw a look of deeply felt responsibility come into Knowles's gray-blue eyes; he knew she wasn't going to make it. She died on the way to the hospital.

At the pub, they drank nine pints each and did not utter a word about it. The next day, they would have to talk with the girl's parents, who would come to collect the body and ask why it had happened. That seemed to weigh heaviest on Knowles. He went hard on himself, as if there might have been something more he could have done. Death in the mountains had a different effect on Taylor: "When you're nineteen, you think you're invincible. You can live forever. Even when we were bringing dead bodies out of the mountains—they hurt you and affect you, but you don't know them. They're casualties. And you think: That'll never happen to me, or to anyone I know. But I think Dave, being a little older, realized how finite this world was."

During their second spring together in Glencoe, Rob accompanied Dave on his rounds as a shepherd. They roamed from glen to glen, among the folds of Highland Blackface, tending to the "drops," the newborn lambs. They talked about their plans for the summer ahead. In August, Rob would go home to America, then return later in the month to join Dave in the Swiss Alps. Dave had a four-week job in Grindelwald as a safety officer and technical consultant for a Hollywood camera crew that would be filming *The Eiger Sanction,* a spy-mountaineering thriller starring Clint Eastwood. Dave would be earning about $500 a week. Upon meeting in Grindelwald, they would set off by themselves on a climbing expedition in the Alps; then, with the money left over from the Eiger job, they planned to make a winter expedition together to the Canadian Rockies, where they would do some extreme-condition ice climbing. Beyond that they talked about going into business together in Scotland and becoming, in Taylor's words, "an entity unto ourselves."

On a hot day in August, three weeks after leaving Scotland, Rob Taylor went down to the large, white, shingled mailbox at the foot of the long driveway leading to his family's farm in Sudbury, Massachusetts. There was a letter from Dave on top of the pile of mail. He was in Grindelwald, having a fine time with the crew from Hollywood, picking out locations on the Eiger: "The circus has started," Dave reported, "and the first work starts on the face tomorrow." Because he was spending most of his time "chasing the filthy lucre," he was eagerly looking forward to Rob's arrival next week and to their expeditions in the Alps and the Canadian Rockies. "When the show ends," he concluded hopefully, there would be time "to put something back into the mountains."

Taylor's spirits were lifted by the letter. Having spent the past several weeks mainly picking vegetables in his family's garden, he was itchy to return to mountaineering.

In the same pile of mail there was a Western Union telegram addressed to Taylor. He casually opened the yellow envelope and found a message from Dougal Haston, a climber whom he had known in Scotland, and who was working with Dave on the Eiger. It was brief: REGRET TO PASS ON BAD NEWS. DAVE KNOWLES KILLED IN ROCKFALL. EIGER WEST FACE. SERVICES TO BE IN PRESTON. A SORRY AFFAIR. Taylor could not believe it. He was sure it was a mistake. This seemed positively unreal: Here in one hand he had a letter from Dave, written the night before the first day of filming; in the other he held Haston's telegram, which he stood reading over and over and over.

He placed a transatlantic call to Glencoe and reached Ian Nicholson, who told him what had happened: On August 13, the first day of filming on the Eiger's west flank (a ridge far less dangerous than the North Face, which Knowles had climbed in 1971), Dave and the cameraman had been shooting sequences of polystyrene "boulders" rolling down the mountain. They were positioned side by side on a small ledge beneath a rock buttress, three thousand feet high on the ridge. When dusk threw the North Face into shadow, they packed up the camera equipment, and waited for the helicopter which had just lifted Clint Eastwood off the mountain. As the shadows lengthened on the west flank itself, there was still no sound of the helicopter. The evening was so quiet that they could hear the sound of cow bells down in the pastures of the Kleine Scheidegg. Then they heard a whistling sound above them. The cameraman tucked himself into a ball. Suddenly, rocks— real boulders—were exploding onto the ledge. When the cameraman looked up, Knowles was lying two feet away from him, dead. The top of Knowles's head—his safety helmet and his skull—had been neatly severed above the eyebrows. His eyes were open, staring at the cameraman. His lips were pursed, as if he were going to say something.

Gradually, over the next four years, Taylor came to terms with Knowles's death and the hole it left in his life. At first, the suddenness of it, the dissolution of their plans, the shock of discontinuity, bewildered him. "The fact that he was gone forever was the most difficult thing for me to understand and accept because I was supposed to see him." Taylor neither went to the Alps nor to Dave's funeral in England. When he returned to Scotland, it was only for a visit. Knowles's absence was a gap that could not be filled: "His dying meant that the place wouldn't be the same, and it wasn't. Even with all the good climbers in Glencoe, he was irreplaceable." Taylor continued to climb all around the globe with a variety of climbing partners, and he became one of the most respected ice climbers in the small world of professional alpinism. Even with partners who were not especially close friends, Taylor still felt the challenge of the mountains. If anything, they now held more mystery than before. Increasingly stoical about Dave's death, he first thought about his friend often—then, less and less. By the time he set off to Africa in January 1978, intending to climb Mount Kenya and to make a direct ascent on the unclimbed southwest face of Mount Kilimanjaro's Breach Wall, he had "buried Dave in my mind."

On the second day of the expedition, at 13,000 feet, Taylor and his partner (an expert rock climber with whom Taylor had little personal association) were stopped by drenching rain on the long approach to the base of the Breach Wall. They encamped in a small bivouac hut. Waiting out the rain, Taylor leafed through the hut's small, tattered register, amused by the dramatic entries left by former climbers of Kilimanjaro's remote southwestern side. One entry startled him. He recognized the handwriting instantly: "August 10, 1971, Dave Knowles. I've come across the Shira Plateau—atrocious weather, rain, sleet, snow, terrible winds. Tomorrow will go across to Mweka then on to Saddle to complete circumvention of Kilimanjaro. Thanks for the hut. As great as my need—is my appreciation." Taylor was incredulous. He had completely forgotten that Dave had trekked around the rim of the mountain alone, the first man to have made the complete circumvention. "It was like opening Pandora's box when I read that logbook," Taylor remembers. "That's what started everything." Before dawn on Friday, January 13, he dreamed about Knowles for the first time since the tragedy.

It was still snowing heavily on January 18, the fourth day since Rob's Taylor's accident up on the Breach Icicle, the third day of waiting for a rescue party to reach him at 16,000 feet. His left ankle and foot were now the black color of gangrenous flesh. With no antibiotics among his supplies, infection was coursing throughout his system. Into the afternoon, he gave up hope of survival. He felt that it was only a matter of time before he would die. His thoughts turned to his family.

And then he became aware of Dave Knowles, standing at the foot of his bivouac sack, silently beckoning him to follow. "It wasn't as if I were imagining it, or dreaming about him being there," Taylor remembers. "I saw, from head to foot, his floppy GI jungle hat, his red neoprene anorak, wool breeches, short red socks, and a pair of boots with holes in the toes, typically. He was there—alive, whole, human, kicking the snow around. And he definitely wanted me to go with him. That is what his purpose seemed to be there."

Taylor recalls that Knowles began to move off into the falling snow, at which point Taylor was no longer concerned about the condition of his ankle, or for that matter, the condition of his entire body. His only desire was to follow Knowles. And then a moment came when he felt himself doing just that. "I felt no connection with that other body lying down there in my sleeping bag except that when I turned back to collect my gear, it looked like me. But it had no bearing on me who was completely whole and alive. I was outside of that shell which was no longer a part of me. It was like two parallel existences, and somehow I just switched from one to another, and I was quite conscious, quite aware that this was going on."

Rob Taylor was just as conscious—some indefinite time, probably only minutes later—when the rescue party arrived. "Certainly there was a gray area between those two events," he recollects, "but not a gray area as in from sleep to waking, or from hallucination to reality. Odd Eliassen [a Norwegian alpinist who was then working in the Tanzanian National Park System] and the rescue team were no less real than Dave. When Odd arrived, I wasn't dreaming or asleep. He didn't wake me up. His calling up to me, and my calling back down to him, was going on for half an hour before he finally arrived on the ledge. If I had been delirious, he never would have found me. The surrounding area was huge. You couldn't see me. I was covered by snow."

The period of Rob Taylor's recovery—after emergency surgery at the Kilimanjaro Christian Medical Center in the village of Moshi, and two months of hospitalization back in America —lasted for over a year. His leg was saved. He slowly regained use of his ankle and foot, the bones of which had been eaten from within by anaerobic infection. He began hiking again in the White Mountains of New Hampshire. In March of 1979, he journeyed to Dave Knowles's grave outside the town of Preston in Lancashire, England. Later that year, Taylor traveled to Norway where he began to climb on ice again.

While in Norway, he also spent several evenings with Odd Eliassen, discussing the details of his accident and his rescue, in preparation for a book he was writing. (It was called *The Breach: Kilimanjaro and the Conquest of Self,* published in 1981, and dedicated to Dave Knowles.) During their conversations, Eliassen remembered two things that had particularly surprised him when he had discovered Taylor on the snow-covered ledge at 16,000 feet. First, he was astonished to find Taylor alive at all. Then, Eliassen had immediately noticed something which he had forgotten during the ensuing two-day struggle to get Taylor off Kilimanjaro, but which had come back to haunt him: Eliassen wondered why the mounds of snow around the bivouac sack in which Taylor was lying moribund appeared to have been recently trampled down.

VI : RIVER-RATS

Leonard F. Picotte / Michael B. Edwards

N o man was more apprehensive about the arrival of the new executive officer than Lieutenant Commander Michael B. Edwards.

During the first week of September 1977, spasms of trepidation had been circulating among the officers at the navy's Surface Warfare Officers School detachment in San Diego, California. The rumor mill had been grinding out the particulars of the new exec's background and career, which had every man going about his duties with a single question lodged in his brain: *If the new XO is really all they say he is, what's life going to be like around here?*

Nobody was saying anything like this out loud, least of all the senior officers, at whose level the anxiety was, in fact, greatest. Up in the small, crowded office of the academic director, the atmosphere of anticipation was not even registering on the outer layer of things. When you had two and a half gold stripes on your sleeve, there was no room to wear your anxiety there, too. So Lieutenant Commander Michael Edwards appeared calm.

Edwards was a big man. Built along the lines of a basketball forward, he had a large head, a broad brown eighteen-nineties moustache, ears the size of Chincoteague oyster shells, fingernails big as nickels. At six feet four inches, he towered over most of his fellow officers. But he was the kind of large man who does not rely on physical endowment for predominance. Partly *because* of his size, he towered in a manner that was somehow gentle. His face was long and pleasant, given to candid smiles and reflective expressions—there was something of the writer in it, suggesting the rawboned thoughtfulness of John Steinbeck. In fact, there was a genuine literary strain in

Edwards's imagination, but this he tended to conceal on the job, hinting that there were more important matters at hand for a thirty-four-year-old career naval officer.

As academic director, Edwards supervised the school's curriculum, a sixteen-week course of study designed to prepare ensigns for every aspect of sea duty, from operations and weapons systems to engineering and communications. To the three hundred ensigns now enrolled and the forty lieutenants working for him as instructors, Edwards was a kind of amiable dean of students. Extremely popular with the junior officers, and also with the officer in charge (the highest-ranking man at the Surface Warfare Officers School), Edwards liked his work, and he considered his the best job in the outfit. After all, he was responsible for all the glamorous academic stuff, while the officer in charge had all the big administrative problems, and the XO had all the petty paperclip headaches of keeping the place operational. Edwards reported directly to the XO, who in turn reported to the OIC. Thus, the arrival of this new XO was going to affect the life and work of Edwards more than any other man in the outfit. Edwards had had a good working relationship with the former XO, though for Edwards's taste the man had been too much of a paper pusher—a dedicated, exceptionally efficient naval officer who nevertheless lacked that quality of leadership that fired torpedoes into the hulls of men's souls. All the same, when you worked directly under an XO, you learned to live with him and his ways.

During his twelve years in the navy, Edwards had never met a fellow officer whose reputation preceded him quite as boldly as this new man's did. The navy was, of course, filled with officers whose personalities had earned them singular reputations, but this man was unusual because he was known by not one but *two* reputations. On one side, he was supposed to be a taskmaster, one of the martinets, with starch in his uniform, starch in his neck—demanding, unyielding, fastidious. On the other side, he was allegedly a "steamer," the unofficial term for one of the yahoos who steam all over the Western Pacific, drinking and wenching—and after all that, the man reports back to his ship and *gets away with it* by securing his pecker, concealing his wriggling liver, and "keeping an even strain," as the navy saying goes.

Edwards was not a little intrigued by what he might expect from this new man. Martinets were rarely steamers—*but*, Edwards recalls, "it turned out he was both."

When Lieutenant Commander Leonard F. Picotte reported for duty, and was introduced around the school as the new XO, Lieutenant Commander Edwards shook hands with a thirty-eight-year-old man who stood six feet three inches and had the goddamndest pair of eyes you were likely to see anywhere in peacetime. Picotte had a tough, athletic body, thick through the shoulders and slim at the waist, almost hipless. His moustache was dark and neatly trimmed. His skin was a deep red-brown color, burned in by months of recent duty at sea. There were regions below his low hairline and along his sharp jaw that were furrowed and intense and a little bit mean. It was a face whose exterior registered interior knowledge of something fundamental about men and war.

Most of all, one noticed Picotte's eyes. What was nervy and resolute in the man at war had now been given to his eyes in an amazing concentration of pent-up intensity. Unmeltable, they had the confidence of dry ice in a warm climate. They were the sort of eyes that wanted to know, right from the start, whether they could look longer at you than you could look back at them. But if you held their restless gaze comfortably, they came forth yet a step farther, now with a hint of regular-guy friendliness, now with mounting curiosity about who you were and what you had to say to the best goddamn lieutenant commander in the United States Navy.

Even with the edginess of all this silent eye contact, Picotte and Edwards exchanged mildly cordial greetings. Then, Picotte made the first move.

"What's wrong with you, Lieutenant Commander?" he asked Edwards.

"No problem, sir," Edwards replied.

"You look terrible," announced Picotte.

Edwards sensed that this remark was aimed at his graying, receding hairline ("Which was the last thing I wanted to hear about," he would later recall).

After a moment or two of sizing up each other's builds and stalwart military appearance (without letting on that each was impressed by the other), they both conducted a guarded investigation, a kind of mutual sniffing around. This was a procedure similiar to the etiquette allowed at tail-end encounters in the dog world, but here in the realm of officers and gentlemen, the locus of interest was the polychromatic bar of awards and decorations on the other man's chest.

Worn over the heart, the decorations were arranged in tiers, by order of seniority, starting in the lower-right corner, with the man's foreign campaign ribbons, and moving to the upper-left corner to the ribbons that corresponded to his most important medals. One quick glance and a well-trained eye could tell where an officer had been, what he had done, where he was going, and whether he was on the fast track of navy life. It did not take any scrutiny to figure out who had been in Vietnam. And of the three ribbons awarded by the U.S. Navy for service in Vietnam, only two were given for service in-country, so one could immediately know whether a man had been cruising as part of a ship's company on a destroyer or an aircraft carrier off the coast of Vietnam, or whether he had seen close action in the Mekong Delta and up the rivers.

Picotte decoded Edwards's four-tiered ribbon bar, and saw that he had done three tours in Vietnam; that he had been in-country for at least one of those tours; that he had been in a unit to which the former Republic of Vietnam had awarded their Cross of Gallantry and two other medals. Likewise, Edwards was discovering almost exactly the same details about Picotte. But as far as Picotte was concerned, there was really only one medal to look for, and it was worn high up on the bar —a blue, yellow, and red ribbon with a thin vertical stripe of red-white-and-blue—the Combat Action Medal.

He had it; Edwards did, too. This meant that both men had been in a fire fight; both had been nose to nose with the enemy; both had actually been shot *at.* A man could have gone to half a dozen deployments off the coast of Vietnam and never gotten shot *at;* and he could have done a hell of a lot of shooting at *them,* but that didn't earn a Combat Action Medal. Now Edwards and Picotte each knew something important about the other, the way members of the same club can accurately make certain assumptions about each other simply by knowing what it takes to be admitted into the club.

Picotte also noted that of the two of them, Edwards was wearing the more senior medal—the Bronze Star with Combat "V" (Valor), which meant that under enemy fire Edwards had performed spectacularly above and beyond the call of normal duty . . . and that he had probably done it more than once. Meantime, Edwards noticed that Picotte had been awarded the Navy Commendation Medal with Combat "V" (one rating below the Bronze Star), which is given for meritorious service, a kind of special nod from the navy, saying, "Good going, mate." But Edwards knew that the difference between his Bronze Star and Picotte's Navy Comm. was probably just a matter of how the recommendations for the medals had been written.

Decorations aside, there was a single item on both men's chests that held for each of them the greatest interest of all. It was a small, round, gold pin, worn just below the ribbon bar —the Small Craft Officer in Charge Pin. Edwards had earned his after serving as assistant officer in charge of a minesweeper boat squadron, patrolling the thirty miles of river between the South China Sea and Saigon, an area known as the Rungsat Special Zone. Picotte had earned his after his tour as the commanding officer of a patrol gunboat, deployed one kilometer offshore and also up the rivers of the Rungsat. For a number of reasons, this little pin was a significant sight for each of the lieutenant commanders.

Edwards was surprised because he had not seen another Small Craft pin in years. He could not remember the last time he had met a fellow "river-rat" officer. As a species, the officers who had served as lieutenants in the River Patrol Forces in Vietnam—known as river-rats—were by now almost extinct in the navy. Some of them had been killed, of course. And some of the senior river-rats were now wearing the Command-at-Sea Pin, so they were not easy to identify. But most of the river-rats had simply left the navy. In fact, they had left in packs, and they had left feeling bitter about the way the navy had treated them. There had been a great deal of acrimonious debate about why this had happened.

In the first place, most of the river-rats had recognized that the navy had lied to them. As Edwards put it: "The big lie was that you could guarantee your career by going to Vietnam. Most young officers were told by their detailers that a combat job would eventually make you ready for flag rank." Furthermore, Admiral Elmo R. Zumwalt, who was then commander of naval forces, Vietnam (before being appointed chief of naval operations in 1970), had taken under his wing what he called the Brown Water Navy—these river-rats who were patrolling all the little rivers, canals, tributaries, and mangrove swamps of South Vietnam. The admiral told them that he personally was going to look after them, and that he was going to make sure that their combat duty would guarantee them a good deal, a special way to get ahead in their navy careers at the conclusion of their river tours.

But, lo and behold, when the river-rats returned from Vietnam, decorated and ready to advance, none of this turned out to be true. Many returning lieutenants, for example, submitted their requests for postgraduate school because they understood that a master's degree would ultimately be a necessity for promotion to the rank of commander, and it was customary for the navy to send qualified men to get a degree in, say, international relations at American University, or Tufts, or even Harvard. But what the river-rats discovered was that there were these *other* lieutenants, "ringknockers," men from the Naval Academy, who had never even been near Vietnam, who had never been shot at, whose Annapolis rings were still bright as babies' peepers—and these guys were being sent to postgraduate schools *ahead of them.* And why? Simply because the ringknockers had better grade-point averages, or they had just lined things up better. It was unbelievable—their old pal Admiral Zumwalt had sold them down the river.

Some, of course, like Edwards and Picotte, had been exceptionally qualified after distinguished in-country tours, in addition to service aboard destroyers at sea, and had received promotion to the rank of lieutenant commander. For them, it was strange not to see other river-rats nowadays. "They're just not around," says Edwards. "We don't share experiences as a group of guys every day at the club, and we don't have an old boy's network of river-rats who are around, drinking and carrying on."

Picotte and Edwards were two of the few river-rats still in the navy. So when Edwards first caught sight of Picotte's Small Craft OIC Pin, there was a happy shock of recognition ("He and I looked at each other and knew we could share our experiences") followed by a quickening sense that things might get pretty interesting around here with a fellow river-rat as his new XO.

During the next few weeks, as Picotte settled in to his new job, Edwards was repeatedly struck by a certain quality of Picotte's leadership. At the Surface Warfare Officers School, one was surrounded by men who had a particular kind of expertise, whether it was in weapons systems, or radar, or communications; the system of specialization ran through the navy, but very few officers were men like Picotte who had it all—who seemed to possess not only expertise in a wide range of operations, but also this certain leadership quality which was hard to define in purely military terms. It wasn't precisely what is known in the services as "command presence." It was much more than that. Yet neither was it the made-in-America and made-it-big aura that great national politicians and movie stars of humble origin exude. His was the presence of a small-town man who could, with this quality, effortlessly adapt himself to a big-world stage. Edwards could find only one word for it, which he rarely heard spoken in the navy: "charisma."

The man had it, and it was the most forceful and arousing quality of his personality. One felt it the second he entered a room because the room itself suddenly seemed to change. The whole center of gravity shifted in order to accommodate the presence of this man who swept in and stood his ground with all his mind and all his strength. It was as if every particle of his being had been harnessed and calibrated to demand one's concentration.

His grin had the warming power of a belt of brandy. It wasn't just some silly dog-snout smirk, there on his face for all the world to see. It was given especially to *you,* awarded like some kind of Major Citation from your good buddy, the "steamer" himself—and no quick write-ups for this award. One had to earn it, in action or by making some insightful remark that evoked the truth concerning all that was brave and important and ideal about being a hard-fighting, hard-working, hard-drinking man in the greatest democracy the world had ever known. At which time, this brandy-warm, good-buddy steamer grin would be granted to you with a citation that read: "Hey, mate, based on that remark alone, I'll go to the ends of the earth for you—whatever it takes. And that's bottom line."

On the job, one mainly encountered the Picotte who was anything but a good-buddy steamer. Here one found a portrait of the commander as a dangerous man. In his own words: "I'm a hard guy to work for. If I tell you I want something done, I want it done. And if I say something, I mean it. If I tell you, Look, I'm gonna do such-and-such for you—you can make book on it. If I also tell you I'm gonna punch you in the nose tomorrow if I see you—well, if I see you, you can make book that I'll probably do that. And my favorite line is: 'No one said it was gonna be easy.' I'm not concerned with how easy or how hard it is. Mission is the important thing. I get the job done— whatever it takes. And you can't do that without breaking some eggs. My philosophy is: In order to make an omelet, you gotta break eggs. Now, if you can't stand that, then I'm not the guy for the job. But if you can, what you'll end up with is an organization that runs well and fights well, and those guys that can't hack it, I'm going to get rid of. Bottom line is: We get paid to kill people. And it takes tough people to do that. I don't train my men in competition with the next ship. The next ship doesn't even concern me. I tell my sailors: Your competition is that Russian petty officer, that Chinese petty officer—put whatever uniform you want on him, I don't care. But you'd better be better than that guy or he's gonna kill you. And that's the business we're in."

This sharp-edged side of his personality cut two ways with the men who worked for him. "Picotte is the kind of guy who generates instant dislike or instant undying loyalty," says Edwards. "And, of course, you need that quality in order to be a great leader because you don't particularly care if your people love you or hate you, but you have to get them to follow you. I'm just the opposite—almost everybody likes me. I guess I'm a big teddy bear or something. I may intimidate people with my size, but I don't have the kind of personality that threatens them."

Their command personae were complementary. Whereas Picotte inspired men with his fiery restlessness, Edwards accomplished the same results with his steady firmness. Picotte could send men into action with fervent allusions to past naval battles and the proudest traditions of the navy. Edwards gripped men's imaginations with his measured sense of perspective. In Picotte's voice there was often a snappy, reedy sound; Edwards voice sometimes contained the tone of a beloved history professor emeritus taking sherry in his study with his favorite students.

To Picotte, Edwards seemed a rare kind of man in these times. He possessed many of the qualities that navy men were losing at an incredible rate. For instance, Edwards was sensitive without being a "sissy," to use a Picotte term. As far as Picotte was concerned, the navy was now full of sissies, officers who had "*only* that sensitive side." These were the guys who could sit down, choose the right bottle of wine, discuss literature, and then, instead of just listening to Beethoven or Brahms, they "responded" to it. Not that there was anything wrong with that kind of refinement—in fact, Picotte himself was quite well read and quite adept at all that officers and gentlemen business. But in his estimation, those guys had lost something important—"They're not a man, in the sense that they won't draw a line with you." When things got remotely confrontational, a little nervy between two men, those men were the ones who invariably backed off, *wimped out,* and took the pseudopsychological approach by implying: "Well, that's all right, that's *your* problem, mister, not mine."

But Edwards—he was not only intelligent, sensitive, well-versed in literature, history, music, and art—he readily drew a line if pushed too far. At such times, the ever-popular and gentle teddy bear would momentarily retreat to his cozy den, then emerge roaring—all six-foot-four-inches of him. "In my mind," Picotte once said of Edwards, "he's what I would call a man's man."

There were other reasons for admiring Edwards right from the start. The officer in charge of S.W.O.S. had briefly filled Picotte in on a few details of Edwards's background, notably that Edwards was a widower with two children. In 1971, Edwards's twenty-eight-year-old wife had died of Hodgkin's disease, leaving him daughters, ages one and three. Since then, Edwards had singlehandedly raised his children, a feat in itself considering the peripatetic life of a naval officer. But to Picotte, who was married and had two sons and a daughter, the amazing thing was that the man had also maintained a *competitive* naval career. Edwards had never done the easy thing. Moreover, he had done all the "right" things to stay on the demanding fast track of Navy life, all the necessary tours of duty; and now he was getting ready for his executive officer tour at sea and going to night school to get his master's degree in public administration. "All that—*in addition to raising two kids*? Incredible! That whole thing kind of overwhelmed me," Picotte recalls.

It also drew from Picotte a kind of respect that was unusual for him to have for a fellow officer of the same rank so early in the game. Here he had begun liking Edwards for his ability to draw a line, to voice an unpopular opinion, to get things done on the job, and then it turned out that the man was also able to tell a bedtime story, to put dinner on the table, to make a good home for two little girls—all without a wife and without squawking about it. And his daughters were among the most polite, thoughtful, self-reliant children one could imagine. "There were a lot of things I really, really liked about Mike right off. But I remember being tremendously impressed with what he'd done with his family, and amazed by what he'd done with his career. I guess a part of friendship is that you've got to *respect* an individual. And I respected him—he knew what was important in life, and he'd put it all together on his own."

For Edwards, "It was the first time in a long, long time that I had met an officer whom I could admire so much—for everything about the guy's character. There was nothing in his character that I couldn't be sympathetic with, that I didn't see an element of myself in. We vibrated to the same tune, and it turned out we liked the same kinds of things." During one of the first occasions in which they spent an evening drinking together, Edwards—already primed with a few beers—positively glowed when Picotte spontaneously burst forth from their discussion with—

If you can keep your head when all about you
Are losing theirs and blaming it on you;
If you can trust yourself when all men doubt you
But make allowance for their doubting too;
If you can wait and not be tired by waiting,
Or being lied about, don't deal in lies,
Or being hated, don't give way to hating,
And yet don't look too good, nor talk too wise;

If you can dream—and not make dreams your master;
If you can think—and not make thoughts your aim;
If you can meet with Triumph and Disaster
And treat those two imposters just the same . . .

If you can talk with crowds and keep your virtue,
Or walk with Kings—nor lose the common touch,
If neither foes nor loving friends can hurt you,
If all men count with you, but none too much;
If you can fill the unforgiving minute
With sixty seconds' worth of distance run,

Yours is the Earth and everything that's in it,
And—which is more—you'll be a Man, my son!

Verses from Rudyard Kipling's "If"! Picotte knew it by heart. And after a few more beers, followed by shots of cognac, there was no stopping him—not that Edwards wanted to; he was a great fan of Kipling's work. Evidently Picotte was, too, for he was soon reciting selections from *Barrack-Room Ballads*. "He would recite endlessly," Edwards recalls. "All the great stuff we warriors like to hear, the stuff Kipling was so good at."

That they both loved Kipling was a revelation to each of them. It was the first time that each man recognized that a friendship with another officer might include the possibility of actively sharing a sense of romance. For both men, the epoch of Kipling and the glory of the military-naval profession in the golden sunset of the Empire was a powerful source of inspiration. For Picotte, who carted around the complete works of Kipling wherever he was deployed (a collection he refers to as "my Kiplings"), the poem "If" was "a gauge of life—a kind of measuring rod to measure yourself against." Once, in a bookstore in Taiwan, he purchased two bronze plaques on which the poem was engraved and brought them home, one for each of his sons. He himself had first taken Kipling to heart as a boy, growing up in the nineteen-forties on the Keweenaw Peninsula, the northern most point of Upper Michigan, a spiky claw of country reaching out into Lake Superior.

There Picotte was raised in Calumet, a small logging and mining village named for the ornamented peace pipe once used by North American Indians, a fact that might have seemed ironic to a stranger upon first encountering the rough-and-tumble folks of Calumet. On Fridays at dusk, the loggers came out of the timber woods, and the miners came up from the copper mines. They filled the thirty-five bars on Main Street, boozed, brawled, then went home. Saturday night, they got drunk again; Sunday, they sobered up; Monday, they trooped back to the woods and the mines. And that was the way things were. ("I didn't understand social drinking until I was thirty years old," Picotte recalls.) When one had trouble with a man in Calumet, you and he settled the score alone: "If you didn't like what the sonovabitch said, you told him, and if he didn't like what you said, well, you both went out into the road, and may the best man win."

Fearless and scrappy, Picotte was among the best of the young men who settled scores out in the road. He graduated from the local high school in 1956, and kicked around for a while, unsure what to do next. Though raised a Catholic, he attended a nearby Lutheran theological college for a year. "Sometimes I wonder why I even went there," he once reflected, "but I guess I was looking for something. I got in my share of trouble as a kid." When he turned eighteen, that something turned out to be the United States Navy. He enlisted, became a seaman, and was assigned to duty as a captain's phone-talker aboard the U.S.S. *Sarsfield.* Ascending to the bridge of the destroyer for the first time, he looked around and told himself that he wanted to command a ship someday. Years later, as the captain of the U.S.S. *Alamo,* with the three gold stripes of a commander on his sleeve, he would look back and realize that he had come a long way to the top of this great citadel of steel. The fact of being there on that bridge, in command of a 12,500-ton ship, confirmed his belief that in America, if one wanted something badly enough, if one were willing to toil and sacrifice, then all goals were attainable. He had inherited this deeply held sense of faith in country from his father.

To Picotte's mother, who had emigrated from Italy at the age of twelve, and to his father, a native French-Canadian who later settled in Michigan, America had been the land of opportunity. "If it's worthwhile living in," Irving Picotte often said, "it's got to be worthwhile dying for." He was a manager of a feed store, a policeman, a janitor, and when his country entered World War II, he became a second-class gunner's mate in the navy. Later, when his son Leonard asked him why he had enlisted at the relatively advanced age of thirty-eight, he replied: "Because I didn't want you and your brothers to have anything you ever had to be ashamed of—to have to say your old man didn't do his part." He became the director of the veterans' program for the entire upper peninsula of Michigan; and he was just as proud that all three of his sons fought in Vietnam: the eldest in the Coast Guard; the youngest in the army's 173rd Airborne Brigade; and Leonard—who had gone back to college after his enlistment tour, graduated from Northern Michigan University in 1962 with a bachelor's degree in economics, and returned to the navy via Officer Candidate School—receiving his commission as ensign and his first deployment to the Mekong Delta with an underwater demolition team in 1963. "My dad was about sixty at that time," Picotte recalls, "and he thought it would be really neat if the navy would take him, too—so we all could be over there."

Talking about his father's pride in America, Picotte quotes Thomas Jefferson ("The tree of liberty must be refreshed from time to time with the blood of patriots . . .") and says: "I'm a first-generation American, and I'm comfortable with the concept that you have to be willing to say, Here's where I stand, and here's what I'm willing to die for. And I got that from my dad. He's a grass-roots kind of guy—God, Country, Family—and those values have rubbed off on me. I guess he's really a jingo in the purest sense of the word. Right or wrong, my country—that's my dad. And that's one of the things I like about Mike. I guess the term is patriot. He really loves this country. It means something to him. The navy means something to him."

Raised in Bremerton, Washington, where his father, a former merchant-marine seaman, worked in the Puget Sound Naval Shipyard, Michael Bruce Edwards was, in a sense, bred to the navy. ("It was in the genes," he says.) During World War II, Edwards's father, then in his late thirties, had enlisted in the army, and had been among the first ashore at Okinawa. Like Picotte, Edwards was a Catholic and a second-generation military son who was determined to become a first-generation career naval officer. "From the minute I walked into the uniform, I felt like I'd sort of found a home. I was a bit of a misfit before—I was a poor kid growing up, although I didn't know it." His parents divorced when he was eight. His mother worked as a bookkeeper for a drugstore chain, earning an annual salary of $3,800. Edwards remembers writing that figure on his scholarship application to Stanford University in 1961, and not thinking much about it until three years later when Lyndon Johnson's Great Society determined that Edwards and his family were below the national poverty line.

After graduating from Stanford University in 1965, with a bachelor's degree in history, Edwards entered the navy through Officer Candidate School, receiving his commission as ensign in December 1965. It was a turning point in his life. "What the navy did for me was to give me a hell of an occupation that I could enjoy, and it gave me status that I wouldn't have had otherwise," he says now. "I have the best of all possible worlds, a perfect occupation. I'm as illegitimate as you can get—I mean, anybody who puts on a uniform and goes off to his job every day is like a Boy Scout, right? We generally leave our scouting days behind when we leave elementary school. But I'm still just a big old Boy Scout. I get to go down and play ship every day. I drive my ship around the world; I have a lot of fun doing it; and, goddamit, they *pay* me for it. They pay me good money for it [a commander's annual salary is about $40,000] and I have the ultimate in respectability—right down to the white suit. Everything that my mother could have possibly wanted, I have. And my father writes me today, envious of the fact that I'm going to a command, and that I was recently halfway around the world sending him postcards from Hong Kong."

The navy also gave Edwards a great deal of responsibility very quickly, very early in his career. After completing Mine Warfare School in 1966, he wanted to be close to the action in Vietnam, so he asked for orders to a minesweeper, one of the two hundred-foot small combatants. Instead, he received orders to a squadron of fifty-seven-foot minesweeper boats stationed in Long Beach, California. When he reported for duty, his superior, a lieutenant commander, told him to hurry up— the boats were getting under way *right now*. Edwards ran down the pier, jumped on the lead boat, and found himself the officer in charge of twelve boats at sea, with the entire responsibility for all twelve vessels, each with crews of seven men who were all waiting for *him* to tell *them* what to do. He was twenty-three and he had never been to sea on a boat.

After a year of training, Edwards and his squadron deployed to South Vietnam, into the rivers of the Rungsat Special Zone. There, in the dense, winding mangrove swamps, which for centuries had been the home of pirates who preyed upon the rivergoing commerce between the South China Sea and Saigon, Edwards first encountered the crude mines that the Vietcong had developed to prey on the U.S. Navy cargo ships carrying munitions and supplies to Saigon. Using a fifty-five-gallon oil drum, loaded with TNT, rigged with a detonator cap, a battery, and two waterproof contact wires, the V.C. had already sunk two U.S. ships in the river by the time Edwards arrived. Though his squadron was fully equipped with sophisticated devices for sweeping acoustic mines and magnetic mines, this gear proved utterly useless against a guerrilla-forces enemy equipped with oil drums and TNT. So Edwards and his boss, a lieutenant, invented and developed a new device.

The river-rats swept the rivers of the Rungsat with nothing more complicated than twenty feet of anchor chain welded to a pair of metal bars that easily disengaged the two contact wires on the V.C. mines. Often, however, the V.C. would swim back out and rewire the mines; when that failed, they simply opened fire on Edwards's squadron, a choice target, being at times only twenty yards off the riverbank. It became routine to take P-40 rocket fire from both sides of the river, day and night, followed by weeks, sometimes months, of eerie silence. Edwards lost a few men and a few boats. But during one especially heavy surprise attack at night, when incoming mortar rounds exploded around the Vietnamese naval base in Nha Be where his boats were tied up like sitting ducks, Edwards "chased my body down to the pier" and managed, through the night, to get the entire squadron under way without a single loss, an action that earned him the Bronze Star with Combat "V."

Edwards enjoyed his responsibilities, and because of his

specialized, firsthand knowledge in the art of sweeping mines that was almost unprecedented in the navy's experience, he became one of the unique junior officers in the entire U.S. Navy. Moreover, as an ensign, he was the most junior naval officer serving in-country. Promoted to lieutenant junior grade before the end of his first tour, Edwards was amazed when he and his boss received a special request to report to Saigon, to the offices of Admiral E. L. Veth. ("Talk about being nervous," he recalls.) This was the first admiral he had ever met, and here he was, a lowly lieutenant jg, going in to *brief the commander of naval forces, Vietnam*—to explain to him everything about this new minesweeping business because, apparently, the admiral knew next to nothing about it, and Edwards and his boss were the only in-country officers who knew anything about the operations in the Delta. This was unbelievable. Edwards's career was off to a fast start.

Picotte, meanwhile, had been seeing a variety of action, first, with his Explosive Ordinance Disposal team, setting booby traps and disposing of bombs in the Mekong Delta; then aboard an aircraft carrier; later, aboard a destroyer; and finally, aboard an offshore and up-river patrol gunboat, of which he was commanding officer. Despite the fact that he earned his Navy Commendation Medal aboard a destroyer under fire during the Tet Offensive, and despite the fact that he was clearly on his way toward eventual command of big ships at sea, it was his double exposure to the in-country war of which he was most proud. "It really was the high point of my life," he later reflected. "It was the epicurean thing. If you're going to live, you've got to live on that outer edge, where it really counts. Out there, everything matters."

Edwards felt much the same way about his own in-country experience. In 1969, during his second tour, steaming off the coast of North Vietnam aboard the U.S.S. *Buchanan,* Edwards viewed the war with new eyes. His job as the destroyer's combat information center and communications officer made him responsible for gunnery control and radar operations, an important position for a junior officer as the ship's primary mission was to carry out gunfire support: In the mornings, a message would be received indicating the ship's coastal targets for the day. These targets, which had been identified by air force reconnaissance spotters who came out of Da Nang and flew up and down the North Vietnamese coast, were supposed to be bridges, railroad crossings, truck parks, intersections on main roads. And there was also another whole group of targets, which were called Potential Mobile Gunfire Sites. A Potential Mobile Gunfire Site was a place on the coast in which the enemy could put a mobile gun if they wanted to shoot back at the U.S. destroyers. It didn't mean that the gun was actually there—just that that was *possible.* So when the *Buchanan* was in range, she would turn parallel to the coast and commence bombardment of these Potential Mobile Gunfire Sites—with no apparent effect, at least none that Edwards could see.

Edwards, who was reading *Catch-22* at that time, became convinced that a Potential Mobile Gunfire Site was the hole that he had put in the ground on the previous mission—a hole that the air force spotters were now perceiving as one of enemy origin. He couldn't believe the futility of this mission: firing five hundred rounds of five-inch ammunition—big gun stuff—at *nothing,* at his own hole in the ground. "I got really negative about the whole thing," Edwards recalls, "which is why, when I came back, I was sympathetic with officers who were very anti-Vietnam, because those guys had only seen the war from that point of view. If all you ever did was ride around on an aircraft carrier, as part of ship's company, and you never got involved in the war in any personal way, it seemed stupid, futile. But because of my experience in-country, I could say that I had been there and that I had taken a big goddamn bite out of it; and, in fact, it had tried to take a bite out of me."

As a survivor of Vietnam, Edwards began to notice a huge gap between himself and many other naval officers. It was as if the men who, like himself, had been in-country, were not *supposed* to have survived. And if they had survived that experience, they were now presumed to be shattered by it. The supposition was that they had lost their sense of morality and reality in-country, so they were now expected to be little more than *lunatics,* walking time bombs disguised as uniformed men, ready to explode at any moment, screaming about *slopes* and *gooks* and *murdered babies.* But Edwards did not feel that way at all. "Hell, I was ennobled by my Vietnam experience, and better off for it, because it made me a better person," he said. "I'm not arguing the right or wrong of the war—because I certainly have come around to a different feeling about the war now than I had then—I'm only talking about me and what I did, what I learned, and what I saw. And this was the thing that set me apart from many of my fellow officers, very few of whom had been in-country or had had any kind of combat experience. So, given the other things I liked about Picotte, this made me closer to him. He knew what I had gone through because he had been there, too. And he knew whereof he spoke."

In San Diego, after work, they had endless discussions about Vietnam and the pieces of it that had each been theirs. They didn't sit around swapping war stories; Picotte recalls that the discussions were mainly interrogatory: "What was that all about? What were we doing there? What should we have been doing there?" For both men, these talks were vital because not only were there very few fellow officers who knew what it had really been like in-country, but very little accuracy could be found in the re-creations of the "Vietnam experience" that had turned up in bookstores and at movie theaters immediately after the war. Edwards and Picotte felt that with only a few exceptions, most of it was utterly fraudulent: "What did those writers know about Contact, about being under fire, about having your sphincter muscle get about *this* tight? My God, no one was telling it like it was. When you had spent months of unending boredom until, all of a sudden, a mortar round came in and missed you by an R.C.H. [an R.C.H. being survivors' lingo for something *very* thin—a Red Cunt Hair] and that sucker had missed you by one of those—followed by another and another and another, then more months of boredom—well, how could you begin to take for the absolute truth what some of these chicken-shit reporters, who had been there for two *weeks,* were now presenting as the suspenseful, spine-tingling, soon-to-be-a-major-motion-sickness, final word on the so-called debacle of Vietnam?"

Picotte, for one, was fond of saying that going to war and making love had one thing in common: "You can talk about it and write about it and make movies about it, but until you've done it, you just haven't been there." With Edwards, here at last was someone to whom he could really talk—who knew what it had actually been like, who knew the frustrations of coming home from in-country with the unreality of the time-space continuum that he had had: Up to his nose in swamp gas at one moment . . . then eighteen hours later, here he was with his wife in some Stateside cocktail lounge, waiting for dinner, and suddenly there was this sound coming from the TV set over the bar (a *color* TV, which he had never seen before) and everybody was cheering and going positively ape-shit because of this sound, this TV theme music, which was going *na-na-na-na-na-na-na-na—Bat-man*!

"I was just lost," Picotte recalls. "I had no idea what this was about." Then, he "wasn't believing this": The people at the bar, grown men, were actually stamping their feet, going nuts over every little bat-gadget and bat-weapon and dingbat bat-enemy, and the TV was asking: *Will Batman and Robin survive the Joker's fiendish riddling bonecrusher?* And Picotte was struck with the thought: *"Are you kidding?* You people are getting excited about Batman and Robin? Do you know what's happening right now? I mean, do you really *know?* There are guys nose to nose. There are guys miserable, afraid, dying. And *this* is what we're supposed to be concerned about?"

So intense was the bond that Picotte and Edwards shared as survivors of the in-country war, that they both agree that their friendship would have had a different beginning, a lesser degree of intimacy without it. "That's just one factor you put in with all the others," says Picotte; "but it's the old story of being a member of a club. You either are or you aren't. And if you aren't, I don't know about you. I mean, I don't *really* know about you. I know how *I'm* gonna react under certain situations of stress. And that makes me a little different, a little more comfortable with myself. So if you get a pair of those guys together, you're a little more comfortable with each other. There's that trust and understanding between you: You've been there."

All the same, just as their friendship was beginning, there was something that made them mildly uncomfortable with each other. At first, they didn't talk about it, but they both had a good idea about what was in store for the friendship of a pair of lieutenant commanders who were working together in the same command. They had both been in the navy long enough to know that the system made it practically impossible for any friendship, once started, to survive.

Sooner or later, a young officer may arrive at the following conclusion: By the time he reaches the top of the navy's great pyramid-shaped promotion citadel—or gets near the top, or for that matter, at almost any step on his way up that obdurate steel superstructure of turrets, bridges, honeycombed crawl spaces, and ladders leading to progressively higher rank and command—he may not have a single *close* friend among his fellow officers. According to Edwards, "Friendship in the navy almost doesn't exist. The navy almost dictates that you won't have a friend. You can't really have a friend because there's no conceivable way that you can beat the competition game. And that's the game we're all playing, making our way toward admiral."

Starting off at the bottom of the citadel, the newly commissioned ensign, fresh out of Officer Candidate School and sixteen weeks at a Surface Warfare Officer School, is assigned to his first ship, the U.S.S. *Competition,* on which he finds himself in the company of perhaps ten or fifteen other ensigns. As part of this fraternal group of young officers and gentlemen, he may think it's safe to assume that he will form at least one close friendship. And, at first, there's a good chance that he will. He probably won't find his friend among that tight trio of Naval Academy guys over there; the ringknockers tend to stick close together, fused by bonds already formed by the alchemy of

Annapolis. But he may find a fellow OCSer with whom to share the pressures from above during their first trials at sea.

Then, when the *Competition* puts into port at, say, Subic Bay, in the Philippines, he and his new friend go ashore for their first liberty, and together they discover the lowdown attractions of Olongapo, the tumbledown, fleshpot liberty port outside the naval base. After a few nights of carousing and "running the alleys" of the infamous "Po," the ensign and his friend are back on the *Competition,* taking an even strain, enjoying the fraternal afterglow of an epic drunk, and planning all the future great times they'll have when they next get off this tin can. But soon it comes time for their captain to write the first set of annual fitness reports, and suddenly the ensign begins to realize that the friend to whom he has pledged undying loyalty during those epic Olongapo nights is one of fourteen guys whom he must now crawl right over to win the highest evaluation on his fitness report.

The navy's officer evaluation system demands that the evaluator of each command—in this case, the captain of the *Competition*—make a series of evaluations based on the performance of each of his junior officers. Before simultaneously sending in all these reports to the chief of naval personnel at the bureau in Washington, where they are kept on record for the duration of an officer's career, the captain is also duty bound to report which *one* of his fifteen ensigns is the best ensign. This means that our ensign, if he's ambitious, must now start playing hardball with his friend and the other thirteen ensigns aboard; he knows that his next promotion, his next assignment, and the next nineteen years of his naval career will depend on where the captain ranks him among his peers. Even to consider eventual promotion up the great citadel to commander, or captain, or the flag ranks above (not to mention the steps he must first make up to lieutenant jg, lieutenant, and lieutenant commander), he knows that he should be ranked number one of fifteen . . . and God help his friend or the poor bastard who gets ranked number fifteen of fifteen.

So, assuming that our ensign has played the game competitively, and has earned his first promotion and a set of good orders to a new ship, he now must bid *sayonara* to his first ship, to Subic Bay, and to the great friendship he began there. After a successful tour as a lieutenant jg, he makes a brief stop at one of the navy's Surface Warfare Department Head schools, and then reports as a full lieutenant to his new ship, the U.S.S. *Rivalry.*

Here aboard the *Rivalry,* the competition game narrows down even closer; and still no one says a word about it. As the Weapons Department head, our lieutenant is now in competition with only two or three other lieutenants, one of whom may very well become a close friend of his as they stand watch together, have long philosophical conversations, and ponder the psychological traumas that have made their executive officer the bastard that he is. But soon enough, out come the fitness reports again, and our lieutenant has to play minor-league hardball. He now has to become the number one of *three.* (As Edwards puts it: "If you and your best buddy are both trying to be the first baseman, and the coach only wants *one*—hell, somebody's got to lose.") On the chance, however, that our ambitious lieutenant values his new friendship at least as much as his next career position, he may resolve not to let the competition game bother him or interfere with his friendship. But, as Picotte puts it: "Even if the competition doesn't bother *you,* if it bothers the other guy, you're out of luck."

By the time our lieutenant has taken the next step up the great steel citadel to become a lieutenant commander, he has probably done better at the competition game than two, perhaps three, friends, and he has possibly even seen those friends bilge out of the navy altogether. And now, as the executive officer of his next ship, the U.S.S. *Cutthroat*—hell, he's not supposed to have a friendship with *anybody.* His job is to keep every aspect of that ship operational, so he can't possibly please the captain and become the captain's friend, too. And God forbid that he would ever associate with his junior officers —who might very well hate his guts anyway.

Then, after a successful tour at sea as the executive officer; after shore duty as an XO, after attending postgraduate school for his master's degree, after passing his Command Qualification Examination—after all that, he's still not even close to the pinnacle of the great steel citadel, but he's at least as high as the bridge, and he has finally reached the rank of commander after perhaps fifteen years in the navy. And if he's lucky, and if he's played the game competitively at every step, and if he's surpassed more than 50 percent of the other commanders, then he is now in full command of a ship at sea, standing on that glorious bridge high up on the ship's superstructure, with three gold stripes gleaming in the sun—the invincible captain of the U.S.S. *Lonely-at-the-Top,* the only man aboard that ship who can turn to no other man in time of crisis.

So it was exceptional for a pair of lieutenant commanders to have developed a friendship as quickly as Edwards and Picotte had. Especially since they were the only two lieutenant commanders at the Surface Warfare Officer School, which meant that despite their mutual admiration and their bond as survivors of the in-country war, despite their enjoyment of each other's company, and despite their mutual fondness for the golden age of Kipling—they were now locked head-to-head in competition. They never mentioned it, but they both knew that the day would soon come when their commanding officer would have to write their evaluations, ranking only one of them as the number one of *two.* Furthermore, both men were aware of the fact that before Picotte had arrived at S.W.O.S., the officer in charge had ranked Edwards *above* the old XO, meaning that in the chain of command, the number-three man (Edwards, the academic director) was nevertheless the better officer, relative to the number-two man (the old XO). This said a great deal about Edwards's performance and future potential, because rare was the commanding officer who wanted to tell Washington that his executive officer was not the best lieutenant commander he had in his command.

As a result of this unholy position of being in direct, silent competition with each other, and yet also being determined not to allow the navy's competition game to capsize the friendship they'd launched, they began competing with one another

in a variety of subtle ways. Three times a week, they ran together—a six-mile circuit around the islet of Coronado, on
which the school was located in San Diego Bay. On Fridays,
they ran eight miles. Starting at the school's gymnasium, they
set a pace that allowed them to chat back and forth for the first
seven and four-tenths miles. These discussions served a number of purposes, one of which was nothing more than as an
elaborate prelude to the final segment of the run.

The distance between the gate of the naval base and the
gymnasium was six tenths of a mile. When they hit that gate,
running abreast, all conversation automatically ceased. The
pace picked up, and by the last two hundred yards, it was a
flat-out dash to the gym. "Whoever won, whoever lost, neither
of us said anything," Picotte recalls. "I guess what we were
doing was just kind of feeling each other out—you know, *How
much sand does this guy have? Just what is he really made of?*"

For Edwards, the runs were the high point of his basically
routine weeks at the school. He looked forward to them, and
enjoyed particularly the discussions in the early part of the
circuit (though, he, too, recalls the adrenal moment of hitting
the gate: "End of conversation; now to the real stuff"). With
Picotte, any conversation—whether it was about a current
movie, such as *The Deer Hunter,* or about a naval battle in the
War of 1812—was bound to get quite lively. During the course
of a single eight-minute mile, Picotte was apt to tie his observations together with quotations from Kipling, General George
Patton, or President John F. Kennedy. In order to keep up
with the intellectual pace, Edwards actually began to prepare
academically for the runs. On nights before a run, the last
thing he would do before retiring was make a quick review of
a subject with which he was familiar, *"something good for the
run."* He would jot down a few notes about, say, the reign of
Charlemagne, which he had studied in college, then commit
them to memory. Naturally, this spurred on Picotte to provide
something even more challenging for the next run. "We did
that just to make it all more worthwhile," says Edwards. "Of
course, it was also the kind of stuff that makes for a good story
later on in life—you know, that *Commander Picotte and I used*

to have these runs *in Coronado, in which we would enliven a good training session by having intelligent discussions.* It was probably utter bullshit. On balance, there was probably more bullshit than there were great discussions, but sometimes they really would be worthwhile, and it was certainly all part of the image we were presenting to the world—that we were something *different,* something better, smarter, faster, stronger, more prepared than the average officer. We worked hard at creating a different kind of image, and that was part of our friendship, too."

Every good naval officer, whether he was the Weapons Department head of the U.S.S. *Rivalry* or the captain of the U.S.S. *Lonely-at-the-Top,* strove to develop a unique personal image that would define his professional style of leadership. The clearer the image, the greater its power to influence an officer's juniors and his seniors, to ensure his footing on the ladders up the great steel citadel, and to extend the idiosyncrasies of his ego and imagination beyond the navy's standard rules and regulations. A certain amount of straying from Rules and Regs was encouraged unofficially, if it served the purpose of maintaining an officer's image. One Vietnam-era commanding officer, for example, brought all his own ham-radio equipment from home and installed it in his cabin aboard his destroyer. When, with all his squelch controls, automatic noise limiters, and modulation indicators, he began receiving Radio Moscow broadcasts out in the Western Pacific, no one thought it peculiar—even though there were equally powerful ship's radios aboard that were picking up Radio Moscow—because this CO was *known* as a ham-radio operator. His equipment was part of his image.

Besides being developed and carefully maintained, the image was also passed on by a senior officer to his juniors. These hand-me-down legacies served not only to preserve the continuity of naval tradition but also to recognize the traits of a junior officer who did not yet have a fully developed image of his own. "Oh, yes, I know that lieutenant," a senior officer would say, "he's a Jones-trained man"—which meant that when the lieutenant in question had worked under Jones's command, the distinctive characteristics of Jones's image and way of doing business had been branded onto the lieutenant's hide.

For an ambitious lieutenant making his way up the steel citadel, this kind of label would be either very helpful or very harmful. There was nothing worse than being trained by the wrong man at the wrong time, thus acquiring the wrong image. For instance, by the early nineteen-eighties, to have it said that you were a Zumwalt-trained man was the kiss of death. This meant that you were a ghost from the bygone era of the liberalized navy of the early nineteen-seventies—the days when Admiral Elmo R. Zumwalt, the chief of naval operations, transformed the navy by initiating over a hundred new personnel policies known as "Z-grams," which upgraded the status of women, instituted human-resources programs, eliminated strict dress codes and the old Mickey Mouse regulations, among other sweeping changes.

Certain officers, such as Edwards and Picotte, abhorred the Zumwalt changes, felt they had weakened the strongest aspects of naval tradition; they resisted them. They didn't want to have anything to do with women in the navy, or with the Human Resources Seminars, or with the "Upward Mobility" crap. That sort of thing was for *civilians,* not navy men. They didn't have time to sit around having namby-pamby discussions about human resources; and they certainly didn't have time to fight the war by "consensus," another popular word of the Zumwalt era. As far as Picotte was concerned, "An officer is not put in charge of a ship to *practice* democracy; he's put there to make the rapid, singular decisions of command in order to fight a war to *defend* democracy."

"And hey," said Edwards, "these psychological counseling sessions for guys who can't hack the navy? Chrissakes, you take a man for what he is—sonovabitch can't hack it, *out.*"

Edwards and Picotte had no desire to be linked with the Zumwalt-trained men, those casually dressed officers who were hiking off to seminars and ding-a-ling encounter groups in love beads and Earth shoes. They even had a name for those men: the "kissy-feely" officers. "God forbid," Edwards recalls, "that we would ever go off to Monterey to some kissy-feely seminar and take off our clothes and blindfold each other and touch each other. . . ."

Edwards and Picotte intentionally created an image that was anti-Zumwalt—whose characteristics were derived from the oldest traditions of the navy: They saw themselves as scholar-warriors, renaissance men who were just as ready and able to fight a war as to discuss great literature and art; men who pushed themselves to the limits of physical and mental endurance; men who could *fill the unforgiving minute with sixty seconds' worth of distance run;* men who could *walk with Kings,* but not *lose the common touch;* men with those virtues described in the 1934 manual of *Naval Customs, Traditions, and Usage:* ". . . strength of character without bombast; dignity, without frigidity; friendliness, without garrulousness; while an appreciation of art, music and the *belles lettres* should not lessen the essential professional qualifications of the officer . . ."; men who took a practical approach to command and seamanship, and whose "promotions had been won mainly by their skill in ship handling and their attention to the drill of their crews, both in seamanship and gunnery."

Consequently, the traits of the Edwards-trained man and the Picotte-trained man were quite similar, and immediately recognizable. Neither one was a high-tech computer whiz kid involved in, say, statistical analysis of retention figures for the navy of the nineteen-nineties. Each was a practical seaman, swiftly meeting operational commitments, pragmatically solving the problems faced when handling a ship at sea. And though each was aware that the front line of the navy's future defense might well be in high-tech computers, supersonic aircraft, nuclear-powered submarines, and guided nuclear missiles, each would probably—because of its links to a glorious past—opt for duty aboard a battleship, the great old ship of the line, which was soon to be reactivated to rejoin the front lines of the surface action fleet.

Grounded in this halcyon image of their profession, Ed-

wards and Picotte's friendship acquired a dimension of romanticism—a sense of the way things ought to be—that was extraordinary for two officers serving in a nuclear navy. Running,
drinking, driving around San Diego, they spent hours talking
about the olden days of naval power—the era before World
War I when the navy was supreme; when national policy was
being made by the navy; when the commanding officer of a
United States naval vessel was an ambassador for his country,
carrying national policy across the seven seas, and *making*
policy by his own judgments, as Commodore Matthew C.
Perry had done when he opened the ports of Japan. "There
were several kinds of romance in which we shared, depending
on mood," Edwards recalls. "Both of us have that military side
of romance, which is that it's an honorable profession, that it's
important, that only certain kinds of people are good at it—
that we're two of 'em. And the sense of romance—that's there,
too, because, for instance, the idea that the turn of the century
was one of the periods when we both would have perhaps lived
a better life—that's the most romantic thing you can possibly
think. We're being silly when we do that sort of thing, but we
did it a lot. It was very enjoyable; it was probably the best kind
of relaxation that he and I would have."

Their sense of romance did have its practical side. Edwards
and Picotte used their discussions of golden-age naval battles
not simply as armchair-and-fireside glory sessions but as useful
lessons in leadership, and as instructive preparation for such
time as they themselves would again have to take action in
combat at sea. Indeed, says the manual of *Naval Customs,*
"Past deeds tend to inspire the accomplishment of future action. . . . When routine duties become irksome, when years of
attention to minute details dull the imagination, when even an
appreciation of great tradition with its inspirational value
waxes cool within us, it is wise to turn to the thrilling exploits
of the officers and men of other days. . . . For what? For what
we all aspire to when the call comes—*preparedness, action,*
and *victory.*"

Says Edwards: "When Picotte and I got together and talked
about the Charge of the Light Brigade, or the action of the

Graf Spee in World War Two, or any of the great naval battles, we were really preparing ourselves for any contigency, for the right action at the right time, making ourselves better officers by talking over these situations. I feel that I'm a better officer and a better person just by having known him."

In May of 1978, the alternating currents activated by the navy's competition game finally began to short-circuit Edwards and Picotte's friendship. For nine months now, Picotte had been the executive officer of the Surface Warfare Officer School. Yet there had been an eight-week interlude during which he had gone to Tactical Action Officer School, as a student, to prepare for his Command Qualification Examination. Meantime, Edwards had filled in for Picotte, performing the XO's duties in addition to his own duties as the academic director. This situation had created some friction between them. For one thing, Edwards did not mind serving in both jobs simultaneously, but he did mind it when, from a distance, Picotte continued to tell him how to run things at S.W.O.S., and to stick his nose into what had become, albeit temporarily, Edwards's business. Now, in May, Picotte was back from Tactical Action School and soon to become the officer in charge of S.W.O.S. Edwards was preparing to receive his next set of orders. At the end of the month, he was to report to San Francisco to become the executive officer of the U.S.S. *Haleakala,* a 16,000-ton ammunition destroyer. Before Edwards was relieved, however, the fitness reports had to be written. So this little matter of which one of the two of them was to be ranked the number-one lieutenant commander had yet to be decided by their commanding officer. "We didn't know how this was going to come out," Edwards recalls, "and he, in fact, as the XO, was even involved in writing parts of my evaluation, and I knew that. And I knew what it was coming to, and I felt that it was wrong or unfair, or that I should be best. So these feelings of both admiration and hostility had reached the point where they were on the edge of the nervous system."

The evening of the fifth began pleasantly enough. Rick Beckhart, a lieutenant at S.W.O.S., had invited several people over to his house. His wife, Sheri, had laid out a buffet dinner. Picotte and his wife, Suzie, were there as were Edwards and his girl friend, a tall, auburn-haired, documentary-film maker named Sandra Nichols. Trouble brewed toward the end of dinner. The general conversation, which had begun as a lively six-way exchange, was narrowing down to a harsh two-way duel between Edwards and Picotte, each man trying to outdo the other with knowledge, argument, and logic.

The logic, however, was soon evaporating. Someone had brought along a bottle of Courvoisier cognac, and this 976-milliliter vial of over-the-counter adrenaline was being consumed exclusively, and in equal parts, by Edwards and Picotte. The argument mounted. "It was like a rubber band getting tighter and tighter," Sandra Nichols Edwards recalls. "They had been under a lot of pressure and tension at work, and Mike had been saying things about Picotte, like 'He's just a damn martinet,' or something to that effect. Then, that night, all of a sudden, he started coming out with this—first a little bit, then more and more. And Picotte was almost goading him. I've always seen Mike as being very much in control and on top of things. And here he was, getting into a situation where he was no longer really on top of it, where he was tumbling into it. And it started to scare me because I'd never seen him that way. The two of them were like Olympic elk, locking horns—these big, strong, male animals getting ready to do battle."

It was late, approximately 0100 hours, when the General Quarters battle alarm sounded. Picotte was in command of the stove in the Beckharts' kitchen. He was making a mushroom omelet, breaking eggs. Edwards was next to him, saying something loudly. The Courvoisier bottle was standing on the kitchen counter, empty.

At 0105 hours, Picotte sustained a broadside shove on his starboard side. He shoved Edwards back. Edwards opened fire, and shoved Picotte again, much harder this time. An eyewitness to the engagement reports that Picotte was sent halfway across the kitchen by one of Edwards's salvos. At 0110 hours, Lieutenant Rick Beckhart bravely entered the battle formation, and separated the two belligerents. All the same, they remained at battle stations. Soon, signals were exchanged, indicating exactly what each lieutenant commander thought of the other at that moment. The combatants erupted into another explosion, caused by internal fires reaching their respective ego magazines. Each sustained another barrage of shoves and body punches. Kitchen vessels were swept aside in their wake. Bowls and dishes were sent down. Chairs capsized. The empty Courvoisier bottle, still on the counter, was listing on her side. A final barrage swept her to the deck. Incredibly, she didn't break. However, at 0120 hours, when Lieutenant Beckhart had again separated the combatants and kicked them out onto the lawn, she finally rolled over and sank. With her went the last of the competitive contumely between two proud officers of the United States Navy.

Today, in Picotte's study at home in Burke, Virginia, among his framed citations, pennants, and cherished mementos, there hang two color photographs which are mounted under a dual-matte in a single frame. One picture shows Picotte and Edwards standing side by side under a tree outside the San Francisco City Hall. This was taken four months, three days after what they dubbed the "Battle of the Kitchen," and only an hour after the wedding ceremony of Mike Edwards and Sandy Nichols, at which Picotte had been Mike's best man. Both officers are wearing dress blues; both are smiling at the camera. Picotte's arm is around Edwards's shoulder.

The other picture in the frame shows an empty bottle of Courvoisier lying on its side on a blue rug adjacent to Rick and Sheri Beckhart's kitchen floor. Pointing to this diptych, Picotte says: "I guess if I were to mark a departure point—the point where we really mattered to each other, or began to become real friends, that was it. I see the famous Battle of the Kitchen as really a break: When all of a sudden he meant enough to me as a person that I wasn't really worried about the competition.

It suddenly didn't matter. It became a secondary thing—I guess it had to. At some point—and I guess you do this with your wife—you establish priorities. And the priority of having him as a friend was obviously more important than where I was going to be ranked with him. When you reach that point, you say, 'Well, that's okay.' We cleared the air, and I guess neither one of us bested the other, and from then on we just had a great deal of respect for each other. With most people, you'll never reach that point."

For Edward's part: "Sometimes I wonder—if I had been, say, a professor at San Diego State, and he had been a naval officer whom I had met through some mutual friend—whether we would have ever had this friendship. And I seriously doubt it. I probably would have disliked him so intensely for his strong image, his strong attitude, that the fight would have been a really severe kind of thing. But because we shared so much that was the same, we were able to get the friendship going, and stick with it, and then after the famous Battle of the Kitchen, it became very good. That was the traditional conflict in which somebody had to win out over the other, and nobody won because you never do in a situation like that. But we had to get that out of our system. Then it passed rather quickly, and we've gone on from there to become much closer. I suppose that could happen again, but I doubt it because I don't think we'll ever again be in the position where we're so close together in the competition game.

"As it turned out, that situation at S.W.O.S. was handled rather neatly by our CO. He had observed us both, and had seen me fill in for Picotte, and he simply refused to compare us. I guess he pretended—beat the system by sort of denying the idea that there were two lieutenant commanders there. So what he did was he made Picotte number one of *one,* and he made me number one of one."

II

In any naval fleet, the events that take place at a Mess Night tend to accumulate, soon thereafter, the cant of seafaring newsmongers, followed by the embellishments of amateur oral historians, thence passing rapidly into the dimension of legend. Edwards hadn't been aboard the *Haleakala* long when he first got wind of a story that was circulating through the West-Pac fleet, making Picotte famous. Apparently, back at the Officers' Club in Coronado, Picotte, as the officer in charge of S.W.O.S., had run an extraordinarily historical Mess Night.

First known as "Dining-In," Mess Night was a formal military dinner ceremony whose stately traditions and strict protocol had originated in the wardrooms and deckhouses of warships in Britain's Royal Navy. The ceremony had evolved over several centuries into an evening of celebration in two parts. Every Mess Night began at precisely 1920 hours when the officers of the Mess, attired in full Mess Dress, gathered for cocktails. At that point the drinking was prudent, for the wise officer did not wish to be heavily laden for the long passage ahead. By 1945 hours, when the bagpiper played the "Officers' Call," a signal to retire to the candle lit dining room, every officer had made his final run to the head; one of the hard and fast rules of the Mess was that no man was permitted to leave the table for the duration of the ceremony without the prior permission of the President of the Mess. At 2000, the smoking lamp was out. The President, seated at the head table, rang his bell once for silence. The Pledge of Allegiance was recited; grace was said by the chaplain; introductory remarks were offered by the President. Then the piper played as the chef rolled in the loin of beef. The President examined the meat, sampled it, and announced: "Gentlemen, this meat is fit for human consumption." During dinner, the President could impose stiff fines for violations of the Mess, which included: smoking at table prior to the lighting of the smoking lamp; foul language; wearing a clip-on bow tie (minor) at an obvious list (major); speaking in a foreign language; rising to applaud particularly witty, succinct, sarcastic, or relevant toasts, unless echoing the example of the President; and so forth. Dinner was elaborately followed by the passing of the port; a series of formal toasts, to the President of the United States, and to the navy, among others; the lighting of the smoking lamp; and the

gradual, but not necessarily inevitable, descent into the second
portion of the night.

If the formality of the dining ceremony and its toasting
procedures celebrated the chivalrous allegiance of officers and
gentlemen to their nation and to their branch of service, then
the institutionalized revelry during the latter part of the evening celebrated the fierce esprit de corps of warriors who now
joined as a band of brothers to make wild the night. In the old
days of Dining-In, the ceremony often degenerated into a
rowdy affair, with warriors smashing glasses into the brick fireplace, insulting the servants, wrestling one another, and competing in various do-or-die contests on the polished surface
of the Mess Table itself—traditions that, for the most part,
had been bled out of the rather tame, anemic Mess Nights
that were now the norm in this age of the computerized nuclear navy.

But being historically minded, and a believer in the powerful sense of romantic identity that could be shared by a band
of warriors on this night of nights, the President of the Mess
at the S.W.O.S. Mess Night ran both parts of the ceremony in
the old-fashioned manner. There were a few modern variations, of course. For one, the dining area of the Officers' Club
was not appointed with a fireplace—just four straight walls
which had recently been redecorated with velveteen wallpaper. So at the conclusion of the final toast, Commander Leonard Picotte, the President of the Mess, saw no alternative but
to throw his empty glass directly at the wall—followed immediately by a cascade of shattering glasses from his fellow
warriors. Naturally, the smoking lamp was lighted, but it was
soon extinguished by one of the junior members of the Mess
who saw fit to vomit *into* the lamp. And while the ceremony
descended toward lathered debauchery, the President himself
ascended to the tabletop, and was soon swinging from the
chandelier above the Mess Table, leading the Mess in the finest
historical traditions.

The next morning, the dining-room chandelier at the Officers' Club was found lying in several parts on the Mess Table,
and there were stems of broken glasses sticking into the new

velveteen wallpaper like pins in a cushion. The overall damage was assessed at seven hundred dollars, a sum for which the President of the Mess took full responsibility. ("I'll cover it," he later told the captain. "Hey, whatever it takes . . .") But at that hour of that particular morning, the President of the Mess was in Yuma, Arizona. He was still dressed in his Mess dress blues, and the sun was frying the lids off his eyes, and it was about 99,000 degrees out here, and Reality was setting in: *What in the hell am I doing here?*

There had been a predawn drive from San Diego across Route 8, through the mesas and the sandhills because one of the warriors had said they could get themselves a Hawk at the Yuma Marine Corps Air Station and fly it on up to Chicago—which had seemed like an outstanding idea. "Hell, you couldn't have come up with a bad idea at that point," Picotte later recalled: *"Wanna fly to Drambuie?—Are you kidding? Hell, yeah!"*

But now, reality was back, in the form of Yuma, Arizona, and the President of the Mess was feeling unbelievably sick, as though he had contracted six forms of cancer overnight, and some chicken-shit marine corporal was standing over him, saying, "Commander, are you all right?"

"All right?" the President replied. "Corporal, *I'm about to die.*" Then he shot that marine a solid-carbon-dioxide look. "This is going to be a first for you, Corporal," he announced in a voice that somehow managed to contain untarnished naval pride, "—having a commander in Mess Dress die right here in Yuma, Arizona. . . ."

By the time the story of the S.W.O.S. Mess Night had reached Edwards aboard the *Haleakala,* Picotte's fame had assumed a dimension even beyond that of a man who had swung from one chandelier and been held responsible for a mere seven hundred dollars worth of damage. The scuttlebutt around the fleet now had the damage up to three thousand dollars, involving the entire premises of the Officers' Club, and an inquiry at ComServPac. To Edwards, the episode seemed quintessen-

tially Picotte. "In the military, you always shake the dice when
you go to the edge of propriety," says Edwards. "Picotte did
that, and he won. He's good at that. And I admire these characteristics that enable him to do things that I wouldn't do myself.
If I were running the Mess Night, I'd probably pull things back
under control when I heard the first glass break—not the way
Picotte operates. That's one of the things I like about him. He
could 'fall on his sword' at any time. More than one officer has
fallen on his sword and been put out of the navy for just that
kind of thing. But, ol' Picotte—he's got an angel sitting on his
shoulder. I'm sure of that."

Yet for Edwards, being Leonard Picotte's friend was not
simply a matter of sitting back and letting that angel on Picotte's shoulder do all the work. There were times when he felt
he could be supportive by offering a cautionary word, and
times of simply keeping a watchful eye whenever Picotte's
sword was unsheathed. For if Picotte was a genius at leading
men into conflict during times of war, he was also a genius at
leading himself into sudden, and sometimes unfortunate, conflicts during peacetime. "He's much more volatile than I am,"
says Edwards. "He's apt to explode and say things he'll regret
later. It takes someone like me to say: 'Pull your head out of
your ass.' But that's always after the fact, and he's not used to
having someone talk to him like that. He needs someone like
me around to at least discuss it with him."

For Picotte, such discussions were the stuff of real friendship, the solid ground that made his friendship with Edwards
different from any other relationship in his life: "That's what
you're looking for in a friend, and that's what's nice about
having a friend. A friend sees you as you are. That's bottom line
when you're talking about a real friend. He understands your
faults. He understands your weaknesses. But in all that he can
still say, 'Whatever you are, however you are, you mean something to me. You're important to me. You're my friend.' And
I think that's the way we are. Mike recognizes me for what I
am, and sometimes I do things he doesn't like. I'm a little more
hyper than Mike; Mike's a little more low-key. I get angry, and
I chew someone out in public, and sometimes I won't do it

properly. And he'll tell me later, 'Jesus, not very good.' The important thing is recognizing the faults. If you can't see the faults of a person, you're really not a friend, are you? Because then all you see are the good things. And Mike sees my faults. He's told me many times: 'You act too fast.' Even knowing that, I can do anything, say anything—be anything I want to be—and I don't have to worry about him judging me. I think one of the important qualities of true friendship is being nonjudgmental. At one time, I didn't know what I was going to do. And I remember Mike said something like, 'Look, I don't know why you're going to do this thing. And I don't think you ought to do this thing. But regardless of what you do, you know I'm always going to be your friend.' And that's what makes our friendship different. You don't have many of those—you don't have many who don't judge you. You just don't. At least I don't.''

Picotte often encountered people who judged him quickly, and who judged him solely on the basis of his fiery command persona. It was not difficult for such people to find grounds for an easy connection between Picotte and some of the more flamboyant military characters of literature and the screen, chief among them Colonel Bull Meecham, the seemingly invulnerable marine fighter pilot, unyielding husband, and strict but loving father in Pat Conroy's novel *The Great Santini.* After seeing the film version, starring Robert Duvall, Picotte was not entirely comfortable. As he puts it, in a measured, quiet tone of voice: "I don't particularly like him—Santini. I recognize a lot of what he did, and I respect a lot of those things, but maybe it just hits too close to home. Maybe I see too much of myself in that. Maybe it's cost too much. I don't know."

Edwards was still aboard the *Haleakala* when he received word from Picotte that Picotte and his wife were getting a divorce. Edwards was glad that, coincidentally, his ship was now coming back into port at San Diego for refresher training. He had a hunch that Picotte would be going through some kind of tailspin. "That was a tough time for him because there were two things that were most important to him: his family and his career, and he'd lost half of that," Edwards recalls. "Just after he got divorced, he was having big adjustment troubles, and I was good for him at that time because of my situation of having been a widower and a bachelor naval officer for seven years. I think he was looking to me for a lot of good solid advice about what it was going to be like to be on his own and how to handle that. And I could give him lots of nice little role models, such as how to talk to women and date them without exploiting them, because that's the quick and easy temptation."

By now, Picotte was the executive officer of the Naval Station in San Diego. He had been promoted to the rank of commander. He called Edwards frequently; they got together for long discussions at night. Picotte remembers: "That was a really hard time for me, but Mike was right there, saying, 'Okay, well, that's okay. How do you feel about it? What's going on with *you*? What do you need? How can I help you? What can *I* do?' Those were the kind of questions I got when I told him that Suzie had just left me. It wasn't: Jeez! *What did you do?* It was: 'Hey, don't lose yourself. Keep it all together.' Totally supportive. It's amazing what happens when you get divorced. All of a sudden, those friends you had, they all drop by the wayside—of course, it's uncomfortable for them."

But here was Edwards, and throughout the entire period of Picotte's divorce, he was standing by, ready to offer a sense of perspective whenever it was needed. Picotte sought his advice constantly. Besides work at the Naval Station, Edwards was the steadiest force in Picotte's life. And in the same way that Edwards had understood Picotte's frustrations with coming home from Vietnam, he was now able to be sensitive to the problems that a man faced when his home had vanished. In fact, Edwards had endured a double-edged crisis in this very department. When Edwards had come home from Vietnam in 1970, instead of finding his wife and daughters waiting for him on the pier as his ship pulled in, he found nobody; unbeknownst to Edwards, his wife was already in the naval hospital in Bremerton, Washington, diagnosed with Hodgkin's disease. Though the initial impact of Picotte's loss was of a different caliber than that which Edwards had faced, the aftermath was somewhat similar. Picotte was relieved to find that Edwards recognized some of the things he was now going through—the feeling of going a little crazy, of disorientation, of finding himself waking up in strange places, strange beds. But Edwards told him: "Hey, that's okay. You're probably going to have to do that to find out where you are and what you're doing." Which raised a very good question actually: What to do with yourself at night, after work, when you didn't have the duty, and you didn't have a family to go home to? Well, you could start drinking yourself into a state of ambulatory stupefaction, and then really go to pieces. Or you could take the positive approach and try to do something worthwhile with those long nights. Picotte began teaching night courses in political science and comparative economics at San Diego Community College.

A year later, he went to sea. In June 1980, he took command of the U.S.S. *Alamo,* a 12,500-ton landing ship whose mission was to carry out amphibious operations in the Western Pacific. Edwards, meanwhile, had been promoted to the rank of commander, and assigned, as executive officer, to the Navy Recruiting District in Buffalo, New York. ("I've never seen a friendship survive shipping out in different directions," says Edwards, "but with Picotte, it did. It's very unusual. For instance, I've never kept up a correspondence with a fellow officer.") Edwards began receiving letters from the captain of the *Alamo.* The ship's special postmark on each envelope was magnificent. Edwards had been a philatelist since boyhood, and he still kept up his collection, which soon included various "naval covers" sent by Picotte from Hawaii, Japan, Korea, Hong Kong, the Philippines, then on to the Indian Ocean, Diego Garcia, Australia, New Zealand. He seemed to be having an outstanding tour, driving that ship, keeping that baby going, making his commitments. "His letters," says Edwards, "struck me like my kids' letters—sort of news-of-the-world. He never got nearly as insightful in his correspondence as he did in our conversations. I'm not sure why. It's a busy life as the commanding officer of a ship at sea, so he was probably just busy doing his duty. Some of his best letters described operations."

The *Alamo* was engaged in an eighteen-month cycle of major exercises, competing with other ships of the same class for awards in procedures such as amphibious assault. Up on the bridge, the solid carbon dioxide in Commander Picotte's eyes was passing through the usual phases, from solid to gas, and then to another phase altogether—the pure steaming joy of command. For a navy man in peacetime, there was no feeling quite as awesome as the sense of power and responsibility that came when his ship was under way and he was meeting his operational commitments without foul-up—putting his marines and his amphibious craft ashore in simulated assault exercises against a beachhead—all of which was proceeding smoothly from his judgment, his orders, his personality, *his ship.* For at such times, the captain became the ship and the ship became the captain, and together they were an invincible, separate piece of their native land, a world unto themselves, surrounded by the wide blue sea.

Picotte was exceptionally skillful at using his own personality, in combination with the historical identity of his ship, to send an inspirational jolt into the spine of each one of his men. In February, on the anniversary of the fall of the Alamo, he initiated and presided over a cake-cutting ceremony on the ship's fantail. Cutting the cake with his sword, he turned to face his men. "The Alamo!" he cried. "Do you realize what that stands for? *Do you?* That stands for men who won't quit. That stands for heroic defense. That stands for dying for what you believe in. That stands for the best ship in the United States Navy. . . . If you realize that, how can you ever quit? How can you not do your best on this ship? . . ." Man for man, the entire crew of the *Alamo* stood frozen, covered with gooseflesh.

For private inspiration, Picotte had a CARE package that Edwards had thoughtfully sent him from Buffalo. Its contents included candy, cigars, and three books that Edwards had selected for him, each for a different reason: *A Passage to India* was for reflective reading; *The Autobiography of Benjamin Franklin* was a book that Edwards knew Picotte would want to have as part of his library regardless of where he was, or what he was doing; *The Adventures of Sherlock Holmes* was for relaxation. And for a little of the old big world perspective, there was nothing like Edwards's letters. "Mike's letters are informative and sensitive," Picotte recalls. "One of them ended: 'Now, get up on that bridge, have a cigar, look at that sunset'—which just put the whole world into perspective for me. My letters to him are not incredibly informative. They're just: 'Hey, I'm thinking about you. How ya doin'? Here's how I'm doin'.' That kind of thing—that reassurance that you're still there and that the world's okay."

When Edwards received word that Picotte's ship had been nominated for several awards, he knew that, for Picotte, the world was looking better than okay—damned outstanding, in fact. Awards such as the Battle "E" (for Excellence), the Engineering "E," and the Amphibious Assault Award were often won by individual ships that had reputations for excellence in a particular procedure. But when a ship was nominated for each of those, in addition to the coveted Arleigh Burke Award, as Picotte's ship had been, that meant that her commanding officer had been able to calibrate every one of her assigned operational procedures better than any other ship in either the Pacific or the Atlantic fleet. Unofficially known as "The Puttin'-It-All-Together Award," it was a recognition of both professional and personal merit—"a hell of an accomplishment," says Edwards, whose ship, the *Haleakala,* had come so close to winning during his executive officer tour that he still felt unhappy about it at times. All the same, when he heard that Picotte had won the award for the 1981 competitive cycle, he telephoned him immediately. ("I was real proud of him. It was great," he recalled. "I gave him a good congrats 'cause that's the kind of stuff that makes it all worthwhile.") Picotte was touched when Edwards called: "Very, very few officers would do that. It's amazing how few people do that because of the competition thing, the zero-sum game—if I'm winning, you're losing. Mike was the only guy who actually *called* me."

In October 1980, Picotte had leave from the *Alamo,* and was flying from San Diego to see his new girl friend in Newport, Rhode Island. Edwards was driving down from Buffalo for a conference in New York City. They agreed that instead of flying directly to Boston, Picotte would take the red-eye flight into New York; Edwards would pick him up at the airport at 5:30 A.M., and they would drive to Newport. ("I was really looking forward to just *seeing* him again," says Edwards. "I miss him when I don't hear from him in a while, so it's nice to get together. And this is the navy way—just grab whatever hours you can.")

Edwards was there when Picotte's plane arrived. They mustered in the airport parking lot for an inspection of stores and supplies. Edwards had a six-pack of beer in the car. Picotte had a liter of Courvoisier stowed in his gear. It seemed like old times. The predawn October air was chilled, and the sky was thinking about turning blue when they hit the deserted northbound lanes of Route 95.

Edwards was at the wheel; Picotte was navigating and dispensing liquid supplies. Somewhere in Connecticut, they ran out of beer. For the duration of the trip, they rationed the cognac by systematically taking a blast or two after passing through the gate arm at each toll-booth island. The conversation was lively as ever. Picotte was full of sea stories fresh from WestPac—all very interesting to Edwards, who was growing desperate sitting behind a desk in Buffalo. He was so frustrated that he had tried to run the 1980 Skylon International Marathon on pure hubris alone. He had not been able to finish the 26-mile, 385-yard course, and was left shattered. Afterward, he'd called Picotte and said, "That ain't gonna happen again." But, next day, there he was, a thirty-seven-year-old prematurely gray-haired naval officer, back at his desk, pushing papers, growing older by the *second*—feeling as if he was going through a midlife crisis that was pointing to the overwhelming question: What do you want to do with the rest of your life, drive ships or drive desks?

That was a helluva good question, Picotte agreed, the intensity of the conversation growing as each toll-gate arm snapped a salute at the dawn patrol Commanders. This business of driving ships was a critical matter. It was the single thing they both loved most—more than the administrative jobs, the personnel jobs, and the other paper-pushing duties that they had to perform if they wanted to climb up the citadel of rank and command. Driving ships was a great way of life, and they were just now beginning to see the end of it. Although Picotte was slightly senior to Edwards (he had entered the navy and received his commission as ensign two years earlier than Edwards), they had both reached a level where there were fewer and fewer ladders going upward, a limited number of which led to command at sea. For rank, and command, and ship type, the citadel was getting narrower all the time. Of all the commanders in Edwards's year-group, for example, only the top 45 percent would be given command of a ship at sea. Then, of that 45 percent, only 40 percent (or 18 percent of the whole) would be screened for major command, making them eligible, at the rank of captain, for one more command at sea on an even bigger ship. Beyond that, only 11 percent of the 40 percent of the 45 percent (or about 2 percent of the whole) would go on to make admiral rank.

So, given the Darwinian process of selection that Edwards and Picotte would encounter at every step, there would soon come a time, probably during their respective twentieth years in the navy, when each would have to assess his chances realistically and decide whether or not he wanted to stay in this fight. By then, they would know the names and qualifications of the men against whom they were competing for each new ladder, and they would know the types of ships for which they were eligible, so they could almost predict what the next steps would be.

Edwards was soon to become the commanding officer of Naval Recruiting District, Buffalo. He would then go to Newport for a year of study at the Naval War College, after which he would be ready for his commander command at sea. Having served as the XO of the *Haleakala,* an ammunition ship, he would now be assigned, as CO, to a similar but larger kind of service ship, probably an oiler. Providing that tour was completed successfully, he would return to shore duty, and after promotion to captain, he would have the option of screening for major command. Successfully screened, he would be eligible for his captain command at sea, which would eventually put him in the running for flag rank.

Picotte, having now almost completed his commander command, was looking toward a future that contained only one more sea tour as a commanding officer. After his captain command, he would have literally used up all the ship-driving jobs. Admirals did not go to sea in command of one ship; they commanded dozens of ships—but that just *would not be the same.* The days of autonomy, of driving his own ship with the pure steaming joy of absolute command, would soon be gone. So what would they do to replace that? As the sun rose over Route 95, and the toll-gate arms continued to trigger swigs of cognac, Picotte wondered aloud about what really counted in his life. His mind zeroed in on an old Buddhist saying: "If you have something you treasure highly, before you give it up, it is best you have something of value to replace it."

They were still considering their future options, while they showered at the Bachelor Officers Quarters in Newport. And still drinking—Bloody Marys now—over breakfast at O'Brien's. And still drinking in the afternoon—now with Picotte's girl friend, Sandy Whitely—out by the sea, at the Inn at Castle Hill where, waxing athletic, they discussed "the good possibility" of mustering at sunset for a run around Ocean Drive. Edwards changed into his jogging togs . . .

And soon thereafter, without having run a yard, he found himself pulling into a rest area somewhere on the Massachusetts Turnpike, still wearing his jogging togs, freezing, miles from Buffalo, with a benign case of the old ambulatory stupefaction. On the long drive home, there was plenty of time to consider the future. No matter what happened, one thing was certain. In Edwards's words: "That guy is going to be my friend for life. That sonovabitch—I'll be having lively discussions with him, if I can ever drag him to my place, or meet him in some mutual ground, or get to his place—hell, when we're old and gray. And that'll probably be some of the best part of it, really."

Picotte felt the same way: "We'll be friends for life, and we'll grow old together—I think that's neat. I suspect we'll always get together wherever we are in the world, whatever it takes. And as we go up—the promotions, the changes of command—that's nice to share. The commonality there is really important. And if we ever have a crisis in our lives, we'd go to each other for advice. I almost can't imagine us not—I can't imagine going through life and not having someone like Mike. I don't know what those people who don't have a friend like that do. I almost find it hard to believe that everybody doesn't. I mean, you gotta have *somebody.* And I mean a non-sexual friend. There's only so much that you'll tell your who-ever, and at that point you need that kind of guy with whom you can just really truly be yourself. That's the purest kind of relationship. There's nothing asked, nothing expected, nothing to cloud it up. There are no pressures from the *biology* of the thing. I accept him as he accepts me."

Two years later, on October 2, 1982, at 0700 hours, Mike Edwards was working in the study of his house in Newport when he heard, not far off, a ship steaming toward the harbor. From the sound that her engine was making he could tell she was a very large vessel. Edwards had been up all night. His wife, Sandy, was away in Sri Lanka researching a new film. He was studying for his courses at the War College, getting enough work done in advance so that, with clear conscience (and time to spare for a Sunday morning hangover followed by a ten-kilometer race in Providence) he could muster for cocktails and dinner tonight at the Chart House at 1930 hours. Picotte was coming to town.

Edwards took his mug of coffee out onto the harborside porch, just in time to see the *Queen Elizabeth 2* cruise by and into the harbor. She was back from the British-Argentine naval war in the Falkland Islands, and she looked magnificent, her scarlet stack sharp and high against the azure sky. As she maneuvered to anchor, her presence suddenly turned the harbor into the big scene, the big hopeful spectacle of ocean passages and the life-spanning connections they make between the long-ago-and-faraway and the hard, bright, here-and-now of a dazzling morning in early autumn. Edwards felt the hair on the back of his head prickle.

Certain ships did that to him—the battleship was another. Now, there was a ship he would love to command—a ship that, more than any other, linked the present and the past. As Picotte had once said: "Talk about romanticism. You give me the *Missouri* tomorrow, and because of its links to history, I tell you, I could motivate that crew. I did it with the *Alamo*—but the *Missouri*! . . . 'This is where MacArthur stood, this is where the Japanese surrendered.' . . . Can you imagine what you could do with that?"

Edwards could imagine. In fact, he could see himself and Picotte serving together on the *Missouri* when it rejoined the fleet—Picotte as the commanding officer, Edwards as the executive officer. Of course, it was highly unlikely that after screening for major command they would receive simultaneous assignment to a battleship. Still, it was something to think about on an autumn day while in close proximity to deep-draft ships and the wide blue sea. "I'd love that," said Edwards. "That'd be fantastic. No doubt about it: We'd be the hottest goddamn team you ever saw."

Then, as an afterthought: "One of the things you don't do very often in the military is reveal your innermost thoughts about your career. Because, see, then you're playing around with your ego. When you reveal to someone what pinnacle you want to scale, you're exposing yourself to the possibility that you could fail. Len and I have never said to each other that we intend to be flag officers, or that we intend to command a battleship, because God forbid that we would ever fail. Neither one of us wants to ever lose or fail at what we do. Along the same lines, it's tough to reveal failures in your personal life.

That's probably why we're so close—because on one occasion, namely in his divorce, he was able to discuss with me his inner feelings. And obviously to get divorced is to admit failure. Nobody likes to do that. So that probably cemented the friendship. But we've done it on that level—we're not going to do it on the professional level. We're just not that kind of guy. Never wear your heart on your sleeve."

Likewise, even though they have talked by telephone at least two or three times a month during the past two years, Edwards has never once asked Picotte for a professional favor. And Picotte has been in a position to help: In his present job as the commander detailer at the Bureau of Naval Personnel in Washington, Picotte is now responsible for writing Edwards's next set of orders and assigning him to the ship he will command after leaving the War College. "So if we had one of those friendships based on serial performance—in other words, constantly demanding the latest proof, or the newest show of friendship—I would have gotten him on the phone two months ago, and said: 'I want a nine-sixty-three class destroyer, a Spruance, and I want it out of San Diego, goddamit. And you can do it. I know you can do it 'cause you're the Man. And I'm your friend, right?' And he would have said: 'Based on your record as a service-ship man, I don't know if I can do it, Mike.' And I would have said: 'I know my record. But you're my friend. And you are where you are. *Get me a Spruance!* Come on, Len, you can do it.' And then, to perform for our friendship, he'd have to do it. And if he didn't? The end of our relationship. But I wouldn't do that to him because that's not right. Nor is it realistic, or fair, or *anything*. He has commanders calling him up and asking for special favors all the time now. Hell, that's not friendship. That's just sucking up."

Edwards and Picotte greeted each other at 1930 with a fast, fierce embrace around the shoulders.

"Hey, buddy!"

"Hey, mate!"

Their voices were affectionate, loud, and full of fun. Edwards was wearing a tweed jacket; Picotte, a blue blazer.

"Who's your tailor, anyway?" Edwards said immediately.

"Hey, where'd you get that gray hair?" Picotte countered.

"Now don't start that shit," Edwards told his best friend, whose dark hair was short, complete, and barely flecked with gray.

At dinner, their conversation moved across a variety of subjects: Notre Dame football; Edwards's sleep patterns; Napoleon's sleep patterns; the ten-kilometer race they intended to run the next day in Providence; Catholicism; the stark-naked marine whom Edwards and his two daughters had seen walking on the road to the medical center yesterday; the *QE 2;* the fun Edwards was having at the War College, getting into inspired arguments with "these wimpy air force boy-colonels"; the official set of orders Picotte had brought from Washington, which, come June, would send Edwards to command a brand new 20,000-ton oiler, the *Merrimac;* the official presentation Picotte was going to make to all the naval commanders at the War College on Monday, unofficially known as a Dog and Pony Show (a term which derives specifically from the days of going to Tijuana to watch the prostitutes take on dogs and ponies, but which, in today's military, refers generally to any uniformed presentation considered to be "a good show.")

They were enjoying themselves, kidding each other, having a great old time until Edwards suddenly mentioned that he had been considering the option of getting out of the navy someday, and perhaps becoming a captain in the merchant marine. Picotte stiffened at the suggestion. It had first occurred to Edwards during his days of desk-bound desperation in Buffalo, but recently he had been reading Christopher Buckley's book about the merchant marine, *Steaming to Bamboola,* and the idea of spending the rest of his life driving a ship, rather than driving a desk, held great appeal.

"I've actually thought about doing that," Edwards admitted.

"Hey, you gotta be kidding?" said Picotte, half question, half declaration.

Edwards declared that merchants were found "where the action is": "Hey, drive into the Persian Gulf today, look around, and see how many navy ships are there, and see how many merchants are there. Can you imagine being more involved in the next twenty years in this world than being captain of a ship sending petroleum products around the globe?"

Picotte didn't answer. The son of a former naval second-class gunner's mate locked eyes briefly, but sharply, with the son of a former merchant seaman.

"Let me ask you this," Edwards continued, aggressively, "Would you rather run a desk or drive a ship?"

After a long pause, Picotte was willing to reply: "Well, there's no question about that. My point is that in the merchants you'd be kind of like an airline pilot. Those guys don't *do* anything."

Edwards pressed Picotte to read *Steaming to Bamboola,* then explained further: "Look, it's an option. It's not *the* option. But you can't stay in the navy forever. And you certainly can't drive ships forever. We're all aware of that. And we all know why we went to sea in the first place. We went to sea because we love it. It's the thing we feel best doing. So you can't just leave it—"

Picotte was leaning back in his chair, eyeing his fellow commander through narrowed lids. He told Edwards that his position was cavalier. "It's very safe," Picotte said in a sarcastic-magnanimous tone, "to sit here on Saturday night, after having five or six drinks, and say, 'Hey, I can go drive a merchant ship.'" Then, in a strident, pragmatic speech, the commander detailer briefly outlined the next ten years of Edwards's naval career, as if setting forth irrefutable evidence of the greater glory, desk or no desk, of the navy man's life. Not to mention the pleasure, the *importance,* of ascending the great steel citadel together.

Okay—Edwards admitted that he had no interest in working for some petrochemical company, and that having spent close to twenty years proudly wearing the greatest uniform in the United States of America, it would be tough to give it up —not to mention *the potential* of becoming an admiral. And yet, he still sounded the more romantic of the two navy men here at the table when he said: "The idea of driving an oiler around the world is very attractive. I could be on a ship for the rest of my life. But the navy doesn't give you that luxury. It splits you down the middle and makes you be the best ship driver and the best goddamn desk driver. And that's very frustrating. Especially when you're sitting in a place like Buffalo, New York, or even Washington, D.C.—"

"I'm not frustrated," Picotte said from behind a fort of elbows and tightly twined fingers.

"Oh, *bullshit.*"

"I'm not!"

"Hey, listen: the sun going down behind the Pentagon, or the sun going down over the South China Sea—which do you want?"

"That's not the issue—what you *want.* You've got to exist within the framework of the organization . . ." Picotte trailed off, heard the dogmatic tone in his voice, checked himself, and broke into a wide, honest, steaming grin. "Jesus, now I'm beginning to sound like a company man."

Edwards started laughing.

"Maybe that's what I'm becoming," Picotte said—amazed —joining the laughter.

"Co-opted! There he is, folks, *co-opted!*"

"Exactly," Picotte agreed, shaking his head.

"The Man with the Dog and Pony Show!"

"Hey,there,hey,there,hey,there," Picotte rumbled, in a very credible imitation of a side-show barker's voice, "see there—*one* stripe across his back, and *two* across his—*cock* your eye over the fence, ladies and gentlemen . . ."

After dinner, they went out by the sea, to the Inn at Castle Hill, where they had once spent a liquid afternoon together.

"Two years ago exactly," Edwards announced.

"Hell," Picotte said, "I don't even remember being here."

"Yeah, well, Len, that was in your youth."

"Obviously it was a problem of ambulatory stupefaction."

"Obviously."

At a table near the piano player, they drank cognac and tried to remember that murky afternoon. It was getting close to midnight, and since they intended to raise a glass in honor of the twenty-fifth birthday of a young man who was drinking with them, they now tried to remember where they had each been on their twenty-fifth birthdays.

"Let's see," said Edwards, " 'Sixty-eight. I was in-country, up the river."

"For my twenty-fifth, I was in the Delta."

They tried to recall the names of places they had been along the rivers of the Rungsat Special Zone, but the names wouldn't come back. "Time, I guess, just lets those things fade away," Picotte observed.

At exactly midnight, the piano player eased in to a slow rendition of "As Time Goes By." It wasn't as good as Sam's original version, but it was doing the trick. Edwards allowed as how he was getting chills up his spine.

Picotte was waxing poetic: "Lookit that there—the moon's almost full." He pointed to the window behind the bar, and sure enough, there was a soft yellow-white globe of light suspended in the glass. "Hey, fall in New England," declared Picotte, his eyes shining, as though he, personally, was proud of, and possibly responsible for, the moon and the light she was casting over the Atlantic coast.

Well, it was apparent that the October moon was, indeed, almost full—but out over the sea, in a different direction. That glowing thing in the window which caught Picotte's eye was just the reflection of a globe-shaped lamp that was mounted on the wall opposite the bar.

Edwards howled with laughter and kidded Picotte about the "moon in the window" for a full two minutes.

Picotte seemed hurt, but mostly embarrassed. "Well, hell," he shot back at Edwards, "at least I didn't jump up and rush over to look at the moon." Then, despite himself, he did stand up to take another look.

This time he saw the moon, the real thing, the mother of the night, and she was out there, making silver of the sea on which they would both command ships for as long as they were given ships to command.

He turned back to Edwards. He had the real evidence now, and in a resolute voice he said: "Hey, Mike. You gotta be *romantic.*"

VII : BROTHERS

John Belushi / Dan Aykroyd

Photograph by Edie Baskin

D an Aykroyd had a plan to change John Belushi's life. The United States Navy had invited the two actors to come aboard a Seventh Fleet ship which was going on a week of maneuvers in the Pacific. Apparently, the ship's commanding officer regularly showed their movie *The Blues Brothers* aboard the vessel. The officers and crew knew all the songs and loved this pair of soul-energized comedians. Aykroyd was convinced that seven healthy days at sea would revitalize Belushi.

"John, I want you to do me the solemn favor of your life—" he told Belushi on Wednesday, March 3, 1982. Aykroyd was in the offices they shared in New York; Belushi was in the bungalow he had rented at the Chateau Marmont Hotel above the Sunset Strip in Los Angeles. Over the telephone, Aykroyd recognized the tension in Belushi's voice. ("I knew he was getting into something. The vermin were out there. He was running with real bad people, and I knew that he had to just relax and cool out and let the pressures of the business off and get away from whatever substances were being pushed.")

"—You've got to come with me on this navy cruise," Aykroyd insisted, his resonant, baritone voice full of energy. "We'll go on seven days of navy regimen. We'll clean out. We'll get ready for the next push, the next season. This is just what we both need. . . ."

A transcontinental pause. Then the reply came back in a shocked, tight, almost robotic voice: "That would be impossible to do," said Belushi.

("Now, half of it," says Aykroyd, "was that he was afraid of being seasick, 'cause he didn't like boats too much. But I think the other half was that—there's-no-turning-back-for-me-now kind of thing. I sensed that in his voice. But these were my instincts: to take him, put him on board a ship where there would be nothing—completely clean him out. He had the will to be clean. He wanted to be clean. Later I heard from our agent, Bernie Brillstein, that after John had hung up with me he talked with Bernie and said, 'Well, I guess Danny's right. That's right. That's what we need—a navy regimen. I'm gonna do it.' So he'd made the decision to do it. And it's so sad 'cause he would have done it. We would have been on that ship the next week. Monday we would have sailed.")

Two days later, Dan Aykroyd was suddenly on his own. His best friend was dead of an overdose of heroin mixed with cocaine. Aykroyd felt as if he had lost a brother. Gone was the business partnership, and the strong friendship which had provided, for both men, an emotional support system as well as a permanent base from which they had launched their careers in tandem. Together they had swiftly risen from obscurity to the stratosphere of American comedy. Together they had earned millions of laughs and dollars. Together they had shared their twenties, and had talked of growing old together. It had been, in Aykroyd's words, "a full friendship. There was no dimension of it unexplored, except the sexual one. This was friendship between two young men, two young Turks, young rogues. We really succeeded and thrived in an interlocking sense, in a true business joint venture."

Like two other interdependent young rogues—Tom Sawyer and Huckleberry Finn—Aykroyd and Belushi understood that romance was the secret of friendship. The romantic sensibility they shared became the invisible bond of a highly visible, multimedia, comedy team. First it was the dangerous medium of late-night, live, national television on which they created folklore wrought from comedy, and formed an intimate, weekly relationship with a whole generation of young Americans. Next came records, concert tours, high-budget motion pictures, and the manic film personae of two down-and-out, rhythm-and-blues hipsters who called themselves The Blues Brothers. Drawing from their own fraternal relationship, Aykroyd and Belushi remade themselves as Elwood and Jake Blues. The result was an original comedic duo whose deadpan humor, lovable crudity, and destructo-escapades projected an image of mutual protectiveness and, most of all, intense loyalty. Set against the backdrop of black rhythm-and-blues music, theirs was white men's comedy; yet the friendship from which it sprang was so affectionate and universally recognizable that it made a deep impression across racial and ethnic lines. Peter Aykroyd, Dan's younger brother, recalls a conversation overheard on a train shortly after Belushi's death: "There were these two black guys talking real loud about this and that. They started talking about movies and one guy said, 'Man, you know, I'm really bummed-out about John Belushi. Shit, I really miss him, man. I *miss* him. You know what I loved about him? Him and his buddy, man, they were so tight. Really *tight.*' "

They had been tight from the start. They met each other in 1973 at the Second City improvisational theater in Toronto. Belushi, who had made a name for himself in the Chicago Second City troupe, came up to Toronto to recruit talent for the new *National Lampoon Radio Hour* and the *Lampoon* road revue, *Lemmings.* He had heard about Aykroyd's work with regional dialects and characters in the Toronto company, and Aykroyd had heard about Belushi's knockout performances in Chicago. After watching the show and joining the cast for the last improvisational set, Belushi went backstage where he was introduced to Aykroyd. Belushi was twenty-four; Aykroyd was twenty.

There was a mood of long-lost brothers finding each other at last. "It was kind of like love at first sight," Aykroyd remembers. "The friendship was almost instantaneous. Clearly here was someone who understood me and someone whom I understood. I made sure that he didn't leave my side during that entire time in Toronto."

Aykroyd showed Belushi around his stomping grounds. The first stop was on Queen and River streets, home of Club

505, an after-hours speakeasy that Aykroyd had been managing for three years. Patronized from midnight to dawn by artists, rock musicians, old blues singers, and underground types, the club had a funky, low-rent odor. It was furnished with old, mossy couches, a rickety barber's chair, a beat-up bar, a cloudy fish tank, and a toilet whose plumbing had once produced a live, scrabbling, sewer-slime rat at the same time that Aykroyd was perched upon the bowl, reading. Aykroyd took proprietary pride in the squalid, go-to-hell atmosphere of his establishment and in the high-quality bootleg booze he poured behind the bar ("I'm proud of being a bootlegger—it's my illicit thing in life"). To Belushi, the place seemed perfect. He felt right at home. As they stood at the bar, tossing back shots of Aykroyd's illegal booze, they discovered a mutual fascination with the first of many romances they would share—the gritty, all-night, low-rent romance of blue-collar squalor.

What Aykroyd knew of blue-collar life and squalor he had gone far afield to learn. Growing up Catholic in Quebec and Ontario, he had been a troublemaker in primary school, and an impious seminarian at the St. Pius X Minor Preparatory Seminary, from which he was expelled for favoring acts of minor delinquency and vandalism to acts of contrition. At Carleton University in Ottawa, he developed an interest in crime and punishment. His studies in criminology, deviant psychology, and correctional policy happened to coincide with his discovery of the Ottawa underworld in which he made the acquaintance of skilled and unskilled criminals, car thieves, hoodlums, soldiers of fortune, acid dealers, bootleggers—men with names such as Ray the Green Beret and George the Thief. But perhaps because his grandfather had been a Royal Canadian Mounted Policeman, and because his father was the assistant deputy minister for research and development at the Department of Transport in Ottawa, Aykroyd managed to find equal enthusiasm for both sides of the law. He was as intensely fascinated by cops as he was by robbers. The joke, later started at *Saturday Night Live,* was that Aykroyd's ideal fantasy was to commit a crime and then arrest himself.

His passion for criminology led him to a summer job working at the penitentiary facility in Ottawa, where he wrote a manual on personnel placement. And there were the blue-collar jobs he loved so much: He worked as a warehouseman, a railroad brakeman, a mail driver for the Royal Mail, a dial reader on a runway-load-testing unit at Toronto International Airport, a road surveyor in the Northwest Territories (where he observed local tension between the Blackfoot Indians and the Royal Canadian Mounties, and learned to like squirrel roasted on a stick). "I explored a lot of different careers," Aykroyd recalled. "That's what I liked about John—he had the blue collar in him, too."

Belushi at various times during his youth in Chicago, and in Wheaton, Illinois, had been a warehouseman, a trucker, a janitor, a cleaning man, and a busboy in one of his father's restaurants. The eldest son of Albanian immigrant parents, he was an outstanding athlete—the Athlete of the Year at Edison Junior High School, and a star linebacker and captain of the football team at Wheaton Central High School where he was elected Homecoming King in 1967, his senior year. Like Aykroyd (who took up blues harmonica at sixteen, and jammed on drums with Muddy Waters at an Ottawa nightclub called Le Hibou), Belushi gravitated toward music, playing drums in various rock 'n' roll bands throughout high school. But what he really wanted to do was to act, and to make people laugh. With his Wheaton friends Tino Insana and Steve Beshekas, he started an improvisational theater company, known as The West Compass Players, and was soon playing improvised comedy to a packed coffeehouse of college kids and hippies in Chicago. His impersonation of the spastic manner of British rock star Joe Cocker became a show-stopping performance that earned him a spot in the company of Chicago's Second City troupe. A year later, Aykroyd auditioned with a straight flush of talent—five characters in five minutes—and earned a place in the cast of Toronto's Second City. The names of Aykroyd and Belushi, and of the comic characters they were creating, began to pass back and forth between the two companies like electric signals.

A tape recorder placed between the two actors when they were finally joined together in Toronto would have picked up the sound of authentic kindred recognition. "That first night was great 'cause we just connected immediately and knew that we were kindred spirits," Aykroyd remembers. "It wasn't as if we told jokes to each other, although John was a great joke teller and raconteur. I can't do it. He appreciated the gift that I had for voices, dialects, and characters, and I appreciated the same gift he had. Our humor fit perfectly together—*perfectly!*"

It also fit in with an eruption of new humor that was beginning to crack open the landscape of American comedy. The seismic epicenter was New York and *The National Lampoon,* a large-circulation humor magazine founded in 1970 by a pair of young Harvard graduates named Doug Kenney and Henry Beard. Written by a team of, mostly, lapsed Irish Catholics, the *Lampoon* seemed to be convincing just about anybody under thirty-five that the Devil—not God, nor Jewish psychoanalysts, nor Polish mothers-in-law—was the preeminent force in the Universe. The magazine's success with black humor and scalpel-sharp satire was soon expanded into a weekly *Radio Hour* and the Off Broadway revue, *Lemmings.* But if on the printed page *Lampoon* humor was subversive, audacious, erratic, and sometimes so smart it was dumb, then it needed for translation to the stage a performer who was visually capable of unleashing every dark impulse man had ever repressed. It wasn't Chevy Chase, or Gilda Radner, or Brian Doyle-Murray, or Bill Murray (though, in *Lemmings,* each proved to be a versatile improvisator). It was John Belushi who embodied the darkest essence of *Lampoon* comedy.

Soon after meeting Aykroyd in Toronto, Belushi called the Second City troupe to ask Aykroyd and Gilda Radner to come to New York to join the *Lemmings* cast. Radner went; Aykroyd declined. He had his hands full with Second City, the Club 505, and a starring role in the Canadian Broadcasting Company's new television comedy series, *Coming Up Rosie.* Nevertheless, Belushi persisted. ("John was a leader, an operator, an organizer, a finagler, a wizard—his intention was always to get me into a group.") Eventually, Aykroyd went down to New York for a social visit. In helmet and leather, he arrived outside Belushi's Village apartment at 376 Bleecker Street, and gunned a greeting with the engine of his old Harley-Davidson motorcycle. From the window, Belushi let out a war whoop, and came down to inspect Aykroyd's prize hog.

Aykroyd loved machines. He was of a particular species of motorcycle fanatic—a Harley man, devoted exclusively to the All-American hog, the big black chopper favored by state troopers and counterculture outlaws. He had the arms of a blacksmith, and the build for long-distance, high-speed, hot rodding. Tall, strong, and beefy (nicknamed by Belushi "the Canadian Oak"), Aykroyd handled the hog with law-enforcement heft. Belushi, evidently, was not ideally suited for the bike. Short, portly, unevenly muscular (nicknamed by Aykroyd, "the Albanian Oak"), he was shaky behind the handlebars when he took off for a neighborhood spin—an outing that made Aykroyd extremely nervous. With his anxiety divided between the safety of his friend and the safety of his bike, Aykroyd ran around the block beside Belushi, yelling instructions over the engine roar, and holding out a protective arm. It was a role Aykroyd would take on more and more often, in different ways, as their friendship developed.

For the moment, though, there was simply high-voltage attraction between them—the kind of interactive electricity that occurs at the beginning of a friendship between two young funny men who illuminate one another's best talents and become each other's best audience. Each was necessary for the other's self-definition as a comic actor. Aykroyd was "nice," mild, and internal; Belushi was "mean," wild, and external. Aykroyd softened Belushi's hardness and Belushi brought a polish to Aykroyd's rough edges. Aykroyd made Belushi vulnerable and Belushi made Aykroyd look tough. The chemistry was combustible. During those first days, in the process of finding out how to make other people laugh, they made each other howl. "I don't know what made us laugh," says Aykroyd, "but, Jesus, we'd roll on the floor. We couldn't talk we were laughing so hard. There were always laughs with

John. He just exuded humor and warmth and the vulnerability that made you want to just hug him."

From then on the excitement they were beginning to share, intellectually and emotionally, intensified for each of them in different ways. "For John, Danny was a wonderful person to find and love as a friend because Danny was so intensely loyal," says Timothy White, a young *Rolling Stone* writer who became acquainted with both men through a mutual friend. "Danny was an inspiration for John about what a great friend is. Danny epitomized the archetypal great friend. He's really a man's man. He's like a character out of the movie *Gallipoli.* He's a true, loyal friend, and he has a strong sense of romance about that. Anyone who's ever been a friend of Danny's is still a friend of Danny's. Above all, he esteemed John, which was a good reason for John to walk around feeling pretty great." On Aykroyd, the impact of the relationship was visceral: "I'm not a homo, and neither was John, but when I saw him come into a room, I got the jump you get when you see a beautiful girl. It was that kind of feeling. It was that adrenaline—that pit-of-the-stomach rush. He was always exciting to be around. One knew that something was going to happen, even if it was just a matter of taking a walk. Being with him was electric, really electric."

The following year, Aykroyd was about to open in the Pasadena, California, company of Second City when he received a telephone call from Lorne Michaels. A Toronto-born, thirty-year-old veteran comedy writer, Michaels was going to produce a ninety-minute television comedy-variety show that would be broadcast live from NBC in New York every Saturday night. The show, which was to be called *Saturday Night* (to distinguish it from ABC's variety show, *Saturday Night Live with Howard Cosell*), would feature comedy sketches performed by a resident company of actors and a weekly guest host. Michaels had received a sixteen-show commitment from the network, and was now selecting the cast. Chevy Chase (later to join the cast for the first season) had been hired as a

writer. John Belushi and Gilda Radner were under consideration. Michaels wanted Aykroyd to come to New York for an
audition.

Aykroyd had doubts about the show. For one thing, there
didn't seem to be a future in *live* television comedy; it hadn't
been done since the fifties—it just didn't exist anymore. For
another, who wanted to make risky comedy in a broadcasting
company that was a slave to Nielsen ratings. Aykroyd didn't
wish to screw up his career with some live show that would
probably be a dead show after three nights of dismal ratings.
At twenty-two, he was doing just fine, thank you very much,
without television and without New York; he had just received
his first part in a Canadian motion picture. "I don't know about
this late night kind of live comedy you're gonna do," he told
Michaels. "I don't think it's going to fly, pal."

There were a few more calls from Michaels; Aykroyd continued to stall. Then, here was Belushi on the phone, madly
persuasive, talking him into coming to New York for the auditions *at least.* Belushi was adamant: They were *actors,* man, so
they wouldn't give an inch to *television*—the kind of pretaped,
canned-laughter, comedy factories on prime-time network
TV. No way, José. He had already met with Michaels, and told
him that he thought television was garbage. But *supposedly,*
this show of Michaels's was going to be a *new* kind of television,
inspired by improvisational theater and spontaneous comic
acting. . . .

After a few minutes of arm twisting, Aykroyd couldn't say
no. (Looking back, Aykroyd sees that his own initial reluctance,
and Belushi's forceful persuasiveness, were constant characteristics of their relationship: "I'm always so reluctant to jump
in. He got me to do things I didn't want to do all the time.
Joining *Saturday Night* was just one.") Though confident of his
own talents, Aykroyd was emboldened by Belushi's fearless-
ness and dazzled by his audacity. According to Michaels,
"Danny absolutely idolized John's nerve. Danny has great respect for courage and bravery, and is, of course, very brave and
courageous himself, but he stood in awe of John's nerve."

They went through the *Saturday Night* auditions together

in the summer of 1975. It was a doubtful business for a number of reasons: Aykroyd still wasn't convinced that he wanted or *needed* this show. Also, the longer the auditions and the video-taped screen tests went on, the more both Aykroyd and Belushi began to fret about all the rigmarole of television. And for all of Lorne Michaels's initial enthusiasm about Aykroyd, he now seemed doubtful about hiring both of them for the cast. ("There was never any doubt in my mind that Danny was going to be in the show," Michaels recalls. "With John, there was what I feared might be an 'attitude problem'—that would be John's phrase. He was the only one that I wasn't absolutely certain of right away. I just didn't know if he would work in an ensemble. Chevy kept lobbying for John, and saying, 'He's a lot of trouble, but he's funny.' ") Finally, word was getting around that the NBC executives were anxious about Aykroyd and Belushi—anxious that this very rough, very cocky, very unruly duo would develop separate channels of authority within the show. Comedic gifts aside, there was something harum-scarum about Aykroyd and Belushi when you saw them together.

But here they were, sitting side by side in Lorne Michaels's seventeenth-floor office at Thirty Rockefeller Plaza, and Michaels was looking at them with fascination and apprehension, as though they were good bad boys, indeed—Tom Sawyer and Huck Finn, reckoning to cause trouble and high adventure in the executive hallways of NBC. It wasn't an inconceivable thought (nor did the eventual reality contradict such a comparison), for here was Aykroyd—this bright-eyed, slingshot-happy, halo-and-mischief twenty-two year-old whose face could spontaneously light up as if he were reading about doubloons in a pirate book, and whose deep, blood-oath voice could erupt into the scariest Cave Hollow cackle this side of the great river— who knew what kind of sly, fence-whitewashing operations he'd set up at Thirty Rockefeller Plaza. And Belushi—bearded, anti-TV, potentially violent—well, it was questionable whether the man could be tamed, *civilized* for a national network TV audience. There *were* limits to what the NBC executives would approve for the cast of even an audacious late-night live comedy show that would be broadcast without censorship devices such as the trusty seven-second delay. And there *warn't* nothing like this harum-scarum Tom 'n' Huck pair in all of television—who knew when they'd slick up their swords and guns, hijack the show, and light out for the territory?

But this much was clear from the auditions and the video screen tests taped on September 17, 1975: They had unusual talent. Powered by a romantic sensibility that delighted in, among other things, mysticism, alien creatures, police uniforms, railroads, and darkness, Aykroyd's imagination was visionary. As a mimic and an impersonator, he was spontaneous and bizarrely original. Like a dish antenna, he seemed to be tuned in simultaneously to all the voices of the planet—and maybe even those beyond. Mid-sentence he could shift from one regional (or galactic) dialect to another with perfect pitch and fidelity. His characterizations (among those presented on videotape for Michaels: a French-Canadian lumberjack; a Louisiana crab 'n' gator fisherman recently held captive in a UFO; a halting Tom Snyder; a smarmy TV salesman for "a very personal product for men—Lloyd Manganero Deltoid Spray") were authentic and startling, chiefly because of the way he disappeared within them. Aykroyd was seamless; when he stepped into a character, he zipped up the front and vanished.

Belushi, on the other hand, unzipped characters to expose himself, to put his own writhing soul on display. Beneath his gruff, marauding-highwayman exterior, Belushi was at heart urgently romantic, and therefore able to create within comedy an emotional life that waylaid one's attention, ambushed one's affection. His face was as beguiling and versatile as Aykroyd's voice. Capable of the facial equivalent of vocal mimicry, it was a protean, transnational visage which might turn up anywhere —on the Sphinx, the *Mona Lisa,* the Statue of Liberty, even Mount Rushmore. His eyebrows seemed destined to become national treasures. Physically, Belushi was an unexpected, brute presence in anyone's life. While Aykroyd was the more cerebral humorist of the two, Belushi was the more corporal. He had a sensual command of full-body comedy which allowed all one hundred and eighty-five pounds of him to become a wild samurai warrior, slashing the air with a curtain rod for a sword—which is exactly what Lorne Michaels saw during Belushi's live audition that summer.

To Michaels, they seemed like fictional boy heroes sprung to life. He was struck by the four-year difference in their ages: "For me, Danny was a boy. He had the best of youth. He had total enthusiasm, total dedication, and honor—all the virtues of the old youth novels. Danny also had the Catholic good boy/bad boy, altar boy/criminal thing, but on the whole he was reliable and honorable and decent, and in no way corrupt. Not that John was corrupt, but next to Danny's youth and enthusiasm, John seemed to possess almost older-boy stuff. He knew his way around. He had street smarts without coming from the streets. Also, he loved Danny—always."

To Aykroyd and Belushi, it seemed that all this auditioning had been going on too long. They were impatient. Did they have the job or not? What was this producer *doing*? (In fact, Michaels had already selected them, but had to wait for executive approval.) They figured that either they were going to be the last members of the cast hired, or that only one of them, probably Aykroyd, would be hired—Belushi had made such a big impression telling a TV producer, who loved television, that television was garbage. ("Lorne dicked us around for so long, and John and I were quite embittered about it, but that was great, too, because it sort of unified the two of us.") As it turned out, both were hired and both were the last to sign their five-year contracts; Aykroyd remained skeptical about the show's longevity.

Saturday Night had its debut in October 1975. During the first two months that it aired, Aykroyd commuted between the set of a motion picture in Canada and the NBC studios, sleeping, when he was in New York, on a foam slab at the foot of the bed in the small apartment that Belushi was sharing with his girl friend, Judy Jacklin. (John and Judy, high-school sweethearts, were married in 1976.) Danny was welcome at the foot of John and Judy's bed indefinitely, so he decided not to get his own apartment until he was sure that this show was going to fly.

* * *

By Christmas, the word was out, mostly among younger New Yorkers who knew what was in and therefore treated it like a secret that the rest of the world had yet to discover: The best place to be on Saturday night was at home in front of your television, tuning in to this hip new comedy show which began at eleven-thirty, precisely the hour when you were supposed to be out somewhere, partying. But that didn't matter now because this show was like a party—a wildly funny, unpredictable, slightly out-of-control party—to which you were invited back every Saturday night. It was also the kind of party everybody talked about the morning after, reciting the most seditious lines of topical satire, so you didn't want to miss out on any of it. Most of all, it was the kind of party that you had to be at because it was happening right now, *live*. Even the established *New York Times* called it "the hottest, hippest, most daring comedy show on television"; the press secretary of the President of the United States (Ron Nessen), of all people, appeared as one of the show's guest hosts; and the Nielsen ratings, which awarded the first broadcast a 23 percent share of the television audience, were climbing every week.

Still, Aykroyd and Belushi were not convinced. Okay, so the ratings and high-priced advertising slots were great for NBC, but for themselves, as performers, they wanted to know if their material was hitting *out there*—in the heartland. Never mind the holy ratings; the only way to get real audience feedback was to go out there themselves . . . *as investigators*. They'd been cooped up all year long with this frantic weekly pace at Thirty Rockefeller Plaza, so when the show's first summer break came around, they decided to light out for the territory—to hit the slab and drive across America, polling every summer-session student in every college town they could find.

From Dependable Driveaway they were loaned a car which they were supposed to deliver to an owner in California in no less than five days. The car was in rough shape. A big blue Oldsmobile 98 sedan, it had beaten-up side panels, chewed-out

upholstery, and a coat hangar for an aerial. Aykroyd, the take-
charge, automotive authority in this pair, tinkered under the
hood, installed a citizens-band radio and a tape deck, and they
were set to go. There was no discussion about who would drive.
Aykroyd didn't allow Belushi behind the wheel once during
the entire journey. For one thing, Belushi was an erratic
driver, prone to multiple distraction. For another, high speed
was essential, and Aykroyd's ability to sustain fast, direct, long-
distance, endurance driving was legendary (he had once
driven from Toronto to Los Angeles, a distance of 2,523 miles,
in thirty-four hours). Anyway, Belushi didn't care who drove
—just as long as the fuckin' tape deck works, man. . . .

So up here on the flight deck of the front seat, Aykroyd was
in command—aviator sunglasses shielding his eyes, a six-pack
of cruising-brewskis resting on the seat, accelerator pedal
pressed to the floor—piloting this slugged-up sedan west by
southwest. Belushi rode shotgun, which is to say, in the seat of
the fearless co-pilot. There would be no idle passengers on this
trip. This was no hokey little sightseeing excursion. This was
a mission. There was important information to be found out
here, local color by the mile, and local characters at every turn
in the road—truckers, waitresses, toll-booth trolls, motel hags,
suburban shopping-mall snoids, and then suddenly, when
Belushi flipped on the two-way radio, there were all these
voices, filling up the car with the sound of gen*uine* American
citizens, drawling back and forth in this new radio language,
the twangy lingo of the road.

Neither one of them had ever used a citizens-band radio
before. It was a romantic revelation, a gold mine for a pair of
professional mimics. Here was this chatty little machine, hum-
ming and crackling with all these gritty, ballad-sad, lonely all-
night café characters who were trying to avoid the law. This
was the Voice of America—the Voice of Blue Collar Squalor!
—and best of all, the two of them could *talk back* whenever
they liked. *This* was the instrument with which to take America's humor pulse. They didn't know the official CB-vocabulary
so they just started yammering away, passing the microphone
back and forth, improvising comic bits, impersonating state

troopers, experimenting with these drawling, twangy voices. This was incredible—better even than the National Broadcasting Company because they were receiving instant feedback from a far-flung audience. Down in Tennessee, for instance, a no-nonsense trucker with a smooth, charcoal-distillery voice cut in on one of their routines to say: "You boys from New York there gon' take trip over side of this mountain you don't stop foolin' around on the two-way." Then they realized: Here they were—*junior* pilots—causing trouble for the senior guys out on the road.

Like campfires and candles, the lights of the nighttime road had a mesmerizing effect, providing the kind of intimacy in which life stories unravel. When Aykroyd wasn't absorbed by learning CB-talk ("Ten-four, good buddy, you got the Black Top Vampire back here . . .") and when Belushi wasn't wound up, singing along with the Allman Brothers tapes (". . . I was born in the back seat of a Greyhound bus, rolling down Highway 41 . . ."), they talked. "We talked about women," Aykroyd remembers. "We talked about Judy and how close John felt to her. He was extremely faithful. He was crazy about her. We talked about our pasts; how come we were in this business; why we liked the things that we did. Our interests were juvenile for the most part—machines, cars, the road, meeting good people, travel, watching for UFOs—everything that any good, healthy, red-blooded North American boy would like. We loved being on the move, in transit. We were always on a UFO watch."

While they drove, Belushi reminisced about the time when he and his mother and sister had seen some kind of unidentified flying object above a drive-in movie theater in Wisconsin. He described the way this thing had hovered over the drive-in with winking lights and chasing lights and glows and hums. Belushi, who was neither an avid UFO researcher nor an embellisher of his own life stories, remembered how he had felt sick to his stomach. Aykroyd replied that stomach sickness was a symptom common to most people who had reported encounters with UFOs. "Oh, yeah—really?" said Belushi, wonder-struck. "That sort of confirms it then, I guess." Awed, they kept their eyes peeled to the wide night sky.

Late at night, they headed for off-road motels, always choosing the scariest, *Psycho*-type Bates Motel, and always taking just one double room (never separate accommodations) and one pastry-soft king-size bed in which they'd "crash right out like a pair of old geezers." (The following year, they chronicled their second cross-country drive for *Rolling Stone*, reporting under a dual byline on such arcane bits of Americana as the recently discovered toxic fumes at the Bellevue-Stratford Hotel in Philadelphia where Belushi, armed with a gas mask, had trouble securing a double room: " 'Full!' Belushi screamed. 'With what—corpses? Isn't this the Bellevue-Stratford? The Legionnaries' Disease hotel?' The clerk quietly mentioned other hotels, but Belushi was adamant. Planting himself in one of the bulky leather armchairs bolted to the lobby floor, he vowed to stay until he got a room. An hour passed. 'Somebody must have died by now,' he suggested to the clerk.") In New Orleans they stayed with Aykroyd's old friend, David Benoit, who had broken away from his illustrious Canadian family to become a merchant seaman, pipe welder, and steeplejack. ("He had that blue-collar thing which I like in people, and John accepted him right away; it was great to see my close friend, Benoit, and this new friend just click and get along.")

From New Orleans, they took off, with fresh six-packs of Dixie beer and a curl of reefer smoke, across bayou roads overhung with Spanish moss. Then up to Arkansas where they pulled in to the University at Little Rock, hoping to scare up some excitement and gauge the reactions of the students to *Saturday Night.* Unannounced, unshaven, unarmed (but resembling, Aykroyd would later say, the two killers from *In Cold Blood*), they prowled around the Little Rock campus, figuring that sooner or later *somebody* would recognize them as famous TV stars. All they were getting were blank looks from kids probably supposing them to be a pair of maudlin alumni back for a nostalgia romp. It was amazing: Nobody knew who they were—*nobody*! Belushi was even resorting to guerrilla tactics: ambushing the cafeteria, sticking his face into classroom windows, bouncing his eyebrows up and down. No recognition. Finally they accosted a group of students—went right up and polled them on the spot. *Hey, do you guys watch* Saturday Night? . . . *Have you ever* heard *of* Saturday Night? (You morons . . .) *But no-o-o-o*—they had not seen it, though a few of them chirped up about hearing something about a Howard Cosell show called *Saturday Night Live.*

Well, that was it! Now they really were convinced that this thing at Thirty Rockefeller Plaza was . . . *just a job.*

During the next two seasons, it all changed. Even the name expanded: *Saturday Night Live* was now so well known that confusion with the Howard Cosell variety show was inconceivable, even in Little Rock. Thirty million people were regularly tuning into the show week after week. The Not Ready for Prime Time Players—Aykroyd, Belushi, Jane Curtin, Garrett Morris, Bill Murray, Laraine Newman, Gilda Radner—were now as well- or better-known than many of the show's guest stars. It had become *a job* just trying to put the show on every week, what with all the extracurricular activities around the studio: the newspaper interviews; the magazine cover-story personality profiles; the autograph maniacs; the skinny-tie and upturned-jacket-collar Studio 54 scones who wanted to hang out till dawn, blowing tootski in the offices after the show.

Aykroyd avoided all that. "He didn't want to be famous," says Lorne Michaels. "He was a little frightened of it all. I kept telling him he was getting the biggest break of anyone because he was just allowed to get better without having to deal with the kind of problems that Chevy first had to cope with—by being on the cover of magazines and being called the next Johnny Carson. So Danny had three quiet years of enormous growth in the shadows because after Chevy left the show, John and Gilda were the next two to catch the glow." Aykroyd continued to live and work as he always had, and to ride his prize hog out on the slab whenever he got the chance. No Lear jets or limousines for this man of the road.

Late one night after the show, Aykroyd strode into Lorne Michaels's office to say good-bye; he was going up to Ontario for two days, driving straight through the night on his motorcycle. Michaels, for the first time, responded parentally: Maybe Danny shouldn't be traveling that way now. Maybe it was too dangerous. He was, after all, an integral part of a hit show on NBC. Aykroyd told Michaels not to worry, and went into a long bit about how "The Lorne Michaels Video Shield" would protect him on the thruway. "I remember just laughing," says Michaels. "We all had this sense that nothing could happen to us. We all just knew that we were the center of the earth—that this was a charmed period of our lives. It was such an innocent time. Nothing bad was going to happen."

To be a performer on *Saturday Night Live* circa 1977 was to be at the center of the hip-comedy universe. The seventeenth floor of Thirty Rockefeller Plaza (known as "Thirty Rock") was where it was happening—*it* being whatever mysterious alchemy turns a combination of base talents into gold. For a time, Thirty Rock had the kind of electrifying aura that momentarily surrounds a hit Broadway play, a victorious political campaign, a World Series championship team. Moreover, it was all happening on *live* national television—to a cast of very young performers.

There was danger here, weekly risks overcome by a willingness to try something new and unsafe—an unheard-of combination on *taped* comedy-variety broadcasts. So intense was the mystique—the atmosphere of a daring, secret society out on a limb—created by the Not Ready for Prime Time Players, that four years later, Mark O'Donnell, one of the second wave of *SNL* writers, described those who replaced the original cast as being like "younger brothers who had inherited the fun, scary tree house which the cool older brothers had made and then abandoned to find fun elsewhere."

One particular tree house at Thirty Rock was built by Aykroyd and Belushi. They took an office together, and moved into it like Tom and Huck building a secret fortress. Aykroyd had bunk beds installed in there. ("I insisted that a shower be installed, too. It was really great. That office up there, man! That shower! There'd be white towels everywhere. It was obviously a place where people felt they could get away from the rest of the show because John and I always represented kind of a satellite.")

Aykroyd also kept a stash of gold coins. Late at night, he'd take them out and make strange, piratical, incantatory sounds; his spooky, cackling, Cave Hollow laugh would float out into the hallway, awakening the other writers on the floor. Sometimes, there were so many people staying overnight at *Saturday Night Live* that the place was like a big sleep-away summer camp with bunk beds and ghost stories and neat activities. ("Working around the clock, a certain kind of bonding happened," recalls Lorne Michaels. "The male bonding was an important part of the show because this was just after the white heat of the women's movement. The women on the show were very strong, and it seemed that it was men who were in disarray at the time, in the sense of not knowing where they were and how they stood. And along came Danny and John who were both very much guys' guys.")

They frequently spent the night there, holing up for days at a time. Hey, it was easier not to go home. Besides, who wanted to go home anyway? This was *fun.* Here you were in your own tree house, with your best pal in the top bunk, staying up late at night, trying out funny gags and sketches on each other (and the NBC camp counselors loved it!—the ratings were climbing like summer fireworks). Why, you could even have wicked fun in the tree house scaring the girl campers: Like the time when Jane Pauley, the prim, trim, cute-as-a-button host of NBC's *Today* show had an elevator encounter with James Downey, one of the *SNL* writers, who was coming out of Aykroyd and Belushi's shower at 5:30 A.M.—half naked, with only a painter's drop cloth covering up his *thang*—scaring poor Jane most to death. ("She stared at me in horror," Downey recalls. "She shrieked," Aykroyd reports gleefully, "she *shrieked!*")

Oh, there was considerable fun to be had in the outlaw tree house with your best pal. Guerrilla stuff and camp hijinks and ambuscades. You could, for instance, lean out the window with a bullhorn and bark crowd-control commands down to the little stick people on Fifth Avenue. And in winter you could order pizza up to the tree house, put the pie outside on the window ledge until it froze hard as a discus, then wing it out over the skating rink and the Christmas tree in Rockefeller Center. ("John and I used to do this—out over the rink! We'd make sure no people were there 'cause it could have sliced somebody's head off. Then we'd aim for the rink—*woozzzzh!*") And if the NBC camp counselors played dirty cabin tricks, there was only one thing to do: scare 'em with some psychic numbers and satanic oaths, the kind of cabalistic stuff that means a man is marked. One time when an NBC executive held back four hundred dollars that Aykroyd had earned by writing for a *SNL* special, Aykroyd got some red paint and nails, and stayed up most of the night outside the executive's office, painting bewitching, diabolic slogans on the walls—I AM THE DEVIL! I AM BEELZEBUB!—which had the entire executive wing of NBC spooked for days. ("They couldn't understand why he would do something like that," Belushi told *Rolling Stone* writer Timothy White, "but I could understand it. And they'll think twice before they take money out of *his* pocket again.")

The tree house was also a terrific place to work. "It just made our friendship better," says Aykroyd. "It was obvious: *This* was where we could work together." During the second year, in addition to their duties as performers, Aykroyd and Belushi wrote sketches together and shared writing credit. In one of their more interactive pieces, Aykroyd played a double-duty radio disc jockey, switching back and forth between AM (frantic voice, bubble-gum music, Wonder Bread commercials) and FM (mellow voice, classical music, whole-wheat health-bread commercials); Aykroyd wrote the AM part and Belushi wrote the FM part. They were a compatible, though not ideal, writing team. "John was never patient as a writer; Danny was meticulous," Lorne Michaels recalls. "The things that John was not good at, which was detailed stuff, Danny was. John had an impatience with detail; Danny once wrote a sketch based on the schedules of freight-train routes in America, which he had memorized. John didn't have the attention span for writing a sketch, whereas Danny would stay there until he died for it."

Aykroyd enjoyed spending long hours alone seated at a typewriter. His ideas took shape on paper. He loved clarity. On a show that required not so much absolute discipline as absolute self-sacrifice, Aykroyd was industrious, prolific, absolutely dependable. "Danny was disciplined, but he was mostly driven," Jim Downey remembers. "It wouldn't be unfair to anyone else to say that Aykroyd contributed more than any other individual to the show, when you take into account his writing and his performing. He was there every week working at full tilt for six days." Though equally fertile with ideas, Belushi was, for the most part, a conceptualist. While Aykroyd liked to fashion comic ideas with clear-cut precision, Belushi liked to keep them mysterious. Some of Belushi's best concepts began in rhapsody or in improvisation, and were put down on paper afterward. "In many ways, Danny and John were opposites," says Downey. "Aykroyd was attracted to words. He was one of the performers in the cast whom you could trust with a long speech. Belushi was different. He didn't like written words; he didn't trust them."

Nevertheless, during the season in which they were writing together, Aykroyd was determined to turn Belushi into a lover of the written word—a disciplined writer who would sit down at a typewriter for hours. "It was a gift I knew I enjoyed so much, and it made me feel good and gratified and deeper than just being a performer, so I really wanted John to learn how to do that himself. I feel so bad about it now because it was the only time I can remember yelling at him. I really gave him hell. It was a sad thing."

And it was a tremendous fight. When Aykroyd was mad, he held back nothing. He went straight to the heart of the problem with direct, confrontational analysis. He didn't go into character or use a mimicked authoritative voice. He was himself—a booming, lashing presence, and he came down hard on Belushi. Aykroyd's position was: Write your stuff *and then* perform it. Accomplish yourself as a writer—that adds a little more respect to the profession if you have to be in show business. Work with pencil and paper—at least it shows you're literate. Do not lose your integrity. *Buckle down, man.* The night mystery, the disco fever, has got to stop—

"—If you're *not* going to be a writer," Aykroyd shouted at Belushi, "then don't pretend you are one."

Belushi suffered visibly during this explosive lecture. He was hurt. Before he lashed back at Aykroyd with a tirade of his own, an expression came onto his face—around the eyes and cheeks, but mostly on his mouth—a look of utter vulnerability that Aykroyd would never forget.

The tension dissolved a few hours later. Belushi was sorry. Aykroyd was sorrier. Both felt wretched about the whole thing. Yet it hadn't been a useless fight. Afterward, Belushi did buckle down somewhat, though it was clear that he had no taste for the long hours at the typewriter. Finally, too, they were both glad that they'd come through a rough patch like that one without causing an irrevocable rift in their friendship. "We got it out quick," says Aykroyd. "It didn't fuck the relationship up. John and I used to have disagreements and arguments, but they were diffused very, very quickly because we both could take a good scolding from each other, which is sometimes what we needed. He snapped me in line, I snapped him in line."

They never argued again about writing. During the third season, they disbanded their tree house and took separate offices because Aykroyd wanted to be alone to write. (Aykroyd was so dedicated to his writing duties on the show that in 1977 when Universal Pictures asked him to join Belushi in the cast of *National Lampoon's Animal House*—and offered him the part of D-Day, the hot-rodding, motorcycle character, which Doug Kenney had written especially for Aykroyd—Aykroyd declined, saying, "I've got to stay here—I love the writing too much.") There was no bitterness about their new office arrangement at Thirty Rock. Aykroyd made sure that Belushi knew he was always welcome in Danny's new tree house: he installed another set of bunk beds. ("The bunk beds were there for *him.*")

It was well known around *Saturday Night Live* that Aykroyd was devoted to Belushi, and vice versa. They expressed their affection for each other in different ways. In front of mutual friends and colleagues, Aykroyd was often more demonstrative than Belushi. Whereas Belushi's love for Aykroyd was understated or expressed directly to Aykroyd, Aykroyd broadcast his affection for Belushi. "Danny could go on and on about John," Lorne Michaels remembers. "His affection came out as praising John in front of John, somewhat backhandedly at times, but always with very high regard and an enormous amount of love. Danny is a very emotional guy and a very affectionate guy. He used to say, 'I love to serve.' He loved to be in a position of the keeper, the trainer: John was the talent and Danny was the self-effacing Angelo Dundee, and everybody knew it wasn't true, including John, of course, and *that* was the joke. That was what made it all acceptable." Aykroyd also showcased the bond he and Belushi shared by acting as an admiring explainer of Belushi's more idiosyncratic moods—a devout, humorous medium through which the Belushi spirit could be passed on to others. "Aykroyd was like the high priest who could interpret Belushi for everyone else," says Jim Downey. "He would get really big and he'd say: *'The man . . . is . . . a . . . god!* He is a living media god. We must *worship* him. We are fit only to stand at his gates . . . *longingly* . . . and to flee when he chooses to . . . *set . . . his . . . dogs . . . upon us.'* Danny would get into these weird rants, and I know that Belushi was twenty percent a comedy prop to him and eighty percent a genuine god. And Belushi needed him, too."

For Belushi, Aykroyd was a source of equilibrium. The force of Aykroyd's personality, his diligence, and his integrity were counterbalances in Belushi's life. Where Belushi was erratic, Aykroyd was systematic. (Before air time each Saturday night, Aykroyd took a one-hour nap.) Compared to Belushi, Aykroyd was organized—in the manner of one who derives existential pleasure from the state of being *in control.* Belushi rarely carried a wallet, and if he did, lost it; Aykroyd often kept his chained to his belt. (In 1976, during their second cross-country drive, Belushi was triumphant with laughter when Aykroyd was stopped for speeding in New Mexico and could not find his wallet or his driver's license—"I *never* lose my wallet," Aykroyd kept insisting as the cop wrote out the ticket.)

Aykroyd's fame-proof, disco-proof work ethic counteracted Belushi's monstrous fondness for revelry prolonged beyond the exhaustion, say, of dawn—seen three mornings in a row. Aykroyd had vices, too, but his carousing usually took him in a different direction: While Belushi would disappear in Manhattan for three nights with his friend the Rolling Stones guitarist, Keith Richards, Aykroyd would disappear into the country for three days of solo, high-speed off-roading on his motorcycle. Aykroyd loved the sensation of speed. Belushi loved *sensations;* he was a man of long nights and huge drinks. His excessive consumption of Vantage blue cigarettes, whiskey or cognac, and a variety of drugs was often more than a nocturnal companion could sustain. Aykroyd was not always on hand for the Long Night of the Wild Turkey.

During one such night, Belushi persuaded Timothy White to come over to his house to kill a bottle of Wild Turkey at 2:30 A.M. White's best friend, Mitchell Glazer, was a good friend of Belushi's; the conversation turned to friendship, a subject that Belushi had a sudden, great compulsion to grasp. He seemed to *need* to understand what made friendships between two extremely different men, like himself and Danny Aykroyd, work and endure. "I can't always figure out Danny," he told White. "But what I love about him is that he makes me feel incredibly safe." Even more urgent was Belushi's desire to know about the dynamics of White's friendship with Glazer. As he turned the inquisition on White (who was, by now, around 5:30 A.M., weary with whiskey), a mean, arrogant, competitive tone came into Belushi's voice, as if he wanted to bully his way into becoming the *best* friend that had ever walked the earth. "I wonder if you've ever figured out friendship," he demanded of White. "Wouldn't you say I'm a better friend of Mitch's than you? *Wouldn't you?*" White began to cry. "John, don't do this to me," he said. Then, Belushi burst into tears. Ashamed, he hugged White fiercely and said, "God, I'm sorry. I'm so sorry. I'm such an asshole. I'll never make you cry again as long as I live." Soon, Belushi was crying harder than White; the balance had shifted and White found himself comforting Belushi. Looking back on that night now, White says, "It gives me goosebumps thinking about the way John said Danny made him feel safe. The gratitude in John's voice was overwhelming."

With Aykroyd, Belushi felt protected; with Belushi, Aykroyd felt protective—for good reason. Belushi had a way of walking without ever looking behind him or to either side. Crossing a city street, for instance, Belushi simply charged ahead. More than once, Aykroyd steered him out of the path of an oncoming vehicle. ("He's Mister Careful and I'm Mister Fuck It," Belushi once told Timothy White.) Only once did Aykroyd submit to occupying the passenger seat of a car driven by Belushi, and then only to offer instruction: "Shoulder check to the right," Aykroyd told Belushi. Every time he changed lanes: "Shoulder-check-to-the-right." ("John always remembered that, too," says Judy Jacklin Belushi, who also recalls that "John's first step into Colorado was out of the car and down a mountainside: he was sleeping, I woke him up, and he stepped out of the car and plunged out of sight.") Although Belushi was agile and weirdly graceful on stage, later when they began acting in motion pictures together, Aykroyd was always on alert for Belushi's accidents.

During the filming of Steven Spielberg's *1941* (in which Aykroyd played a U.S. Army 10th Armored Division tank sergeant, and Belushi played a crazed National Guard airman), Aykroyd watched helplessly as Belushi stepped backward off the high wing of a grounded P-40 fighter-bomber—an unintentional fall which finally wound up in the movie. When *The Blues Brothers* was in production, Belushi fell off a skateboard and hurt his knee. ("John just got on some kid's skateboard," Judy Belushi recalls. "It was typical—'No, don't do that!'—and he steps on it.") While production was held up for two days, co-star Aykroyd telephoned Belushi and fabricated a story about how he himself had fallen off his motorcycle and hurt his hip. "I did that to make John feel better," Aykroyd later explained, "and to alleviate some of the guilt he felt for stopping this multimillion-dollar production. It was like: 'I'll jump in there with you and be injured, too!'"

Aykroyd's dedication to Belushi was reciprocated with generosity and affection expressed during the few comparatively calm, private moments they could share in the increasingly pressurized, public life of live television comedy. According to Aykroyd, "John would talk about our friendship. He talked me up all the time—how much he depended on me and my support, and how we were partners. He always said we were partners. And this just made me glow."

Although Aykroyd and Belushi were the dominant performers on *Saturday Night Live* during the second, third, and fourth seasons, the configuration of their personal friendship was probably not recognized by most television viewers as an on-screen partnership until April 1978. Individually, they had both earned TV cult followings of varying intensity—Belushi for his slashing samurai routines; Aykroyd for his Jimmy Carter caricature and his interplanetary creation, Beldar Conehead, among many other characters through which Aykroyd diverted attention from himself. ("The Nazis could get hold of Danny and he wouldn't break character," Lorne Michaels once said of him.) Aykroyd was often seen in tandem with Bill Murray as the shoot-first-ask-questions-later cops, or with Steve Martin as the Czech Brothers Festrunk—"two wild and crazy guys." Belushi, even in ensemble pieces with the whole cast, had achieved singular superstar status.

Few sketches exclusively paired Aykroyd and Belushi. "It wasn't easy to write two-character sketches for them because they were different kinds of performers," explains Jim Downey. "Aykroyd lost his personality in characters; he was cool and brilliant, a thinking man's performer. To the audience, Belushi was more accessible and warm, because there was always something of Belushi's own personality in everything he did, and in some cases, it was mostly Belushi." Aykroyd agrees: "That's part of the secret of his charisma and his stardom: He opened up part of his soul a little bit and let you see what was really inside. With me, it's a strict character. I put on a disguise when I go out there."

Then came the Blues Brothers.

For the first time, they were together in deep disguise. Not only were they sheathed in darkness—black suits and ties, midnight fedoras, and Ray Ban No. 5022-G15 sunglasses—but they were unrelentingly in character and incognito. At first, their act was startling, and not a little confusing. In comedy-variety terms, it trumped both an ordinary music number and an ordinary comic sketch. It drew laughter in three dimensions. Viewers were mesmerized: Belushi singing the blues? Aykroyd on harmonica? ("When Danny first played blues harp on the air," Lorne Michaels recalls, "I don't think people even knew that it was him playing—that's how subtle it was.") No one knew how to respond. Was this musical satire? A takeoff on the white man's fascination with the irresistibly cool, all-black cultural medium of rhythm and blues music? No, these guys seemed strangely serious. One couldn't tell what was going on behind their very dark shades, but apparently they believed that they actually *were* a pair of blues musicians—two incredibly soul-energized white brothers named Jake and Elwood Blues. Dan Aykroyd and John Belushi had vanished.

Considering their fraternal affection for one another and their romantic admiration of the old Blue Collar Squalor, it was not surprising that Aykroyd and Belushi chose for their alter egos the identities of two juvenile delinquent brothers from Chicago. Jake and Elwood allowed them to act out fantasies they had had since early youth. As Aykroyd dreamed up the details of the Blues Brothers' background he was finally able to unleash all his knowledge of criminology, Catholic education, recidivism, police procedures, and general human dereliction. Belushi was at last able to be what he'd wanted to be all his life—a singer.

The musical dimension of the brotherhood had begun during the fifth show of *SNL*'s first season. Appearing in bee costumes, Belushi sang the blues classic "King Bee" and Aykroyd played harp. But after the excitement of that first night had worn off there seemed to be no medium in which to develop the act further. Then, one day in 1976, in the process of looking for an old car to revive, they began reviving old blues tunes: Here they were, out on Long Island, being shown around an automotive graveyard on a misty, foggy afternoon. Belushi spotted it first: a 1953 Oldsmobile 88 with the most beautiful chrome graphic he'd ever seen—an "88" with a rocket roaring through both numerals. *"Wow,"* Belushi said, "look at that." Aykroyd ran his hand over the chrome. "It's a Rocket 88, man. Don't you know that James Cotton song? 'Step in my rocket, baby/ Don't be late/ Gonna take a little ride/ In my Rocket Eighty-Eight/ In my Rocket . . .' "

Belushi had never heard that, but he loved it. They bought a 1967 Dodge Monaco, which they painted black and dubbed The Blues Mobile. Soon they were riding around, putting together a repertoire of blues classics which they performed to warm up the *Saturday Night Live* studio audience before air time. "It was a perfect synthesis," says Lorne Michaels. "They were two of the greatest comedians of their time, and they both got to do the things they loved to do most. John got to come out and do three cartwheels, and Danny got to come out with the briefcase and the handcuffs. And then, when Danny finally danced it was the most exhilarating thing in the world because you'd never seen him move."

Passionate about the music itself, both knew they weren't superior musicians. Aykroyd called himself "the George Plimpton of blues harmonica." He had no anxiety about the quality of the humor they would scare up onstage, but he was doubtful about his own musical nerve. "John opened up that whole stage to me. He gave me the gift of being able to jump up onto a stage anytime, with any band in the world, and sing 'Kansas City.' He really *made* me play the harp. That's one thing he forced me to do, 'cause I would rather have just stayed the thinker, the writer."

"Don't worry—this is gonna be great," Belushi kept telling a reluctant Aykroyd after the mixed reactions to their first professional gig with Roomful of Blues at the Lone Star Café in New York in June 1978. "We're gonna get our own band, a great band. It's gonna be great. We're gonna have a great time. We're gonna have a great audience."

"I don't know, man," was Aykroyd's constant refrain up until the night they opened a show for Steve Martin at the Universal Amphitheater in Los Angeles in September 1978, and then recorded their first album on Atlantic Records, *Brief-case Full of Blues,* which went straight to the top of the record charts and eventually sold over three million copies.

The Blues Brothers act was more than an ideal outlet for their professional partnership; it also deepened the sense of brotherhood which had been growing in their friendship. They were now spending more time together than ever before, and they both became involved with each other's families. Elwood and Jake Blues were orphans, but Aykroyd and Belushi were not. Whenever Belushi was on the telephone, talking to his mother, he would put Aykroyd on the line, and Aykroyd would do the same when he was talking to his mother. "John's mother is kind of soft for me and my mother was soft for John 'cause we really were brothers in a sense. We would have always had that with each other and with each other's mothers. With John's mother, Agnes, I'll always feel a closeness just 'cause she was John's mother. My mother just loved him, and that was great."

When Dan first brought John up to the farm in Canada to meet his parents, John stepped out of the car and executed a running somersault in front of Peter and Lorraine Aykroyd, as if to say: "Here I am! I'm Danny's friend! If you're his parents, I love ya!" Magnanimous and irresistible, John was loved by all the Aykroyds. "John had a lot of time for everybody," recalls Dan's younger brother, Peter, who was then twenty-two. "Dan and I were always pretty close, so John immediately became close to me." As an auxiliary brother to Danny and Peter, John was ready and willing to take part in any and all activities— swimming in the lake; driving around in the 1941 Chrysler pickup truck; robbing an Ontario marina (as it turned out, they didn't steal anything, but Aykroyd was touched that Belushi would go along on any caper, no matter how crazy, as an act of friendship); and spending the night in an old farmhouse on the Aykroyd property, waiting for spirit entities which had been known to appear in ectoplasmic form during the formally documented séances that had been regularly conducted there by Grandfather Aykroyd. (None appeared for the new generation.)

After the visit, Aykroyd was sorry that Belushi never made it back to the farm. He always wanted John and Judy to come up together. The three of them—John, Judy, and Danny—had been growing ever closer since the days when Aykroyd had slept at the foot of the Belushis' bed. Judy, an award-winning graphics designer and a warmhearted woman who had the patience and soul of an angel, was involved in both the personal friendship and the professional partnership. She accompanied them in every Blues Brothers venture, giving general business inspiration, and designing each of the album covers and a book titled *Blues Brothers: Private.* Just as Belushi had brought Aykroyd into his marriage, so, too, did he bring Judy into his friendship. "It was a wonderful thing," says Aykroyd. "Here I had a friendship with this man, but his wife was not excluded at all. That's very rare in male-to-male friendships. Extremely rare. I told Judy everything that was going on, and I used to talk her up to him when they went through their domestics—periods of personality estrangement, alienation, whatever. The woman is often excluded in male-to-male bonding, and it just didn't happen in this case because we would have been shortchanging ourselves, both of us, if we had done that."

Although Belushi wasn't always fond of Aykroyd's girl friends ("which wasn't really a problem," says Aykroyd, "because I just told him, 'John, I'm sorry, I'm with this woman—there's nothing you can do' "), Aykroyd was—and is—intensely fond of Judy: "She was sort of a surrogate wife/mother to *me,* as well. That's one of the gifts John gave me—a friendship with her that will last forever."

Dan also had a special fondness for John's brother, Jim, who was then beginning his acting career at Chicago's Second City troupe. When John was too busy for a phone call to his brother, Dan would keep in touch with Jim, and John would do the same with Dan's brother, Peter. John took an interest in Peter's career as an actor, musician, composer, lyricist, rock guitarist, and lead singer, giving active support as the drummer in Peter's two rock groups, The Stink Band and The Mini-14s. "John changed my attitude toward my little brother," Dan

Aykroyd would later recall. "I've always loved Peter, but I've always felt that he should not have gone into show business because it's so hard. I thought he would have more potential doing other things—and John was the same way about his brother, Jimmy. But John encouraged Peter to do his music. When I had no time for my little brother, John always did. Theirs was such a tender friendship, and it warmed me so much. It was such a love, such a valuable thing. It made me so happy. That's the one thing that makes me cry now—that my two brothers *got along so well.*"

After four seasons of successful television comedy, Aykroyd and Belushi decided to leave *Saturday Night Live* together in 1979. Aykroyd had considered staying with the show for another year, but when production dates for filming *The Blues Brothers* had been set, his allegiance to his script and his partner finally won out. Though Belushi's mind had already been made up, there must have been relief in knowing that he wasn't going alone. "Chevy's departure in 1976 had been a trauma for us all," Lorne Michaels recalls. "John had seen Chevy leave, and had seen the perception of Chevy in the press be that he was leaving his friends for Hollywood and for bigger things, which was, to a certain extent, true. So I think John was uncomfortable about leaving by himself, particularly after the cover of *Newsweek,* and *Animal House* breaking all the box-office records, and then with the Blues Brothers record at number one."

The success of *National Lampoon's Animal House* (the largest-grossing comedy of all time) paved the way to Hollywood. The studios, particularly Universal Pictures, were now willing to risk millions of dollars on comedy epics—the more outrageous the better. The generation, now in their twenties and early thirties, that had subscribed to *The National Lampoon* and religiously tuned in to *Saturday Night Live* was just as eager to shell out their dollars at the cinema box-office if there was comedy from the same sources inside. On the cover of *Newsweek* as the toga-clad, eyebrow-arched Bluto Blutarsky, Belushi had become a mascot for this generation. For Universal, he was a national emblem of the lucrative new genre of destructo-comedy on the big screen. So it seemed logical that with Belushi, Aykroyd, and *Animal House* director John Landis signed up, Universal would invest over $30 million in *The Blues Brothers,* one of the most expensive movies ever made. By the time Jake and Elwood Blues appeared on the cover of *People* magazine on August 4, 1980, they had become literally (and facetiously) "part of the Gross National Product."

The new headquarters for Aykroyd and Belushi's joint ventures was a suite of offices on lower Fifth Avenue in Manhattan. Set up by Judy Belushi, ably manned by Karen Krenitsky, this new tree house unified the personal as well as professional aspects of their friendship. The two were now practically inseparable, and thus, Phantom-Black Rhino Enterprises Ltd. was born. Here they discussed career decisions and gave each other daily support. Belushi became the organizer and promoter of their post-television partnership. Distrustful of the ways of Hollywood, Aykroyd was sometimes uncertain about their new projects. "John *made* me write *The Blues Brothers.* I didn't want to do the movie. The script was three hundred pages of images and thoughts. John made me go to Hollywood and deal with John Landis, and he made Landis deal with me; there was friction between us immediately. John made us work together on the script. He turned the key that made it happen. He did that with all our projects."

Increasingly reclusive, Aykroyd holed up alone in his apartment when he was working. To obtain privacy during the writing of *The Blues Brothers,* he hired an assistant to screen all telephone calls and intrusions. Once, the assistant threw up the screen when Belushi called, and it drove Belushi crazy. He later told Aykroyd that if the assistant was going to work on the production of the film, he, Belushi, would not. "We have to have complete two-way communication," he insisted. Yet Belushi recognized that Aykroyd also had to have complete privacy. "John did depend on me for support," says Aykroyd, "and I on him, but him a little more 'cause I was able to be alone much more than he. I'm an ex-seminarian, and I'm used to Catholic retreats where they lock you in a room alone for two weeks. I like that solitude. John respected that about me. He never taxed that. He knew he could come to my apartment any time of the day or night, but I don't think he came over more than three times. I would go to him and spend time with him in his sphere. He knew that I loved being in my home alone."

Belushi loved to have people around him. He was a generous host and companion; his status and income as a movie star enabled him to indulge himself and his friends in a variety of nocturnal luxuries, including Courvoisier and cocaine. Aykroyd's indulgences were comparatively prosaic; he was more often happy with a six-pack of Moosehead Canadian Lager and maybe a joint or two. Unlike Aykroyd, Belushi gravitated toward friends in the fast-paced, bicoastal world of show business. Aykroyd was more comfortable with a different breed of coastal men—fishermen, lobstermen, merchant seamen. He was also more comfortable with anonymity. ("Danny had more fun being Belushi's biggest fan than in being a celebrity himself," says Jim Downey.) Though cheerful and generous if stopped by a fan in public, Aykroyd was genuinely pleased not to have the kind of notoriety that had become Belushi's burden.

After 1978, Belushi was recognized wherever he went. Yet lurking by his side on the street, Aykroyd often escaped recognition. ("I was able to just stand there and look like the Secret Service," Aykroyd recalls. "That was one thing that was really fun about the relationship. I could really protect him. I always observed him. I was always one step back from him 'cause I didn't want to be too close to the flash. I wanted to see the whole picture.") As they would exit the stage door after a Blues Brothers concert, Aykroyd often walked literally a step or two behind Belushi. The fans screaming—"Jawn! Jawn! Hey, B'lushi!"—presumed Aykroyd to be some kind of rough-trade bodyguard. Naturally, he acted the part flawlessly. ("When someone is as flamboyant as John was, you have to be around it, or do it yourself, to know how vulnerable that makes you," says Lorne Michaels. "Part of the nerve of being John Belushi was that there could always be great humiliation and failure with it. And Danny, who was sensitive enough, and astute enough to know that—to know what it was to be that vulnerable—would naturally protect him.")

Yet no matter how talented Aykroyd was at playing the bodyguard, there were limits to the protection he could offer Belushi—from the world, from himself, from those who would make drugs available to a star of Belushi's stature: "The people who were giving him this shit—they thought they were doing him a favor," Aykroyd would later say. "Just from a pure business and insurance standpoint, the company should have protected him more. He should have had two or three bodyguards, the way a Saudi prince does, because the enterprises that John was involved in—more than three hundred million in gross sales already. *The Blues Brothers*—gross sales of one hundred and twenty million; sales of the records at six million; *Animal House* is over two hundred million; which is not to say that other people weren't responsible. But here he was part of a team that was just a money-making charger."

To alleviate the pressures of public life and the tensions of their expanding role in the motion-picture industry, Aykroyd and Belushi sought private surroundings. In New York, they could retreat to the Blues Bar, their private clubhouse in a dilapidated building on Dominick and Hudson streets where the faces were familiar, the whiskey unlimited, the juke box stocked with the best R & B tunes in town. And when New York was too frantic they could retreat to the new locus of their friendship—Martha's Vineyard.

In 1979, Belushi bought a house near Vincent Beach which had belonged to former Secretary of Defense Robert McNamara. Judy Belushi negotiated the purchase (for approximately $435,000). Meanwhile, she telephoned Aykroyd to tell him about another property that was for sale (for $500,000) nearby. Aykroyd said he wanted a house that was up high, with a good view. The view was the important thing. Judy told him that there were lovely views—three of them, in fact—one on each side of the house. *"How* lovely are the views?" he wanted to know. She told him they were the loveliest she had ever seen.

"Three of the loveliest views, eh? And John's moving there —well, okay then. Sure. Fine. No problem."

He bought the house, views unseen. "I knew," Aykroyd says of his investment, "that here was a friendship and a professional relationship that was forged for years to come."

The summer of 1981 was idyllic. It was just an extraordinarily good time because Aykroyd managed to talk Belushi out of going to Europe in August. Belushi was restless; but this was the worst, hottest month to go abroad, Aykroyd kept telling him. "Nobody's in Paris anyway. What's there to see? Half the place is shut down. You're *here.* You've got the best house on this beautiful beach. You're not going to find a spot in the world that's going to assuage you and take care of you in a spiritual, physical, and mental sense. There's just no way. Europe would just wear you out." Belushi hemmed and hawed, and finally stayed.

It was a little bit of heaven. They fished, they swam, and they surfed at six every evening, like a pair of California beach boys—Aykroyd even had the platinum blond surfer-boy hair (it had been dyed for the filming of their last two-guy movie, *Neighbors*). They loved the seclusion of their beach, which they called Skull Beach. Any one of their friends who wanted to come down to the beach had to present a skull insignia to the police guard at the road. Aykroyd wore a headband with skull and crossbones all summer. Even the guard wore skull and crossbones.

In preparation for "The Crunch Three," an annual demolition derby for year-round islanders which takes place on an oval track near the Gay Head cliffs after the summer season is over, they began fixing up the X-13, the original Blues Mobile. They put a heater on the back of the car (to make it resemble a rocket engine), and painted on red triangles and jet-fighter stencil graphics—NO STEP, RESCUE, EXIT—and, of course, a large skull-and-crossbones death's-head. "We did this as a celebration to John," remembers Aykroyd, "as a celebration of death and death-defying stunts and jet pilots and all of that mystique—which is a heavy premonitory irony."

In the summer afternoons, after being out on the water with his friend Walter, a lobsterman, Aykroyd would come back to his multiview home where he would find Belushi napping on the couch in his living room. Aykroyd covered him up and let him sleep. It was, in Aykroyd's words, "a ritual": Whenever Belushi was crashed out, Aykroyd would put a blanket over him. ("I loved to see him sleep. I knew he couldn't get into trouble. I knew he was in peace when he was asleep.") Aykroyd would watch Belushi's slumbering form, listen to his breathing—the heavy rise and fall of three-packs-a-day—and feel a momentary sense of ease himself. At times like these, the turbulence of the business, the jangled, overheated, cocaine pulse of Hollywood at night, seemed far away. This summer, John was clean.

Sometimes, they walked along Skull Beach and talked about growing old together, about what their lives would be like. It was going to be great: Even if they weren't working together when they were sixty, they would see each other. Sure, listen: Danny would be up on his farm in Canada, a crotchety old hermit with a shotgun ("Who in tarnation is comin' up the way now?") and John would be his portly, gray American friend, and they would go fishing like the old men from Jersey who drive up to Canada every year, and they would sit around the lodge, farting and geezing together. And there would be time for all the things they were too busy for now.

Then, other times, Dan and John wondered if they would even make it to *forty*. They knew they were living fast. They talked about early departures. According to Aykroyd, "There was this Ring Lardner thing that we enjoyed bantering around —live fast, die young, leave a good-looking corpse. We *knew,* man. Listen, if I make it to forty, I'll be really thankful. But I certainly don't expect to. I'd like to see forty. John would have, too. But then again, there was this little favorite thing of ours —*live fast, die young, leave a good-looking corpse*—grab it all now. That's the left hand's thinking. The right hand's thinking is to do right by your life, to fulfill and accomplish yourself." If Aykroyd tended to be right-handed, even when he gripped the handlebars of his motorcycle going 80 mph, Belushi was now clearly ambidextrous.

One late-summer afternoon when the island was beginning to smell of September, they were driving around in Danny's Jeep, listening to tapes. Danny put on an instrumental tune by the Ventures. It was called "The Two-Thousand Pound Bee." It was full of such bad, buzzing electric-guitar bee-sounds that it was fantastic. They both loved it. *"Man,"* said Danny, "wouldn't it be great when we died to force this song on a church full of people—so loud it'd hurt?" They laughed and thought about that for a while—"The Two-Thousand Pound Bee" hovering around all those mourners. It'd be a great, monstrous joke.

Then Danny said, "Listen, John, if I die first, man, you've got to promise to play this at my eulogy or my funeral."

John pledged that he would, and they made a pact as they drove around in the last amber light of that summer day: Whichever one of them died first, the other would play "The Two-Thousand Pound Bee" at the funeral.

On Friday, March 5, 1982, Aykroyd was alone in his office at Phantom-Black Rhino in New York. He was writing a script called *Ghostbusters* (in which he and Belushi were to play "paranormal technicians" who exterminate ghosts and spirit entities from suburban homes). Along with *Spies Like Us, Never Say Mountie,* and *Moon Over Miami,* it was one of several two-guy projects that were scheduled for production. Aykroyd was mid-sentence, writing a line of dialogue for Belushi, when the phone rang. Bernie Brillstein was calling from Los Angeles. John was dead.

Six seconds passed before it sank in. "Well, how did it happen?" was Aykroyd's first question.

"He died in his sleep this morning."

"Drugs?"

"They don't know at this point," Brillstein replied. "It was respiratory."

Another pause came in.

"What are we going to do?" said Brillstein.

Aykroyd took charge. He felt himself going into his "pragmatic robot mode: *Don't think now. . . . Gotta give the man a decent burial.* I'm gonna do my part." There were arrangements to be made. But he couldn't help thinking how it all could have been reversed. John could have gotten the call about *him* being killed on the highway in a motorcycle crash. He wondered how John would have reacted, and what John would want him to do now: *"Carry on. . . . Be a little robotic about it."*

He remembered the last time he had seen John—just the week before, at the Blues Bar. John had not been in the best of shape; he looked tired, exhausted. Danny begged him: "Don't go back to L.A. Let's go to the Vineyard."

"But John had to get out there," Aykroyd recalls, "had to solve something, had to have that excitement—those dwindling dawn hours on Sunset Strip." Then the phone calls through the week, the navy cruise plan, the tight jangled voice, the talks with Judy about going out and bringing him home if he didn't come back East by Thursday night . . . then the coroner's report, saying that he'd died of a drug overdose due to intravenous injections of heroin and cocaine. *"Intravenous injections?"* Aykroyd thought. "The man hated even getting his finger pricked *for a blood test—"*

"I think if I had it to do over again," Aykroyd would say later, "I would have taken two or three of my friends and handcuffed him and put him in an institution just to turn him around, clean him up. It was mainly the cocaine he was interested in, like everybody else. He had the money to do it. He just fell in with some bad people. I'm not saying that he didn't ask to be hit up, but I don't think he could have hit himself up —he was not that good a mechanic. The last days were pretty sad, but if I'd cuffed him, that would have broken his heart: his best friend taking him and putting him in an institution."

Now Aykroyd had to put him in the ground. Up on the

Vineyard he was handling all funeral arrangements, and comforting John's parents and Judy. He made sure that no fewer than three state police cars were there on the tarmac when John's body was flown in on a stretcher in a Lear jet. John was wearing the clothes he normally wore. This was the way he would have come home to the Vineyard anyway—in a private jet. When the body was taken to Sylvia's Funeral Home in Vineyard Haven, Aykroyd finished planning security logistics for the following day. This was going to be, in Aykroyd's view, "a funeral fit for a goddamn Head of State."

That morning, Aykroyd dressed himself in motorcycle boots, blue jeans, and, in honor of John's (and Jake's) hometown, a Chicago police scooter jacket with the city's flag patch sewn on the right shoulder. He wore a carnation in a buttonhole. Wrapped around his neck like a scarf was a Confederate flag (" 'cause John was a rebel"). With the hearse, the Blues Mobile, and the family cars behind him, Aykroyd led the cortege to the West Tisbury Congregational Church. On his motorcycle, he gunned the engine, making as much noise as possible—just in case John's soul could hear it. The churchyard was like a carnival midway, crawling with gawkers and cameramen and reporters. Two helicopters whirred around overhead. Aykroyd thought: *Oh boy.* Adding to this spectacle, the guys in the Blues Mobile suddenly jumped out and began watering a pine tree in the churchyard; they'd been drinking, and didn't want to get stuck in the church service with a full bladder. Meantime, the helicopters were circling like buzzards, and the cameras were clicking like a swarm of locusts, recording this unholy micturition for posterity, and the guys were waving, and who knew how many cartwheels John's soul was turning.

During the service, which was presided over by a priest from Boston's Holy Trinity Albanian Orthodox Church, Aykroyd was thinking he really did not want to be here at all. He was sitting in the back, wondering whether John would have been here if this were *his* (Danny's) funeral. ("I knew that he wouldn't have sat through a church service like that.") It went on for almost an hour. Aykroyd tried to bolt, but reconsidered when he discovered that the back door was, in fact, the front door, through which was waiting the swarm of photographers. He sat it out and was glad, after all. It was, he thought, a beautiful service. By the end, he was weeping.

In Abel's Hill Cemetery, snow fell during the burial. Family and friends crowded around the grave, and James Taylor sang "That Lonesome Road." Everyone wept as the solid oak coffin was lowered into the ground. Aykroyd remembered that John had once talked about having a Viking funeral on Skull Beach; he'd wanted his body set on a pyre heaped with boughs and set aflame and floated out to sea. . . . "Well, *that* would have been a circus," Aykroyd was thinking. "There would have been a flotilla of press boats, and what if the fire had gone out too soon, and . . . *Forget that.*" Aykroyd didn't feel too bad about not fulfilling John's wish for the Viking funeral on the beach. But he found himself telling John what was going on here, murmuring in a low voice: "Now, John, relax now. The Viking funeral is out. Just relax. We're putting you here in Abel's Hill with the whalers and the Indians and the pirates and the smugglers. You'll be fine. There are so many ghosts on this island. Good bones here, man. You're gonna be with good bones. . . ."

Three days later, Aykroyd stepped up to a microphone in the pulpit of the Cathedral of St. John the Divine in New York City. He took from his blue knapsack a cassette tape recorder, turned its speaker to the pulpit microphone, and pressed the play button. The large crowd that had gathered in the chancel for John Belushi's memorial service sat stunned, then rocking with laughter as "The Two-Thousand Pound Bee" suddenly soared upward, buzzing into somber places where no tribute of this kind had ever gone before.

Two months after the service, New York City makes Aykroyd restless. He wants to go up to the Vineyard, to see what's doing at John's grave. "I think about him every morning when I get up, and I just sigh," says Aykroyd, his eyes still glistening with tears from a momentary surge of grief brought on by remembering John's devotion to Dan's brother, Peter. "That's the first time I've cried since the grave and the funeral. See, there's a lot of grief there, a *lot* of grief, 'cause it's your best friend. I don't weep for the tragedy . . . I cry because I miss him."

Aykroyd says he just has to accept the fact that John's bones are lying nearby. He often muses about going up to John's grave and eating some chickens and drinking some beer to commemorate the dozens of chickens and beers they used to polish off together. So he'll bring a six-pack and eat those chickens and spend a little time with the whalers, the Indians, the pirates, the smugglers, and John.

Even now, whenever Danny Aykroyd drives by that graveyard, he always honks his car horn—long and loud—on the good chance that somewhere, somehow, in some form, John can hear it.

VIII : LOURIE-LOVES

Epilogue

A n urge to recapture the past by revisiting the scene of old friendships is displayed everywhere at Princeton University on this Reunions Weekend.

All across the campus, bands and orchestras are playing in each of the brightly colored tents that serve as headquarters for the decades of returning classes. The music—teens ragtime, twenties jazz, thirties Broadway melodies, forties swing, fifties rock 'n' roll, sixties rock, seventies disco—offers an aggregate impression of *hearing* time accumulate, as if every bygone era of this century is simultaneously alive in 1982, filling the spring air with the particular tribal rhythms that have, decade by decade, led each new class out the gate to some unknown future.

But the classes always come back: Each June, alumni from nearly every year of the century, dressed in the particular costume of their respective class, return to the campus for a three-day celebration. The climax is a three-hour march known as the One and Only P-rade. It begins on Saturday afternoon when the 25th Reunion Class passes through the FitzRandolph Gate on Nassau Street, followed by, in ascending order—1907 to the present—the oldest living alumnus, the rickety Old Guard classes of 1907, 1912, 1913, 1914, 1915, and so on, rank upon rank, year by year; the march winds around Nassau Hall and then through the campus and down Prospect Street, gaining speed as each successive class, stronger and more youthful than the one before it, falls into line, until finally —with a burst of exuberance—this year's graduating class closes the ranks and sets off down Prospect Street, following its predecessors into life.

For even the most jaded observer, there is something incredibly optimistic about this spectacle. Seen from a fixed point along the parade route, the procession creates an overall effect like that of a time-lapse movie in reverse: alumni grow *younger* as the years go by. From front to back, a historical perspective is offered (notice the placards they carry, displaying the popular slogans of their respective eras) which seems to say that no matter what happens in the world, *this* will endure; this is where the continuity of the generations will be perpetuated for all time. Better than any mythical fountain, this is where people come to *see* youth renewed eternally.

This year, the surviving, active members of the Class of 1922 have returned to celebrate their 60th Reunion. And there they are—sixty-four old men and one Seeing Eye dog—slowly ambling up to the FitzRandolph Gate, ready to march in the P-rade. They're all dressed in their class costume: white golf hats encircled with an orange and black '22-insignia band; spanking-clean, white blazers with the class coat-of-arms on the breast pocket. If they had angels' wings on their backs, they would look like a Peter Arno *New Yorker*-cartoon vision of Heaven. Milling around, they're waiting for the scores of men in '57, the 25th Reunion Class, to march through the gate and begin the P-rade; but in a sense, just by virtue of the fact that they are here at all—in their eighties, standing, moving, *breathing*—they're already on parade.

Part of the P-rade mystique (some say the best part) is the revelation of age: Before the procession gets under way, the youngest Princetonians stand around marveling at the oldest Princetonians, appraising the relative fitness of the geezers to see how senescence is going to affect their own minds and bodies someday. (The young men seem to be full of wonder: *Will I look that good when I'm eighty-two?*) The Class of 1922 is looking pretty good.

Donold B. Lourie is looking great. He is identifiable from a distance of fifty feet: His ears seem more prominent than ever. He is chatting with one of his classmates, grinning the famous Lourie grin: All-American, but modest. He seems not to have aged so much as *evolved*. Besides the fact that Lourie is from the Midwest, there is about him something that suggests the heart of a once-innocent America. Elected president of his class yesterday, for the fourth time since 1919, he is enjoying the leadership and fellowship of his classmates as much as he did sixty years ago. Stooped slightly forward and wearing an expression of affectionate curiosity, he moves with the gentle gait of a beachcomber. Here and there he finds a hand to shake, an elbow to clasp, an audience for a sly joke. The grin, which lights up his own face, makes the faces of those around him positively glow.

Then, for a few minutes, he is standing alone near the gate, regarding the slim ranks of the Old Guard classes, grinning amiably at either nothing in particular or the spectacle of Time itself. His wife, Mary, is already stationed with the other wives in parade-side seats over on Prospect Street; unaccompanied, Lourie seems almost, but not quite, bereft. One wonders why Cupe Love isn't here. (He's not on the list—printed for yesterday's Class Memorial Service—of the eighty-six classmates who have died since the 55th Reunion.)

The class secretary suggests that Love's absence is the result, in part, of Love's impatience with "the lack of discipline at Princeton nowadays." But Don Lourie explains differently: "Old Cupie couldn't make it on account of an abscessed tooth. The doctor ordered him to stay home in Pittsburgh. He's getting worse and worse, but he says he can still beat me in golf."

Is this true? ("My golf handicap increases annually," Love has written for the 60th Reunion Class Directory, "and now the only one I can beat is my old roommate Lourie.")

"Don't believe a word he says," Lourie advises, grinning— a bit of linksmanship with his absent partner.

Talking about the most recent years of their friendship, Lourie describes a relationship that has remained, in its essence, unchanged by time. But surely old age has put limitations on their friendship? "No, heavens no," says Lourie. "We're still as close as ever—" and he goes on to recall their visit at Love's place in Florida last year. "We still have lots of fun together," Lourie explains, adding matter-of-factly: "Never had a fight once."

The remarkable endurance of their friendship seems

hardly surprising to Lourie. It's simply part of a world in which certain important things remain reassuringly in their place. He will no more readily identify the elements of his success as an athlete and businessman than he will identify the elements that have preserved a friendship for more than half a century. "I think probably it was humor as much as anything," his son, Donold, suggests later. "They both consider what the other one says very funny—they have identical senses of humor. Their sense of humor about other people tends to be rather cutting, a bit biting on outsiders, and they even kid each other with a bit of the knife, but always very happily. They're very warm people, and they both cared a great deal about each other right from the beginning. The friendship was a very powerful thing, and it still is—it very definitely is. They're getting old now, and they have to take care of themselves, but there was a time when I doubt that either one of them would go anyplace, such as a reunion, without being pretty sure the other one would be there. But now they're getting along, so they have to take care of themselves first."

Yet by his absence, Cupe Love has created a presence here, signaling a motion toward memory. Lourie suddenly recalls whole episodes from the past. The campus offers itself as a museum of their friendship; Lourie can literally point to the artifacts: Their old room, 181 Little, which abutted on the gymnasium (before an archway was tunneled through the walls) where they used to sneak local kids through the gym window for a free admission to the basketball games . . . and the time they were back for their 25th Reunion when a big policeman stopped them over there on Nassau Street ("I wondered what I'd done now, but this cop only wanted to thank us because he was one of the fellas we'd slipped into the gym") . . . and the times when Cupe wouldn't crack a book until just before exams, staying up all night, memorizing texts with a pot of coffee while Lourie slept ("The son of a gun had a wonderful memory") . . . and Dopey Miller's bottle of gin during Prohibition . . . and Cupe's sprint to retrieve Lourie's lucky dime before the Yale game of 1920 . . . and the handcuffs sunk in the cornerstone of Lourie-Love Hall . . . and the dormitory itself.

Although Lourie-Love Hall continues to accommodate ninety-three students (thirty-eight of whom are freshmen, living in the hall's nineteen double rooms), it is now a building in which the names of Lourie and Love are only mentioned in a single breath. Without a trace of recognition of the friendship for which it stands, one of today's freshmen will tell you: "Yeah, my roommate and I live in Lourie-Love," and he, or she, will enounce this fact using the same number of syllables as, say, a student who lives in Witherspoon, a dormitory that was named for one man. ". . . I am absolutely sure that the legend of Lourie-Love Hall will go resounding down the corridors of time," Russell Forgan had declared at the building's dedication ceremony in 1964, "and that it will warm the hearts and enrich the lives of untold generations of future Princetonians. . . ."

Yet today, one discovers that not a single current resident of Lourie-Love Hall—not even one of the seniors—has the faintest idea that Lourie and Love are a pair of living men, as old as the century, whose friendship began when they were roommates at prep school, and continued at college, and endured throughout their lives, ultimately being memorialized in a house full of roommates, the cornerstone of which has made their names inseparable—forever linked in stone and steel.

None of this seems to faze Donold Lourie in the slightest. It's time to march. The Old Guard classes are already inching their way up the path. The Class of '22 is falling in behind '21 and a band of bagpipers. Lourie ambles over to join the white-jacketed ranks, and for some reason (this is one humble class president) he chooses a spot at the tail end of his class. One bystander calls to him over the squealing of the bagpipes: "Too bad Cupe Love isn't here to march!"

"Don't worry," Lourie replies with a big sock-'em grin, "we'll give him hell!" Then, on second thought, he calls over his shoulder: "It won't make a difference, though."

And they're off: Up toward Nassau Hall, past the procession-swelling classes of the thirties, the forties, the fifties. Around Cannon Green—where sixty years ago the handcuffs were slapped on Lourie and Love—'22 moves at shell-fancier's speed. The classes of the sixties and the seventies, arrayed on the perimeter of the green, are giving '22 a major reception, full of cheers and locomotives: "Tiger, tiger, tiger, sis, sis, sis, boom, boom, boom—*boom*—22! 22! 22!—rah!"

Marching by himself, the caboose of the class, Lourie smiles at the crowds and occasionally doffs his hat. Down tree-lined McCosh Walk he goes, with a big grin and a hat-tip for the roaring locomotive from the Class of 1982; then into the cool, vaulted, 1879 Arch, through which light breezes are blowing, and the din of the bagpipes echoes out to Prospect Street.

Out here in the sunlight, the spectators form a wild, congratulatory congress beside the steps below the mouth of the arch. Packed shoulder to shoulder, obliterating the sidewalks down along the leafy corridor of eating clubs, standing on tiptoes, perched in the big elm trees, they clap and wave and cheer on the Class of 1922. Lourie waves back—a little wave with a weary wrinkle in it—the pace is faster now; the ranks in back are cresting over the steps of 1879 Arch, surging onto the street, rolling ahead, their intensity increasing by the year.

Down in front of Tiger Inn, a curious thing happens: Lourie quietly breaks from the formation. His class continues on to the rally down on the athletic fields.

Spotted with shade, Lourie wanders over to the eating club where he and Love used to take their meals. He parks himself on the path, and removes his hat—with no apparent plan of immediately rejoining the generations. And yet, Don Lourie seems to have stopped for something more than the refreshment of shade. He is peering at the men who keep getting younger and younger as the years pass him by, as though somewhere in that eternal parade he might catch a glimpse of a younger pair of Lourie-Loves as they march on, side by side, borne out of sight under the tall tired trees.